FROM CONTROL TO DRIFT

From Control to Drift

The Dynamics of Corporate Information Infrastructures

Claudio U. Ciborra

and

Kristin Braa, Antonio Cordella, Bo Dahlbom,
Angelo Failla, Ole Hanseth, Vidar Hepsø, Jan Ljungberg,
Eric Monteiro, Kai A. Simon

OXFORD
UNIVERSITY PRESS

OXFORD
UNIVERSITY PRESS

Great Clarendon Street, Oxford OX2 6DP

Oxford University Press is a department of the University of Oxford.
It furthers the University's objective of excellence in research, scholarship,
and education by publishing worldwide in

Oxford New York

Auckland Bangkok Buenos Aires Cape Town Chennai
Dar es Salaam Delhi Hong Kong Istanbul Karachi Kolkata
Kuala Lumpur Madrid Melbourne Mexico City Mumbai Nairobi
São Paulo Shanghai Taipei Tokyo Toronto

Oxford is a registered trade mark of Oxford University Press
in the UK and in certain other countries

Published in the United States
by Oxford University Press Inc., New York

© The several contributors 2000

The moral rights of the author have been asserted
Database right Oxford University Press (maker)

First published 2000
Published new as paperback 2001

British Library Cataloguing in Publication Data
Data available

Library of Congress Cataloging in Publication Data
From control to drift: the dynamics of corporate information
infrastructures/Claudio U. Ciborra . . . [et al.].
p. cm.
Includes bibliographical references.
1. Information technology. 2. Management information systems.
3. Organizational change. I. Ciborra, Claudio.
HD30.213.F76 2000 658.4'038—dc21 00-021846
ISBN 0-19-829734-3
ISBN 0-19-924663-7 (pbk.)

3 5 7 9 10 8 6 4

Typeset by Hope Services (Abingdon) Ltd.
Printed in Great Britain
on acid-free paper by
Biddles Ltd.
Guildford and King's Lynn

Preface

The international research project called 'Infraglobe: The Dynamics of Global Infrastructures' began in the autumn of 1997. The research team came from three European universities, Bologna, Göteborg, and Oslo, and from two participating companies. It was composed of ten academics, of which three were junior researchers and two were members of industry. Six company case studies were undertaken, in each of which an average of twenty people (top managers, middle managers, users, and specialists) were interviewed, in sessions lasting for more than two hours, in seven different countries, including the USA. Three joint sessions between industry partners and researchers were held to discuss the research.

The launch and execution of the project—the field study, the feedback meetings, and the theory seminars that accompanied the various work stages before the writing of this book—and the actual writing itself spanned over a period of three years, starting in 1997. The chapters of the first part contain the syntheses of our thoughts at the end of this period (late 1999). The cases are dated between 1997 and 1998, but for stylistic purposes the texts are not always written in the past tense.

We would like to take the opportunity to thank the multiple funding bodies for this project: the Italian IBM Foundation, and the 60 per cent research grants of the Italian MURST Ministry and University of Bologna; the Swedish Transport and Communications Research Board (KFB); the Swedish National Board for Industrial and Technical Development (NUTEK); the KTK (Knowledge, Technology, and Culture) Research Programme at the University of Oslo; the Internet project of Göteborg University; the Norwegian Research Fund (Social Aspects of Information and Communication Technology Programme); the Department of Information Systems at the London School of Economics; Astra Zeneca; Hoffmann La Roche, and Statoil. David Musson of OUP helped us greatly in shaping the idea of the book and bringing it to a successful completion. Hilary Walford carried out the excellent editorial work.

Contents

List of Figures and Tables

Figures

Tables

Notes on Contributors

KRISTIN BRAA is Associate Professor at the Department of Informatics at the University of Oslo, Norway. She has been project leader of the Internet Project (internet.informatics.gu.se), in which the research of this book has taken place. She has for several years undertaken research within participatory design, digital documents, integration, and geographical dispersed information systems. She has edited the book *Net Society* (in Norwegian) and *Planet Internet* (with Bo Dahlbom and Carsten Sørensen). She has had recent journal publications in *Information Systems Journal*; *Accounting, Management, and Information Technology*; the *Scandinavian Journal of Information Systems*; and *Systèmes d'Information et Management*.

CLAUDIO U. CIBORRA is Professor of Information Systems at the London School of Economics and the University of Bologna, and a leading researcher in the areas of information systems, management, and strategy. His earlier work dealt with transaction costs and information technology (his *Teams, Markets and Systems* is in its third printing with Cambridge University Press). In the 1990s the focus of his research shifted to the issues of learning and the implementation of IT systems. He sits on the Editorial Board of the most important information systems journals in Europe, and also in journals in the domain of organization theory. He has been keynote speaker at various international information-systems conferences, and has worked with many corporations, public authorities, foundations, and intergovernmental bodies worldwide.

ANTONIO CORDELLA holds a Laurea in Political Science from the University of Bologna and is currently writing his doctoral dissertation on IT infrastructure at Göteborg University. Since July 1997 he has been a research fellow at the Viktoria Institute in Göteborg.

BO DAHLBOM has a Ph.D. in philosophy, is Professor of Informatics at Göteborg University, Sweden, and director of the Viktoria Institute. Among his books are *Dennett and his Critics: Demystifying Mind* and (with Lars Mathiassen) *Computers in Context: The Philosophy and Practice of Systems Design*. He is an editor of the *Scandinavian Journal of Information Systems*.

ANGELO FAILLA is Research Manager at the IBM Italy Foundation. He has managed and co-authored research projects in the area of computing in schools and education for the Italian Ministry of Education, and other projects on the impact on work and management issues.

OLE HANSETH has worked most of his career in industry and applied research before moving to his current position as Associate Professor at the Department of

Informatics at the University of Oslo. He also held a part-time position at Göteborg University. The main focus of his research has been comprehensive, integrated, and geographically dispersed information systems—information infrastructures—in both the private and the public sectors. Recent journal publications on these issues have appeared in *Computer Supported Cooperative Work*; *Information Technology and People*; *Accounting, Management, and Information Technology*; *Science, Technology, and Human Values*; and the *Scandinavian Journal of Information Systems*.

VIDAR HEPSØ is a Senior Scientist and anthropologist at Statoil R & D in Trondheim, Norway. He is currently taking a Ph.D. in the anthropology of science and technology at the Norwegian University of Science and Technology (NTNU) in Trondheim. His current work evolves around how visions, concepts, and solutions related to IT-based collaborative technologies are developed and spread within organizations. He has worked within the field of CSCW (Computer Supported Cooperative Work) in Statoil since the early 1990s, both as a researcher and as project manager.

JAN LJUNGBERG is a research director in the research group IT & Organization at the Viktoria Institute in Göteborg. He is also Associate Professor in the Informatics Department at Göteborg University. He received his Ph.D. in 1997. His current research interests include knowledge management and the role of IT in processes of communication and organizing.

ERIC MONTEIRO is Professor at the Department of Computer and Information Sciences, Norwegian University of Science and Technology, Trondheim, and holds a part-time position at the Department of Informatics, University of Oslo. For some time he has studied comprehensive, integrated, and geographically dispersed information systems (that is, information infrastructures) in both the private and public sectors. Recent journal publications on these issues have appeared in the *Information Society*; *Accounting, Management, and Information Technology*; *Science, Technology, and Human Values*; *Scandinavian Journal of Information Systems*; and *Information Technology for Development*.

KAI A. SIMON has been studying Economics and Information Systems at Duisburg University, Germany and Göteborg University, Sweden. He was the Managing Director of the Viktoria Institute during its start-up phase and now holds a position as Research Director of IT & Organization at this institution. He has also been working as an assistant researcher and lecturer at Göteborg University where he is currently concluding his Ph.D. studies, and has several years of experience as a consultant in the field of IT and management.

Abbreviations

AC	Andersen Consulting
AC/DC	alternating/direct current
ANT	actor-network theory
ATM	Asynchronous Transfer Mode
BCG	Boston Consulting Group
BPR	Business Process Re-Engineering
CISR	Centre for Information Systems Research
CRF	case report form
CRM	customer relationship management
CSCW	computer supported cooperative work
dp	data processing
E & P	exploration and production
EDI	electronic data interchange
FASTRAC	Fastest and Smartest to Registration and Commercialization
FC	formative contexts
FDA	Food and Drug Administration
FIST	Fastrac Implementation Steering Team
GFSS	Global Forecasting and Supply System
HAE	Hydro Agri Europe
HTP	Hydro Technology and Project division
ICSS	International Customer Service System
IND	investigational new drug
INF	information unit
IS	information system
IT	information technology
JIT	just-in-time
KFB	Swedish Transport and Communications Research Board
KIT	corporate IT
KOT	coordination technology
KTK	Knowledge, Technology, and Culture [Research Programme]
MCSS	Manufacturing Customer Service System
MEST	SKF Electronic Message Transmission
MIS	Management Information System(s)
MPSS	Master Production Scheduling System
NEDS	New European Distribution Structure
NMFC	New Material Flow Concept
NTNU	Norwegian University of Science and Technology
NUTEK	Swedish National Board for Industrial and Technical Development

OCR	optical character recognition
OPEC	Organization of Petroleum Exporting Countries
OTC	over the counter
PFS	Product Forecasting System
PWC	PriceWaterhouseCoopers
R & D	research and development
RDC	remote data capture
RFC	Requests for Comments
SAM	Strategic Alignment Model
SCOT	social construction of technology
SCSS	Sales Company Service System
SData	Statoil Data
SDC	Single Distribution Centre
SMTP	Simple Mail Transfer Protocol
SSK	sociology of scientific knowledge
STS	science and technology studies
TU	Therapeutic Unit
WAN	wide area network

I

Introduction: From Control to Drift

CLAUDIO U. CIBORRA AND OLE HANSETH

An Alternative Perspective

The reader will find in this book a set of alternative views on the role and dynamics of global information infrastructures deployed within the corporate context of large multinationals. By alternative views we mean that the reader is presented with both empirical material and scholarly interpretations that diverge, at times substantially, from the current wisdom contained in the management and information-systems literature. Certainly, there has been a designed, intentional element in the way the book has been written; but there has also been an element of crafting interpretations and theoretical conclusions along the way, as the empirical evidence came pouring in from the field studies. Thus this book can be looked at as a research report, where the ideas and interpretations reflect the empirical evidence emerging from six case studies of large companies engaged in implementing complex information infrastructures (i.e. integrated sets of equipments, systems, applications, processes, and people dedicated to the processing and communication of information), but also as an (alternative) textbook that indicates and explains the important aspects of corporate infrastructure implementation and management. Ideas and frameworks stem from the authors' backgrounds and shared theoretical orientations, but also from what has been observed in the field. Alternative vistas and theories intermingle and provide a different, emerging profile of what an infrastructure is, and how it is implemented and managed. At the same time, our project was not conceived at its beginning as, nor can it be said to have ended up being, a 'critical view' of information infrastructure management. It was not the initial aim of the research project to unveil the management games that govern the deployment of infrastructures in large bureaucratic organizations or the assessment of the role played by technology in reinforcing existing power structures. Our research agenda was more to look closely at the prevailing business practices and the ideas driving them. We were intrigued to study the multiple ways in which managerial prescriptions coming from consulting and theoretical models in good currency were being followed and what outcomes they would deliver. In particular, we focused on the discrepancies between initial goals, visions, plans, and models, and the actual outcomes. What also attracted our attention was the range of initiatives taken by management, specialists, and users to cope with deviations and variance

The authors wish to thank Frank Land, Susan V. Scott, and Edgar A. Whitley for their suggestions.

in outcome, the ensuing organizational learning processes, and their quality and effectiveness. The cases, selected on an ad hoc, informal basis, were far from showing a common pattern of behaviour. But their emerging variety offered enough discrepancies and learning processes to provide a fertile ground for interpretations. Multiple, fruitful marriages have emerged between interpretations that had to leave the current management frameworks and the empirical evidence disclosed by our field interviews and observations. The sequence of cases and their outcomes is arranged to support a more general discourse on the dynamics of global infrastructures. Here, we want to share with our readers what we, and some of the managers who have accompanied us in our efforts, have learnt, and specifically what differs from the current literature. At the same time, we want to share those theories that selectively have helped us to make sense of the empirical evidence.

The result is a 'hybrid' book—hybrid, we think, in a good sense. Cases contain interpretations, but also pose questions and remain ultimately open-ended. Theories are used to revisit some of the key concepts of the management literature, such as globalization, strategic alignment, and the economics of infrastructure, leading to a quite different light being thrown on these topics. Thus, empirical evidence, interpretations, and theories overlap and mingle with each other, and leave room for further analysis and questioning.

The 'message' emanating from this composite content can be captured in a nutshell by stating that the complex process of 'wiring the corporation' cannot be understood, let alone managed, by applying approaches that were effective for mechanical organizations, and assembly-line type of technologies and processes. Information systems are often analysed and designed as highly decomposable; bureaucracies are also decomposed along hierarchical lines. Extant information infrastructures, we claim, are deployed within ramified webs of externalities and interdependencies. It is too simplistic to cut through such interdependencies with the old, industrial-age models shaped by the principle of functional, hierarchical decomposition, and the six cases seem to confirm that. As a consequence, while admitting that management and designers need and will continue to act and intervene in the practical world, we hesitate to provide them with (the illusion of) easy solutions, and deceivingly deployable agendas and recipes. Managerial action is management responsibility and rests on the seizing of the opportunities provided by upcoming business and technological circumstances. Our contribution consists in enriching the premises of managerial choice and action with stories, interpretations, and what we have found as the most useful theories to explain the dynamics of infrastructures coming from a variety of fields: from economics and complexity theory, to the social studies of science and technology.

Corporate information infrastructures are puzzles, or better collages, and so are the design and implementation processes that lead to their construction and operation. They are embedded in larger, contextual puzzles and collages. Interdependence, intricacy, and interweaving of people, systems, and processes are the culture bed of infrastructure. Patching, alignment of heterogeneous actors, and bricolage (make do) are the most frequent approaches we found in the company cases, irrespective of whether management was planning or strategy oriented, or inclined to react to contingencies.

Here we diverge most from the current management literature. In fact, the latter easily acknowledges that the state of infrastructures in many companies resembles a somewhat messy collage, as a result of deals, improvisations, and layers of sedimentation. But this is seen as a situation that should be abandoned in favour of a more integrated and controlled approach aimed at streamlining the infrastructure, fitting it into the corporate strategy, and extracting more value from it. Basically, collage is there, but it is bad, dysfunctional, and ought to be avoided. The value added by the management models and methods would consist precisely in moving infrastructure from a thrown-together institutional backbone to a value-generating, integrated set of technologies, applications, and processes. Substantial gains in productivity are promised, together with the general shared and legitimate concern for achieving an increasing level of control on a resource that is complex, expensive, long-lasting, and critical for running the business in the information society.

We agree that control is an overarching issue for business organizations. According to Beniger (1986) and Yates (1989), most technologies and organizational forms have had as their main objective the creation of more advanced control instruments—instruments that enable us to enhance and extend our control over processes in society and nature. Correspondingly, most of the management literature continues to provide models and tools to enhance and support control over business processes—production, distribution, marketing, sales, and so on.

But we submit that control is difficult to achieve. Nature, society, and the economy have always been unpredictable and uncontrollable. Although technology allows us to sharpen our governance capabilities, we seem to end up deploying technology to create a world that resists control (Postman 1992). This is what globalization is all about: not just extended transactions or higher cross-border investments. We experience governance in the age of globalization as more limited than ever. We are creating new global phenomena (global warming and greenhouse effects, nuclear threats, global production processes, and so on) that we are able to control only in part. Information infrastructures are important instruments for controlling global phenomena. But they share such an ambiguity. They are themselves difficult to control and, as such, they may curb our governance capabilities just as much as they enhance them.

The map contained in Fig. 1.1 portrays the 'vicious circle' that leads businesses from the tight, top-down control of the information infrastructure to the actual drift of the infrastructure itself. The 'formative context' (Ciborra and Lanzara 1994) within which this circle takes place, is centred around the credo of 'management *is* control'. Besides the turbulence of the environment and the business, implementation tactics, the power of the installed base, the difficulty of second-guessing the final user behaviour, and the sheer complexity of the new infrastructure are all factors that make for a different outcome: drift (see below). Individual and organizational limits to learning and the power of the pre-existing formative context make it very difficult for businesses to leave the vicious circle. On the contrary, they

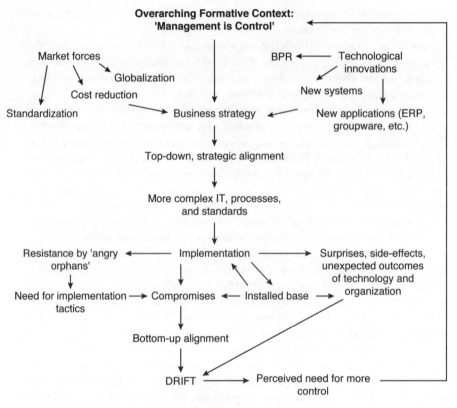

FIG. I.I. Mapping the dynamics of infrastucture

reinforce the perceived need for even more control: this never-ending need and its consequences seem to be the hidden engine of our modern world of business and technology, a runaway world (Giddens 1991).

Our storyline, then, unfolds in a different way, perhaps more troubling, but also more open-ended. Since we are successful in operating through more complex, global organizations and are able to learn new things by tapping larger amounts of information, the number of new opportunities emerging is getting larger and larger, and all our previous beliefs in planning and control processes and systems are becoming outdated at an increasing speed. The information infrastructure, being one of the backbones of such processes, is a true citizen of the runaway world. Hence it shares its main surprising aspects: it is open-ended and in part out of control. We capture these features by saying that infrastructures tend to 'drift', i.e. they deviate from their planned purpose for a variety of reasons often outside anyone's influence. The management literature privileges the ideal image of organizations as pyramids—the orderly, top-down process of strategic planning, the prescriptions on how to measure and control resources. Thus it reproduces within organizations the fundamental principles of a positivistic thinking that was making the industrial world turn for more than a century: the centrality of measure and control; technology as a powerful set of tools augmenting human action and thinking; the need to pull the messy everyday world towards an almost geometrical or mechanical view of the business organization, characterized by measurable and representable forces, linkages, and dynamics. Our cases and theories move forth from a different paradigm, which suggests that those very principles that were supposed to govern the emergence of the industrial society are even less applicable to the information society, without significantly changing those very principles. The terms may be the same, because one society gave birth to the other, one economy still feeds upon and is fed by the others. However, their deep meaning can diverge radically.

Consider, for example, the terms 'globalization' and 'strategic alignment'. The industrial view of globalization is certainly revolutionary, but also narrow: it focuses on the expanding markets, on the design of global products and global enterprise structures, cross-border investments, and technology transfer. In reality, it is a view that ends up being confined within one discipline or two: business policy and industrial economics. One needs to be global about the study of globalization too: where does globalization come from? What are the key points where global business gets linked to a global society? What is the dialectics between local moves and macro effects? What are its global implications? And so on. With the notion of a runaway world we put the globalization of business into a wider context, the one of modernity (Giddens 1991) in order better to understand its origins, dynamics, and ramifications.

A similar approach applies to the notion of strategic alignment. In an industrial vision the challenge is about how the top of the pyramid can plan and steer the large infrastructure at the bottom. In our vision alignment is a long, tortuous, and fragile process whereby multiple actors and resources try to influence each other to constitute a new socio-technical order. A number of forces, feedbacks, and self-reinforcing actions are at play. It is hard to be able to predict an outcome: an aligned infrastructure is a rare event that triggers an ad hoc explanation. Presenting it as the ideal goal to be reached through a supposedly 'best practice' is illusionary. It is a fragile equilibrium kept alive by the interlocking of multiple processes. Each one has to be accounted for in a highly circumstantial fashion. In sum, if the current management literature views the dynamics of the information infrastructure from the 'high grounds' of methods and control systems, we think that the companies we studied urge us to adopt a different paradigm, more attuned with the characteristics of modernity (not industrial modernity, but the more recent one caused by globalization—see further Part One, and especially Chapter 3) and at the same time more attentive to what happens in the organizational 'swamps'.

We intend to use the study of infrastructures *in situ* as an occasion for reflection and debate about how to make management models and methods in the information-systems field more attuned with new awareness of the implications of modernity. We leave the necessary development of new approaches and solutions to the practitioners themselves. With the materials collected here we want more modestly to enrich their reflection and learning when they (can) retreat from the action front. We will continue to be attentive observers, listeners, and diffusion agents of their discoveries.

Structure and Content

The research project itself moved back and forth between theory and empirical evidence, but we present the material in a sequence that places the theory first (Part One) followed by the cases (Part Two). We suggest that different audiences adopt distinct reading strategies when approaching this sequence. Thus, managers and consultants can go straight to the details of the cases for a preliminary check to ascertain whether the evidence collected in the cases is similar to theirs, or whether these are special situations. Then, since some of the interpretations we provide are rooted in theoretical premises that lie outside the conventional literature, practitioners should turn to the chapters contained in Part One. These will lead them from a critique of the existing literature to the socio-economic underpinnings of our interpretations. Students, and possibly academics, not fully familiar with the specific issue of corporate information infrastructure should follow the opposite approach. Specifically, Part One will make them acquainted with both the conventional definitions and models, and those economic and sociological issues not hosted by the mainstream literature. The chapters on globalization, economics of infrastructures, and actor-network theory also work as tutorials on these subjects and approaches that we, at the end of our study, repute as fundamental background to an understanding of the complexities of infrastructures in large corporations. At this point the readers will be prepared to penetrate the case studies and their various facets in a way that should be fruitful, at both an intellectual and a practical level.

Part One contains four chapters. Chapter 2 (by Ciborra) is dedicated to a focused review of the management literature, and expands some of the themes and references contained in this Introduction. It first presents and then discusses critically key concepts related to the main management concerns for the information infrastructure: strategic alignment, value and investment, learning, and change. The chapter pivots around two contrasting definitions of infrastructure: as a powerful tool or as an embedded collage of other infrastructures. These definitions accompany the reader in confronting the different treatments that the same issue—for example, strategic alignment—can receive. Since some of the cases examined here have also been objects of study in the current literature, the chapter contains a few remarks on the use of case studies for the progress of the field, in both business and academia. Certainly, the literature is full of tools enabling management to control the information infrastructure. Implicitly, it is assumed that, if management uses the new powerful tools 'properly', it will be in control. The chapter contains a preliminary discussion of a number of issues that invalidate such an assumption.

The next three chapters present theoretical approaches that indicate the different ways in which global information infrastructures are hard, if not impossible, to control. They set the stage for developing our understanding of infrastructure as an embedded and drifting institution.

In Chapter 3 Hanseth and Braa introduce the context of globalization. Departing from a narrow vision of globalization, they identify its social and technical drivers as the main features of modernity: the loosening-up of time–space constraints; the diffusion of systems that process information and knowledge; the increasing pace of learning by economic and social institutions. Globalization appears to be confined neither to the description of market transactions that cross nations and extend their linkages all over the globe; nor to the articulation of a firm's structures to encompass more territories and business. Globalization is not only about the architecture of transactions and the standardization of interfaces; it is a runaway process (Giddens 1991). Correspondingly, the corporate context should be looked at as a runaway learning organization: dynamic and unpredictable. This leads to the paradoxical image that looms large over the chapter, and the book as a whole: the main side effects of globalization will be higher risk and less control. Beck's (1992) notion of 'risk society' is important in this respect. The ubiquitous integration at the core of the ongoing modernization and globalization processes leads to an increasing importance of unintended side effects. All actions imply side effects. Higher integration implies that side effects 'travel' faster and longer. Their role widens. In Beck's (1992) terms, globalization means more than anything the globalization of side effects. Unintended side effects are unpredictable. This leads further to higher levels of unpredictability and risk: in general—to a risk society.

Chapter 4 (by Hanseth) introduces the economic analyses that back up the sociologist's views of globalization. Certainly, in the management literature discourses about value, investment, and productivity are paramount. They would suffice if the information infrastructure was just another piece of 'production equipment'. But is such an analogy correct? The study of large infrastructures suggests a quite different agenda: externalities; increasing returns and self-feeding mechanisms; battles of standards; and the paradoxes of the economics of information. It soon appears that, from a sound economic point of view too, control over an infrastructure can be only partial. The diffusion of an infrastructure has its own accelerations or slowdowns, in ways that are only indirectly correlated to the decisions made by the resource-owners: there are delays; there are unintended consequences; there are sudden oppositions; and there is an always imperfect attempt to align all the stakeholders. The interplay between the intervening factors is too complex and no model can capture the dynamics and their final outcome, which remain open and highly dependent upon local circumstances.

In Chapter 5 Monteiro further extends the analysis of the complex negotiation processes that surround the building and implementation of a corporate infrastructure. Specifically, he helps us understand why and how infrastructure, and technology in general, can 'act'. The previous chapters show how one important characteristic of infrastructure is to be 'recursive': it feeds upon existing infrastructures and represents the platform for further infrastructures. Infrastructure is always 'behaving' as an installed base and a platform. Actor-network theory (ANT) has recently been imported into the information-systems field as an interesting way to understand the influences and the 'actions' performed by technology. It is a way of looking at infrastructure that reduces the taken-for-granted asymmetry between 'management as an actor' and 'technology as a passive tool'. Such asymmetry, whereby management plan and decide while technology follows, proves to be unrealistic: indeed the irony is that all the talk about strategic alignment often leads to a mirror reality: technology (the installed base) 'pulls' the organization (Ciborra 1998). Actor-network theory has the advantage of restoring symmetry: it invites more creative analyses and interpretations of the dynamics of global infrastructures. The theory contains a set of specialized concepts, such as the ones of translation and inscription that can help us in specifying the ways by which infrastructure is managed, drifts in multiple directions, or even becomes an autonomous agent.

These three theories have distinct origins and have been developed to describe or explain different phenomena. However, they all point out important aspects of information infrastructures, and the challenges related to their development and governance. Actor-network theory can be looked at as a theory upon which Beck's and Giddens' ideas about modernization and globalization, as well as the economics of information, could be based. It can be used to describe in detail and in a consistent way how large heterogeneous networks are built through the ongoing modernization and globalization processes, and also how these networks can be interpreted as actors, as side effects propagate through the networks themselves, and new events—in their turn also having side effects—are triggered.

Network externalities can be looked at as nothing other than side effects, and self-reinforcing mechanisms are specific patterns of side effects. Large systems, like the Internet, show some of these features: they are built by many independent actors over time; given the very high number of actors who contribute to shape the network, changes are unpredictable; side effects bubble up and these become new changes leading to further change (see also T. P. Hughes 1983).

Part Two consists of six company cases. They are specifically ordered to show the variety of approaches, from the first case, which reports on a way of managing an infrastructure that is closest to the paradigm of industrial modernity, up to the last, which portrays the business context of the runaway world.

Chapter 6, by Dahlbom, Hanseth, and Ljungberg, contains the case of SKF. SKF is a global production- and distribution-focused company, selling the same type of products all over the world. The chapter outlines the successful co-evolution of SKF and its infrastructure. It is shown how, over a period of twenty years, the Swedish company has relied on a strategy for building infrastructures focusing on standardization and stability, on inertia, and the cultivation of entrenched infrastructures. For example, in the 1970s it had already begun to secure its own communications infrastructure (based on the SNA protocol). In the 1980s it standardized its information systems into an integrated set of Common Systems. In the 1990s it introduced a process orientation in production and distribution. The infrastructure built over the decades allows SKF to run global forecasting and supply systems through a variety of corporate applications, message transfer systems, and satellite links. For example, the International Customer Service System, installed by 1981, provides a key global interface between the sales and manufacturing units. Other systems are dedicated to master production scheduling, manufacturing, and finance. What is striking is that SKF always seems to have focused on production, and has developed its infrastructure as a Management Information System for global production and control. Sometimes, ambitious applications, expected to provide very rich information on processes and products, have been abandoned in favour of more basic versions. SKF was born global, and, thanks to its hefty market share throughout the decades, has been able to grow gradually and build its infrastructure accordingly. On the other hand, its information systems do not strike the observer as sophisticated or state of the art. When SKF adheres to the infrastructure strategies in good currency, aligning business and infrastructure strategy, following a top-down, centrally controlled, approach, it does so by developing slowly, without radical breaks with its past. Still, at the end of the study a few questions emerged. How long will such a conservative approach be possible? Can SKF meet an increasingly global competition by simply making its production and distribution organization more efficient? Or is there finally a need for more radical changes?

The second case (Chapter 7 by Ciborra and Failla) is of a redesigned process, and the IT tools to support it, in IBM. Since the mid-1990s IBM has been formulating and deploying an extensive fabric of new processes and tools in order to be able to operate efficiently on a worldwide basis as a global company. One of the most important is customer relationship management (CRM). CRM consists of an array of processes that streamline all the activities between IBM and its customers across markets, product lines, and geographies. It affects many thousands of employees worldwide and it is based on a variety of existing and new systems and applications. CRM is supposed to be the backbone for the completion of any business transaction, from the early opportunity identification to the order fulfilment and customer satisfaction evaluation. The main components of CRM—processes, roles, and IT tools—represent the comprehensive infrastructure of the new, global IBM. Various organizational units and practices are dedicated to the strategic management and operational deployment of CRM. Backed by full top management support, its implementation had been going on for four years at the time of the study. From the initial top-down approach, management has shifted over this period to a more opportunistic attitude, trying gradually to fix the sources of resistance that emerged during the long deployment phase. The IT platform was slow in delivering the expected support because of the huge installed base of pre-existing applications. While the development from scratch of a totally new IT infrastructure is out of the question, new hope comes from commercial applications such as groupware and enterprise resource planning (ERP) systems.

In the following case (Chapter 8) Hanseth and Braa report on two main interlinked infrastructures at Norsk Hydro. This is a diversified Norwegian company, founded in 1905. Apart from its original fertilizer business, it produces light metals, oil, and gas. The business divisions have enjoyed a significant level of autonomy. The case reports on the management's efforts to introduce a standard infrastructure made up of multiple components: the Bridge. Standards are widely considered as the most basic features of information infrastructures—public as well as corporate. This view is expressed by a high-level IT manager who said: 'The infrastructure shall be 100 per cent standardized.' Separate standards should fit together—no redundancy and no inconsistency. The case illustrates that reality unfolds differently. The idea of the universal standard is an illusion, just like the treasure at the end of the rainbow. Information infrastructures are not a closed world defined by a closed standard. They should rather be seen as open networks—that is, as networks that are linked to other networks, which are again linked to other networks, almost indefinitely. Larger and more interconnected networks imply that effects—including unintended side effects—of events are propagating more quickly and across longer distances. This is leading to less predictability of actions outcomes, and, accordingly, the role of unintended side effects increases. This chapter will illustrate how the role of side effects has broadened as infrastructures in Norsk Hydro have been deployed. Through this process, the company's control over the infrastructures as well as the business processes they are supporting has decreased. The story of the implementation of an ERP package (SAP) in one of the main divisions shows how the trend towards higher complexity and uncontrollability gets reinforced.

Statoil is the State of Norway's oil firm founded in 1972. The case study in Chapter 9 by Monteiro and Hepsø discusses a six-year effort to develop a flexible Lotus Notes-based infrastructure facilitating the company's further evolution towards globalization of its business processes. The early adoption of Lotus Notes was due to mere chance. The period after the Gulf War and the ensuing recession in the oil industry triggered major reorganizations in Statoil to cut operational costs. Cost savings also affected IT, at the time seen as an expensive item. Lotus office automation software was chosen mainly for price reasons. The initial small-scale diffusion of Notes grew to the point of making Statoil one of the largest users of that group-ware application worldwide at the time. The case further shows that the establishment of a Notes-based infrastructure needs to be recognized as a broad, socio-technical mobilization process characterized by a high degree of improvisation and opportunism. This deviates significantly from more planning-oriented descriptions of how technology strategies are formed and implemented. Finally, the case study offers the opportunity to contrast the notions of strategic alignment (as portrayed by the mainstream management literature) and the 'bottom-up' alignment tactics described by using actor-network theory.

Chapter 10 reports on the experience at a dynamic pharmaceutical company described by Cordella and Simon. Astra Hässle is a relatively small (about 1,500 employees) research company belonging, at the time of the study, to the Swedish multinational Astra (since then, the company has merged with Zeneca, and is now called AstraZeneca). It was a newcomer in the pharmaceutical industry, but extremely successful, thanks to its leading drug for ulcers. The company was undergoing major BPR initiatives aimed at speeding up the product development process. IT was seen as a key component of such redesign. For example, a major project was launched aimed at reducing time during the clinical trial process. A new infrastructure comprising hand-held terminals and sophisticated networks supported remote data capture in 500 centres in twelve different countries. Though conceived and planned centrally, the project suffered from an ineffective initial analysis model that failed to represent all the facets of the remote data capture operations. Formally, all the projects were ongoing and successful; however, at the time of the study, deployment was characterized by a number of unplanned developments. Local circumstances during implementation seemed to influence the final use of applications, so that the global infrastructure model drifted. The study tries out an interpretation of this process based on the notion of technological and organizational inscriptions, borrowed from actor-network theory.

In Hoffmann-La Roche (henceforth referred to as Roche) two different infrastructures in Strategic Marketing were the objects of a study carried out by Ciborra (Chapter 11). During the 1980s, Strategic Marketing championed the establishment of the first corporate network. The purpose of the network and its applications, which went under the name of MedNet, was to support the new, centralized marketing function. After eight years of development, there was a very low level of acceptance of the main applications (consulting medical literature, accessing clinical trials data, office automation); the only exception was e-mail. The experience had also generated considerable frustration: 'we would never do it again, had we to start it today'. Some affiliates were even developing systems of their own, on separate platforms. Eventually MedNet was discontinued. Its negative aspects, especially the costs, dictated its end. However, it did survive as a network infrastructure: what was phased out was the application portfolio. From the ashes of MedNet a second infrastructure was built by Strategic Marketing composed of various web sites based on the Internet protocol. Here, the governance of infrastructure is totally different. With minimal coordination and direction, each therapeutic unit within Roche developed web sites for external (Internet) and internal (Intranet) communication. One striking feature of the sites is their interaction with constituencies outside the corporation. Thus, for some diseases, external constituencies such as associations, lobbies, doctors, even individual patients exert their voice and have a relatively high degree of horizontal communication on the Net. As a consequence, the network applications have many users, but their development and diffusion are runaway processes. No master plan was in sight at the time of the study.

Finally, in the Postface (Chapter 12) Dahlbom rejoins the themes of infrastructure and modern society, showing how the notion of infrastructure itself may be tied to an 'industrial' understanding of IT and organization, very much geared to the paradigmatic cases of railways, motorways, or water pipes. Is this a correct way of proceeding? Should we focus instead on the lighter dimension of IT, so that the underlying infrastructure of it all, if any, would be rather the web of human networking moves and acts? In a way, the author suggests that we should have a 'runaway conception' of infrastructure too, leaving the old one behind. By offering this provocative piece, which may even contradict some of the ideas presented in Part One, and which also finds the research team divided, the authors transfer the adventure of further questioning, interpretation, and reflection to the readers.

PART ONE

Theory

2

A Critical Review of the Literature on the Management of Corporate Information Infrastructure

Claudio U. Ciborra

The purpose of this chapter is to look at the basic ideas, models, and recipes that the current management literature recommends for the building, implementation, and management of information infrastructures within corporations. The literature stretches from the emerging area of 'global information systems'—the analysis and design of IT systems that support a global enterprise (Ives and Jarvenpaa 1991; Roche 1996; Peppard 1999)—up to the technical and consulting manuals dedicated to the management of corporate computer platforms. Despite such a large spectrum, the fields of global information systems and IT infrastructures are still in their infancy, and therefore offer a rather limited body of models, prescriptions, and case material that may be used as a reference to identify key concepts and approaches. On the whole, as we shall try to show, the literature lacks originality. It mostly consists of attempts to extend the current approaches and models in the information-systems (IS) field to the new idea of global information infrastructure. This review, then, offers an opportunity to present and criticize some of the principles, models, and recommendations that are already in good currency within the more established IS literature.

We divide the presentation and discussion into two main parts. First, we present a selection of key concepts and approaches. Secondly, we criticize the existing literature mainly from a methodological point of view. We believe that, for such an emerging discipline, it would be of little value to the reader and for the advancement of the discipline itself to engage in lengthy discussions about the fine detail of definitions. In any case, given the turbulence and innovativeness of the field, definitions and frameworks are going to change. Rather, this review offers an opportunity to criticize and deconstruct some general approaches to the study of the role of IT in organizations.

Key Concepts

What is an infrastructure? What are the main types of infrastructure? How is an infrastructure (or how should it be) linked to (global) business? And, more generally, how should its deployment and use be managed? These questions point to some of the fundamental concepts in the management literature.

Definition of infrastructure

What is a global information infrastructure? As we enter the new century this is a question that is receiving multiple and evolving answers. But we do not consider that this is a severe problem, since the field is relatively young.

Corporate infrastructure as a concept emerged in the 1980s in relation to the planning of large corporate information systems. It emphasized the standardization of systems and data throughout the corporation as a way to reconcile the centralized IS department and resources, on the one hand, and the distribution of systems and applications, on the other. More recent developments in networking focus on the aspects of infrastructure that deal with communication (of data, documents, and so on). Given the association of infrastructure deployment with Business Process Re-Engineering (BPR) projects, some authors also include in a broad definition of infrastructure those chains or sequences of processes that are directly supported or enabled by the IT infrastructure. More generally, in relation to BPR, there can be an overlap between the 'systems and applications' infrastructure and the lighter 'process' or BPR infrastructure. Fig. 2.1 shows that there are cases that fall in the overlapping area (where the 'hard' infrastructure is present with the 'process' one), cases where infrastructure is not accompanied by any special redefinition of processes, and cases where the new processes are the existing infrastructure, while the tools to support the processes are still being developed. In the area of overlap, some authors introduce the concept of 'inscription': the execution of a certain business process gets 'inscribed', frozen into, the infrastructure (see Chapter 5).

Typical representations of infrastructures may be pyramidal, as the one provided by Weill and Broadbent (1998),[1] or multilayered, as suggested by Hanseth (see Chapter 4). Weill and Broadbent point out the following main layers:

- IT components;
- human IT infrastructure (people, skills, etc.);
- shared IT services;
- shared applications.

The diagrams provided by Hanseth have a different emphasis. They are derived from the 'layering' of different technologies, as discussed in the software field (think, for example, of the ISO model of communications standards): no pyramid is envisaged here. But the differences are not just in the ways of representation.

---

[1] We will draw many ideas and definitions from this recent book. We do this for two main reasons. First, we follow Thomas Davenport's advice, according to which, 'This book contains most of what the world needs to know about this critical topic.' Secondly, the models, principles, and normative prescriptions contained in the book are based on an extensive set of empirical material, both qualitative and quantitative, and a long list of scientific publications, including award-winning ones.

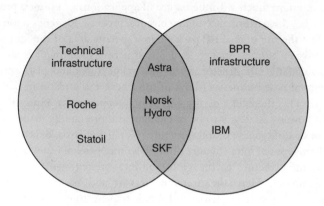

FIG. 2.1. Technical and process infrastructures: how the cases qualify

They are more profound. There is another perspective, which is very much at the core of this book.

The managerial definition echoes in form and substance the traditional definition of Management Information Systems (MIS) (see Davis and Olson 1985). The pyramidal view suggests that the contours of infrastructures are fairly well delineated (it is possible to argue about *where* to draw the boundaries, but not to question the fact that they *can* be drawn). Infrastructure components may be difficult to evaluate, but their services are not: so it is possible to price them—for example, by looking at how much the market values them. Finally, the infrastructure can become a firm's capability if management is able to deploy it in a way that is unique and strategic for the firm.

In the second part of this chapter, by contrast, we examine an alternative definition, which puts an emphasis on the openness, multilayering, and inertia of infrastructures.

Relationships with the business

The boundaries and organization of an infrastructure, and specifically the services it can provide, are set by defining the value of variables such as *reach* and *scope*. Reach is the number of activities or processes actually touched by the infrastructure, while scope refers to the type and variety of applications running on it (that is, the range of processes being partially or totally automated through the infrastructure) (Keen 1991). Depending upon these two variables, and especially the strategic intent of the firm, infrastructure can play different roles: *utility, dependence, and enabling* (Weill *et al.* 1996). In the first role, infrastructure is a utility aimed at reducing the costs of processing and communicating information throughout the organization. Here, the emphasis is on achieving economies of scale. A utility architecture maximizes efficiency in processing and transmission but does not necessarily interfere much with the nature of applications or business processes. In the second case, the performance of key business processes depends upon the infrastructure, like the use of an ERP package in a specific area of the business. Here, the link between business strategy and infrastructure investment is apparent and conscious. Enabling infrastructures provide architectures and platforms for new applications and new businesses (think of the Internet as a platform for electronic commerce). 'The flexibility of the infrastructure permits a number of as-yet-unspecified business strategies to be implemented more rapidly than in firms with a dependent or utility view of infrastructure' (Weill and Broadbent 1998: 101).

These three types of infrastructure point to a more general issue: how to link the information infrastructure to the global business strategy—that is, the issue of strategic alignment. Here the literature is vast and has various origins and ramifications (see e.g. Henderson and Venkatraman 1993; Earl 1996; Peppard 1999).

Peppard provides a summary scheme of the major interdependencies between infrastructure and strategy when addressing specifically the issue of globalization. The scheme highlights in a new 'diamond diagram' four interconnected bubbles: global business strategy, global business model, global business drivers, and global information strategy. Despite the variations among different authors, the basic idea of strategic alignment still dominates the theme of the relationship with the business. 'It is sensible and desirable for management to focus on aligning the information technology portfolio with the business strategy' (Weill and Broadbent 1998: 40). Strategic alignment was originally defined as concerning the inherently *dynamic fit* between external and internal domains of the firm—such as product/market, strategy, administrative structures, and business processes—with IT (Henderson and Venkatraman 1993). Economic performance, it is argued, can be enhanced by finding the *right fit* between external positioning and internal arrangements.[2]

IT infrastructure as an investment portfolio

Information technology includes a firm's total investment in computing and communication technology. Within this encompassing investment different components can be distinguished according to the hierarchical view of information systems, applications, and technologies. The IT portfolio of a firm represents such an investment in people, machines, and services, in whatever way they are

---

[2] Among the results of the MIT research programme 'Management in the 1990s', a framework was set out, whereby information technology (IT) was regarded as a variable linked with others such as strategy, organization, and culture in a so-called diamond diagram (Scott Morton 1991). Strategic alignment inherits that representation. In 1993 a special issue of the *IBM Systems Journal* featured a series of articles on the concept of 'strategic alignment', including the leading article by Henderson and Venkatraman (1993). Another paper, by Broadbent and Weill (1993), reported on an empirical study on strategic alignment in the Australian banking industry. The aim of that study was to identify organizational practices that contribute to alignment. The authors present a model of strategic alignment based on fifteen propositions, concluding that enhancing business and information strategy alignment will remain a key challenge in the future.

employed or outsourced. Weill and Broadbent (1998) suggest the following major classifications of the IT portfolio:

- infrastructure: the largest component of systems and applications, which are reliable, shared, and usually centrally managed;
- transactional systems dedicated to the processing of the routine transactions of the firm;
- informational technologies to support or automate the main management and control functions;
- strategic applications aimed at gaining competitive advantage.

Each class of technology contributes in varying degrees to generate value and has a cost component (the infrastructure being the major cost item). The authors recommend that, in order to use IT adequately, an IT investment portfolio should be managed in the same way as a portfolio of financial investments. 'Individuals make different decisions about personal investments based on their commitments, aspirations, experiences, values and attitudes to risk. Managers make decisions about information technology investments based on a cluster of factors, including capabilities required now and in the future, the role of technology in the industry, the level of investment, etc.' (Weill and Broadbent 1998: 24). The largest component of the IT portfolio is the infrastructure, which involves investments that are large, shared, and have a long planning horizon. In general, the composition of the portfolio must be driven by the objective of increasing shareholder value and by demands of business strategy. The latter requires a constant alignment of the portfolio with the business strategy. The IT portfolio needs to be managed in the same way as financial portfolios, balancing risk and return for each selected strategic objective. Analytic tools like the Balance Scorecard (Kaplan and Norton 1993) can help to identify indicators for high-risk, longer-term returns (customer satisfaction; new-products generation) with safer, shorter-term, or lagging indicators (return on investment; cost-cutting applications): 'A balanced scorecard approach encourages a firm to change the balance in good times and bad, just like bull and bear markets for financial investment . . . as with personal investment portfolios . . . a little needs to be invested with a longer-term perspective' (Weill and Broadbent 1998: 33).

How to deploy and manage an infrastructure

Managing an infrastructure to deliver effective IT capability means dealing with problems such as: aligning strategy with IT architecture and key business processes information requirements (Luftman 1996); universal use and access of IT resources; standardization; interoperability of systems and applications through protocols and gateways; flexibility, resilience, and security. Ideally, the infrastructure reconciles local variety and proliferation of applications and uses of IT with centralized planning and control over IT resources and business processes.

A typical management (and consulting) agenda concerning the creation and governance of a corporate infrastructure would entail the following activities:

- analysis of the firm's strategic context so as to elicit the key business drivers;
- a joint consideration for the need to improve or transform existing business processes and infrastructures (various combinations are possible in the sequence and significance of the change in both areas);
- formulation and implementation of a relevant BPR and technical change plans;
- envisioning the related changes in roles, responsibilities, incentives, skills, and organizational structures required by BPR and infrastructure reforms.

Again, by way of example, and not being able to survey all the normative suggestions and prescriptions that the management literature provides, we report here only on a typical approach to implement strategic alignment and, more generally, develop an infrastructure: the 'management-by-maxim approach', presented by Weill and Broadbent (1998). Quoting the authority of Aristotle, the authors see in maxims (a 'practical course of conduct to be chosen') a means to express strategy in a way that is actionable and that can be coordinated centrally. In a given company, management has to focus on both firm-wide maxims and IT maxims in order to capture the essence of both in an interdependent way.

Examples of the former are statements such as 'relentless cost reduction' and 'continuous innovation'; examples of the latter are 'data must be accessible through common systems', 'to develop a firm-wide infrastructure', and so on. The point of translating strategies, or IT portfolio choices, into maxims is to articulate complex propositions in phrases that can be easily 'understood and communicated'. Senior management are recommended to pay ongoing attention to the fact that IT maxims are in line with business maxims, and that at all times the business maxims reflect the strategic positioning of the firm, or what changes are required.

There exists, however, another way to build corporate infrastructures: the 'management-by-deals' approach (Weill and Broadbent 1998). The deal-making stems from a variety of factors and business circumstances, such as the will to satisfy short-term needs, or being servant to the more powerful groups in the organization: 'the deal-making process is the free market of information technology infrastructure formation', the same authors suggest (ibid. 159). This means, at best, an uneven establishment of the infrastructure. The management-by-deals approach seems to be frequent: it is present in about 50 per cent of cases. According to the authors, however, by 'dealing' one can hope to achieve only certain types of infrastructure, ranging from 'none' to 'dependent'. An 'enabling' infrastructure can hardly be the outcome of fragmented deals.

Shifting from a management by deals to management by maxims depends ultimately upon senior management's consideration of the way business and technology strategies should be integrated. Leadership, supported by a due attention to governance, is the essential ingredient to achieve the results of the management-by-maxims approach—that is, to gain the most out of the IT investment portfolio and develop an infrastructure according to the current strategic intent and vision. In this respect, Weill and Broadbent (1998: 250) claim that, by adhering to their Ten Leadership Principles, it is possible to gain up to 40 per cent premium for the same level of investment. These principles capture in a nutshell what the management literature prescribes for the optimal governance of an IT infrastructure, for example:

- to manage the IT infrastructure in the same way that a financial portfolio is handled, continuously changing the mix between risky and less risky investments, trying to maximize returns; this principle obviously requires a centralization of the supervision of the overall IT investment in the firm;
- to achieve strategic alignment by the strategic maxims approach;
- to agree on business value indicators and responsibilities;
- to learn from the mistakes made during implementation and to keep the process of evaluation transparent, so that the memory is not lost of what has been achieved and what has not and of which are the successful best practices;
- to pay attention to the dynamics of information politics: 'Appreciating the dynamics of information politics is essential when planning the development of IT infrastructure capabilities, as destructive behaviours can make the investment not worth the effort' (Weill and Broadbent 1998: 252).

Let us now turn to a more critical analysis of the principles and recommendations contained in the management literature. This will provide an opportunity to deepen and extend our review, but also to begin to show some of its limitations and contradictions. This exercise should enable the reader to appreciate better the scope and content of the case studies presented in Part Two of this volume, and indicate the validity of a more interpretative (that is, less immediately concerned with modelling and prescriptions) approach to studying the dynamics of global corporate infrastructures.

Problematic Issues

Empirical studies, and insightful thinking related to the actual management of infrastructures, point out some problematic aspects of the management agenda just presented. For example, empirical findings suggest that, the more firms undergo change, the higher the need for investment in infrastructure. One may ask, however, are there decreasing returns to infrastructure (Cordella and Simon 1997)? Does more investment mean more sophisticated infrastructure or does it just mean facing maintenance and adaptation costs of an existing, rigid infrastructure? Relatedly, is it better to have a highly flexible infrastructure that enables the firm to seize a wide range of future, unplanned business redesign options, or a highly consistent (that is, aligned) infrastructure with the current strategic intent? Thus, should one aim for alignment, as repeatedly suggested by the literature, or for flexibility? Extensive review of top managers' opinions does not seem to lead to any clear-cut conclusions (Duncan 1995; Peppard 1999).

Certainly, the cases in this volume add more empirical evidence to the fact that the issue of how to design and especially implement an infrastructure is much less clear-cut than the management literature wants us to believe. Our cases show that, for one reason or another, management by deals is a far more common approach than other authors suggest, and that at least in one case (Roche) the opposite is true—that is, the abandonment of a top-down, strategic alignment approach has been the precondition for the take-off of a corporate infrastructure. It is not intended here to compare contrasting empirical results—a comparison that to date would be bound to be inconclusive—but to enquire whether certain basic definitions, assumptions, and research approaches typical of the current management literature might bias the data collected and the ensuing models and normative prescriptions. To wit, enquiring how infrastructure has been studied may offer an opportunity to reflect upon the basic tenets of undertaking (managerial) research on IT use issues (Dahlbom 1996).

Contrasting definitions

We have seen above that the definition of infrastructure given in the management literature is non-problematic. There might be doubts related to where one draws the boundaries (at the applications level or at the business processes level?), or arising from the confusing technical terminology that sometimes refers to platforms, architectures, or simply systems and networks (Peppard 1999). But the relative 'straightforwardness' of the definition can be welcomed only if one confines oneself to a purely managerial perspective. As soon as one looks towards other disciplines interested in the study of infrastructure, the definitions change, and so do their implications for research and normative prescriptions. Consider, for instance, an alternative definition that comes from the domain of science studies (Star and Ruhleder 1996). The authors characterize the information infrastructure by maintaining that it is 'fundamentally and always a relation', and that infrastructures in general tend typically to emerge with the following dimensions (see also Chapter 4).

- *Embeddedness*. Infrastructure is sunk into, or is inside, other structures, social arrangements, and technologies.
- *Transparency*. Infrastructure is transparent in use, in the sense that it does not have to be reinvented each time or assembled for each task, but invisibly support those tasks.
- *Reach or scope*. This may be either spatial or temporal: infrastructure has reach beyond a single event or one-site practice.
- *Learned as part of membership*. That artefacts and organizational arrangements are taken for granted is a *sine qua non* of membership in a community of practice. Strangers and outsiders encounter infrastructure as a target object to be learned about. New participants acquire a naturalized familiarity with its objects as they become members.
- *Links with conventions of practice*. Infrastructure both shapes and is shaped by the conventions of a community of practice—as, for example, the way that cycles of day–night work are affected by and affect electrical power rates and needs.
- *Embodiment of standards*. Modified by scope and often by conflicting conventions, infrastructure takes on transparency by plugging into other infrastructures and tools in a standardized fashion.

- *Built on an installed base.* Infrastructure does not grow *de novo*; it wrestles with the 'inertia of the installed base' and inherits strengths and limitations from that base.
- *Visible upon breakdown.* The normally invisible quality of working infrastructure becomes visible when it breaks.

The bundle of these dimensions forms 'an infrastructure, which is without absolute boundary on a priori definition' (Star and Ruhleder 1996: 113).

In contrast with the one seen previously, the definition stresses the heterogeneous character of infrastructures as expressed by the notions of embeddedness as well as its socio-technical nature by being linked to conventions of practice. These aspects also mean that, although information infrastructures are enabling and generic, they are not completely independent of their use. Certainly, the notion of service put forward by the management literature also captures the dimension of use, but in a different light. When service is well defined, it becomes a commodity on a market for services and has a price. Instead, Star and Ruhleder (1996) look at infrastructures as 'institutions', norms, and conventions that provide the 'often implicit' context, for the performance of practices.

In Chapter 4 Hanseth points out that information infrastructures are larger and more complex systems, involving significant numbers of independent actors as developers as well as users. Further, information infrastructures grow and develop over a long period of time, new parts are added to what is already available, and extant parts are replaced by improved ones. An information infrastructure is built through extensions and improvements of what exists—never from scratch. It is open in the sense that any development project, independently of how big it is, will just cover part of an infrastructure. The rest is there already and will be developed by others who are out of reach of the project and its control. What is developed by a defined, specialized activity will have to be hooked into an existing infrastructure. Eventually, what exists has significant influence on the design of the new. Certainly, the focus on infrastructures as open systems raises some questions. Are the boundaries between open and closed systems absolute and predetermined in some sense? Is the crucial role played by the installed base a unique feature of infrastructure and systemic technologies or is it a more general one? Focusing on information infrastructures as an open installed base (see again Chapter 4) means that such infrastructures are never developed from scratch: they *always already exist*. If so, when and how can an information infrastructure be built, acquired, or dropped at all?

As mentioned at the beginning, there is no point in ranking these two alternative definitions. However, maybe a deeper lesson can be learned by pointing out the difference in the perspectives, beyond their provenance from the managerial and the science studies literatures. Our empirical evidence casts a vote in favour of the latter. We submit that, despite being more open-ended and less structured, it addresses some issues and puzzles that the other leaves unexplained. And, perhaps more importantly, the definitions point to alternative perspectives in approaching empirical research, handling qualitative evidence, and coming up with normative indications. We now turn to these issues, which also explain the philosophy underlying our empirical research.

The case-studies approach: two styles of rhetoric and interpretation

It may be not by chance that Weill and Broadbent (1998) refer twice to Aristotle's *Treatise on Rhetoric*. In fact, the way they use short case studies to argue for selected ideas, principles, and prescriptions on what are their main views on infrastructure—how management should lead the effort to build a corporate infrastructure aligned with the business strategy, and so on—owes much to the art of rhetoric. Their qualitative cases are snapshots to persuade the reader about the realism of the statement, model, or advice contained in the text. Certainly, there is no point in requiring a quantitative survey to settle the matter. It would be too pristine at this point for the scarce knowledge we have of the phenomenon. We want neither to engage in the debate about the rivalry between qualitative and quantitative research methods, nor to feel guilty about the superiority of quantitative hypothesis testing, representativeness, and statistical generalizability. These are all positivist concerns relevant in the IS field, especially in the USA, which sometimes unduly distract European researchers. Still, the gathering and use of qualitative data can lend themselves to different styles of presentation. Without getting into the nitty-gritty of how to carry out case-study research in organizations (Yin 1994), it is useful in this context to contrast the two styles of qualitative research in the area of infrastructure. Of course it would make little sense to compare the eighty (qualitative) cases mentioned in Weill and Broadbent's book with the bare six contained in this volume. Looking at the sheer size of the sample would indicate to the reader which study should be trusted. But such a conclusion would be misplaced for a number of reasons. First, we are not given enough 'evidence' to evaluate the nature, depth, and scope of Weill and Broadbent's company cases. We are provided only with short synopses, which tell a striking story or convey a telling message on how a certain infrastructure issue was dealt with in a corporate context. Still, there are oddities in the way some of these stories are reported or not told at all. We were struck in particular by two stories that refer to companies that also figure in our very limited sample: IBM and Hoffmann la Roche (see Chapters 7 and 11). In Weill and Broadbent's book (1998: 197), Roche is mentioned briefly in relation to a knowledge-management application in R & D, presented as an undisputed, inspiring success. However, the sources mentioned are second-hand, coming from the business press and from a manager who had since left the firm. It turns out that the story is somewhat more complicated and the outcome of those KM and CSCW projects is much more open, as already reported elsewhere (Ciborra 1996*a*). Moreover, Roche is such a complex and varied company, and the infrastructure initiatives are so many and disparate, as to warrant a thorough, attentive analysis. The Roche case study in this volume, for example, offers to the reader a first glimpse on the evolution of the infrastructure deployment in just one tiny section of the corporation: Strategic Marketing. The lessons to be learned are exciting, but a full coverage of the Roche infrastructure dynamics would require one or more books in itself. Instead, one snapshot of a project—discontinued at the time of writing (and in any case one that was never based on IT, but rather on paper support)—is presented to the reader to demonstrate (or, better, to argue in a rhetorical fashion) that such a knowledge-management programme is 'still thriving and delivering benefits', indicating a successful way for harnessing the information infrastructure to enable knowledge management. It may be persuasive, but it is not accurate.

Secondly, part of the infrastructure study carried out by Weill and Broadbent over a number of years has been funded by the IBM Consulting Group (see p. xi in their book). We are not told whether IBM is included among their sample of eighty companies: it does not seem so from reading the anonymous company vignettes dispersed in the book. In comparison to what happened to our research . group, this looks strange: we also enjoyed the generous funding of IBM (this time through the Italian IBM Foundation), in our case aimed at studying IBM's current gigantic efforts to provide itself with an infrastructure geared to its key business processes. In this volume the case of one of these major processes is reported, the Customer Relationship Management (CRM) (see Chapter 7). The reader will have the opportunity to appreciate the maze of initiatives, projects, moves, advances, and setbacks that the implementation of CRM has created, and the finale is not yet written after more than five years of progress. Why, then, does IBM, with its achievements and problems in building a new worldwide infrastructure to support a new global enterprise model, seem to have eluded the authors of the 'best book on the subject'? Certainly, access should not have been a problem.

These remarks are put forward not to trigger a polemic, but to underline the divergence from tradition in the case studies the reader is going to find in Part Two. It is impossible to escape some kind of rhetoric when writing such a text, but we trust this is a different one. Our cases seldom point to solutions: rhetoric is aimed at talking the reader into a relentless effort of interpretation, appreciation, and questioning. Our cases are *interpretative*, in the sense that they are 'aimed at producing an understanding of the context of the information system, and the process whereby the information system influences and is influenced by its context' (Walsham 1993: 4–5). Thus, despite our cases being close to 'quick and dirty ethnographies' (Hughes *et al.* 1993), we still want to provide enough context to put any infrastructure initiative into perspective, and thus create a 'clearing' for readers to make their own judgement next to ours. We agree with Walsham when he puts forward the idea that the best prescriptions for an implementation strategy follow from a thorough diagnosis of the organizational setting in which the infrastructure is going to be used. The context and the longitudinal analysis contained in the case studies of this volume move in such a direction. The methodological approach, as in Walsham's book, focuses on the exploration of the 'multilevel context' of interesting, complex infrastructures, and the processes of technical, organizational, and economic change within which the infrastructure is a key element.

The role of empirical evidence in the case of strategic alignment

There is another methodological issue separating our research on and interpretations of infrastructure from those contained in the literature. Our research is not just a matter of contrasting gathered empirical material supporting different styles of rhetoric to attract the (limited level of) attention of the management audience. It deals, more fundamentally, with the status of the abstractions—that is, the models, the principles in both their descriptive and their normative functions—one so frequently finds in the management literature in general, and in the infrastructure literature in particular, and how they are related to what happens on the terrain. There is no better way to show this difference at work than by looking at the genesis and use of the notion of strategic alignment (Bloomfield *et al.* 1997; Sauer and Burn 1997).

We have seen above that in the 1990s the various research programmes on strategic alignment claimed to be able to draw a much-needed connecting line between strategy and IT planning and solutions.

Despite the attractiveness of the idea of strategic alignment, the managerial literature warns us today that it 'will be always difficult to achieve'. Indeed, the models of strategic alignment, the agendas that spell out what to do in order to extract the maximum IT capability from corporate infrastructure and the empirical studies of how corporate infrastructures are developed and used in practice, all seem to include some caveats. Typically, researchers and management authors make the following suggestions:

- Aligning business and technology strategies is an ongoing executive responsibility: 'strategic alignment is a journey, not an event'.
- Managers must be ready to learn and adapt, no matter what the alignment pattern selected at one point in time.
- There are expression barriers that prevent the clear articulation of the strategic intent of the firm, and thus hamper the effort for an explicit strategic alignment.
- Other barriers are due to political, cultural, or economic factors impeding the smooth implementation of any strategic plan concerning infrastructure (Luftman 1996).

Certainly, at the end of the 1990s the 'classic' scholars of strategic alignment suggest that the two-way link between business and IT strategies is 'an old question', since the term alignment describes a static equilibrium. They agree that what is needed is an innovative approach to design effective new business platforms (Venkatraman and Henderson 1999). Before adopting their newer, 'multi-vector' model, it may be worthwhile taking some time to reflect on why the concept of strategic alignment was, after all, static and limited. Without such a reflection, the risk is to jump on yet another bandwagon, only to realize the limits of the new fad when it is too late.

Thus, in a more reflective and interpretative spirit, let us consider a couple of issues that have been accompanying the frenzy of research and consulting activity on strategic alignment, and that researchers are eminently responsible for having carefully avoided in the recent past:

- IT strategic plans have been around for years, and their link with the business strategy should have brought, however indirectly, some form of alignment. Often they have not, so there must have been a problem all along related to the difficulty or impossibility of alignment.
- Many cases of successful Strategic Information Systems seem to show that tinkering, not conscious alignment, was behind successfully aligned IT applications (Ciborra 1994).

Think for a moment. Alignment, as a conceptual bridge, urges us to reflect on the true nature of the foundations on which it lies: management strategy and technology. The researchers of the original theory took these concepts for granted. Perhaps that research programme is judged 'old' after ten years, because those very concepts should not have been taken for granted, but rather as problematic (see Ciborra 1997). For example, ethnographic research about groupware technology in large multinationals hints at the facts

- that leadership is often missing, and
- that technology is often drifting, as if out of control (Ciborra 1996*a*).

How come researchers privilege the geometry of the ideal lines connecting abstract concepts in a model, but remain blind to the blurred reality of connections that any, even 'light' ethnographic study would present them?

Here we encounter the general problem of management research regarding the relationship between management models (and their geometric representations, with lines and boxes) and everyday phenomena, which concern people at work.

What happens when we link the boxes of strategy, organization, and IT on the famous 'diamond diagram'? It changes our view of the interdependencies between some key business variables. We obtain a new 'geometrical' representation that materializes the idea of 'alignment' in front of our eyes. Thanks to such a representation, management scholars can raise the awareness of practitioners simply by showing them the diagram, as a reminder of what should be the new map with which to venture into the world of business and IT.

But how do these (newly traced) geometrical lines translate into a new management performance? Awareness and espoused theories may not be enough to learn new behaviour (Argyris and Schön 1996) (see below). Indeed, despite the research discoveries and their translation into new management models, the news from the field has constantly been that alignment is not easy to implement, awareness does not suffice, and the two main poles of alignment, strategy and technology, are actually drifting apart for one reason or another. The aim of our interpretative approach is precisely to get closer to the 'of course', the obvious dismissal of the intricacies of 'real life' that 'naturally' cannot be captured by a model, to that 'business savvy' to which the caveats implicitly make reference. It is this long journey towards the sources of obviousness that gradually makes our perspective on infrastructure very different from the one contained in the management literature.

For us, a representation like the one of strategic alignment that does not work provokes a breakdown. From an interpretative perspective, this breakdown offers an opportunity to encounter the world, possibly with different eyes (Dreyfus 1994). Indeed, the grey world of organizations, always there with its pasted-up sets of arrangements, people, machines, which are not aligned according to the models, reminds us of the following: when focusing on the geometrical representations of business variables and interdependencies we tend to grant them essence and existence. It is an ideal, perfect world to which the 'real' world has to conform. According to the conventional wisdom, thanks to a careful and rigorous method researchers can discover the 'objective' world, and then extract the relevant models. Once they have learnt them in the literature and executive courses, managers are supposed to steer the world towards the models.

We argue, instead, that operating in this way may be a source of deadlock and ineffectiveness, and even crisis in the IS field (Ciborra 1998). Look more closely at what happens when we follow the line of argument and reasoning in the management literature: the messy world that we encounter daily, already there, largely outside our control and that we know by pre-scientific evidence and intuition, provides us with the raw materials for our abstract representations. We intentionally take such raw materials, we sanitize them, elicit (through some measurement method) a limited number of connections, and build models by fitting empirical data. However sophisticated, the models remain a de-worlded image of the organization. They are granted essence and existence in the domain of abstractions. Outside that domain they are not 'indexed' by the same degree of reality as the 'world-out-there'. Thus, for example, we can understand the very notion of alignment only thanks to our (tacit) knowledge of the messy corporate world. But the reverse relationship does not hold: from the notion of alignment we cannot reconstruct, let alone intervene in, the everyday world of business.

The world-out-there is the precondition for our understanding of the models and methods, and thus the latter presuppose it, while the former is far from being presupposed by them (Husserl 1970). It is our pre-scientific understanding of and participation in organizations that give to the notion of alignment its existence as an abstraction in our discourses and representations about the world. This is precisely the scope of the alternative definition of infrastructure given above.

We should regard the geometrical models as a superstructure world, as outcomes of an idealization process. But in order to manipulate the raw materials of what has been idealized, we need to go back to the foundations of the superstructure: the lifeworld and the immediate evidence of our lived experience. (A similar urge to value the 'non-logical processes' of the mind engaged in everyday affairs was also expressed in the management literature by C. I. Barnard as early as 1936.)

If we pay attention to the evidence provided by recent cases of automation and work organization, we conclude that in the world-out-there alignment does not obtain because *strategy* is not such a clear concept or practice, because, owing to turbulent and unpredictable circumstances, managers are busy in muddling through, betting, and tinkering (Mintzberg 1980). Furthermore, the use of the *tech-*

nology itself is characterized by improvisations of various sorts (Ciborra 1996*a*; Orlikowski 1996*b*) and by many unexpected outcomes (see Chapter 10).

We are now in the position to explain the trajectory of the formerly promising research programme on strategic alignment. Those researchers made multiple abstractions out of the muddling-through and drifting. They idealized tinkering and called it strategy; idealized technology as a controllable set of means and called it IT; granted to these concepts existence and essence, transformed them into boxes and traced a line between them. Then, they started the difficult journey back to the real world, and found difficulties in measuring 'the strength of the line' or formulating prescriptions that would be followed by practitioners when walking along the line on the field of practice. They provided more and more sophisticated representations of alignment, as more analytical and detailed maps for the actors to 'measure' the real world (see, for example, the Appendix on 'checking your level of alignment' contained in Weill and Broadbent 1998: 257–9). To no avail: the higher conceptual detail remained confined to the world of idealized abstractions. But, we submit, it has only a limited impact on the lifeworlds of business and organizations.

Consider now the alternative path. We stick to basic evidence, and encounter the world as it presents itself in our everyday experience. We rely on evidence, intuition, and empathy. We listen to practitioners and participate in their dealings with puzzles and riddles, and we do not confer any particular relevance to words such as 'strategy', 'processes', or 'data'. In this way, by suspending our belief in the models of management science, we approach the everyday life of the manager, made up of frustrations, accomplishments, confusion, joy, and desperation. We can be discouraged: all this is too close to the world we live in! Can we come up with any sense of this blurred reality and address some of the issues raised so far?

Certainly, if we listen to the everyday conversations of practitioners, we hear the familiar terms of strategy, product/markets, and even alignment of systems and administrative structures. These practitioners can be interviewed on such topics, and some of their statements even lead to empirical measurements on a Lickert scale. But, beyond their espoused views, we can observe phenomena such as: plans that keep being diverted, surprises that arise constantly, opportunistic adjustments that must be carried out on the spur of the moment. Planning may be espoused, but circumstances may compel managers to improvise (Ciborra 1999*a*). This is the organizational, 'primordial soup of anonymous practices and events' (De Certeau 1984), in which every well-running infrastructure will float, as the second definition of infrastructure here provided tries to suggest.

Infrastructure implementation is punctuated by unexpected outcomes and side effects, turns that require frequent adaptations if not reinventions of the initial solution (Rice and Rogers 1980; Bikson 1996; see also Chapter 3). We have called this phenomenon 'technology drifting' (Ciborra 1996*a*).

At this point, we can do what management science suggests—that is 'to realize' these 'surprises in implementation' as exceptions, build an ideal world of 'how things should be', and try to operate so that the messy reality in which practitioners act moves towards this idealized model (where surprises are absent or under control). Alternatively, we can *suspend belief* on what we think we know about strategy, structure, markets, feedback mechanisms, and so on, and reflect upon what we observe. If we stick to this second approach, we encounter the structure of business phenomena that may enrich our geometric notion of alignment and infrastructure deployment, such as care, hospitality, and cultivation.

Care

Henderson and Venkatraman (1993) note that seeking the fit between strategy and the other main business variables is a dynamic exercise. Our research shows that the driving force behind alignment in action, as opposed to the one on paper, is a great amount of caring performed by the various actors involved in the design, implementation, and use of IT infrastructures. What is striking is that there is nothing special in this caring: it is just familiarity, intimacy, and continuous commitment, from the initial needs analysis through the construction of the infrastructure, training the users, introducing the systems and applications into practice, modifying them as new practice emerges, and so on. Care itself has a 'structure' linked to how we are-in-the-world, articulated in perception, circumspection, and understanding processes (see Ciborra 1996a).

Hospitality

What calls us to align technology? First, the general need to cope with and understand the world. Secondly, alignment presupposes acceptance and hosting. To wit, previous empirical research has shown that technology can be both fragile and ambiguous (Grudin 1988; Ciborra 1999b). Fragility derives from the ubiquitous presence of substitutes at the automated workplace, usually tools that are better 'understood'. Often, new applications—compared to those that already exist— appear to be incongruous, an obstacle in the workflow. They require circumspection and to be worked at (or 'work-arounds') in order to be embedded in the workflow and to deliver their potential. They require an extra, subtle effort of acceptance. Secondly, because today's infrastructures enable multiple uses, and since shifting in the practices of coping, use, and reinvention occurs continuously, they often lead to surprising outcomes. Thus, a groupware system designed to enhance transparency and knowledge sharing can instead raise fears among users of being a 'Panopticon' for centralized control (Zuboff 1987). Technology is in a state of flux in organizations, and it is highly ambiguous. Acceptance has to face ambiguity: coping, thus, becomes hospitality. In its turn, hospitality is an unstable way of coping with the stranger: it can suddenly turn into hostility. Behind the technocratic idea of planning and alignment, the phenomena from the field make us encounter one of the oldest arts of mankind: hosting a stranger.

Certainly, if the technology were totally 'disambiguated', univocal in producing its effects and impacts, hosting would consist of straightforward adaptation and alignment. The latter is precisely the picture of the world of implementation as portrayed by both the structured methodologies and the management literature: systems are objects, infrastructure is a well delimited pyramid, knowledge is data, work is business process, and people are emotionless decision-makers who have to align their preferences and adjust to the changes rationally planned for them. It is the world of business re-engineering models, where designers, consultants, and managers juggle around boxes and arrows to come up with solutions that optimize pre-selected performance criteria. The intricacies and uncertainties of ambiguity, hospitality, and hostility are ruled out from such a world of abstract organizations, but equally ruled out is the 'organizingness' of everyday business life (that is, the essence of the experience of operating in an organization), or, better, what Walsham (1993) calls the multilayered context in which infrastructures are embedded. It is precisely such 'organizingness' and rich context that help infrastructures become integrated in the workflow, 'aligned', and 'understood'. Unfortunately 'organizingness' cannot be represented geometrically: it is made by real-world participants from their experiences of coping and caring, of being there amidst ambiguity and intimacy, and of sporting hospitality as well as tamed hostility towards what the new and the unknown disclose.

Cultivation

The intricacies of the relationship between strategy and technology, hidden by the deceptively clear management-science concepts, can also be captured by the notion of 'cultivation'. Itami and Numagami (1992) see cultivation as the dynamic interaction between current strategy and *future* technology—a process by which technology is accumulated (often in unplanned ways) with a much greater future potential than is necessary to meet current needs. For example, Toyota's lean product system was the outcome of technology investments made out of necessity to cope with short-term problems, such as small production runs for small market volumes. But, in retrospect, those investments helped Toyota's later strategy to become an internationally competitive manufacturer.

To wit, cultivation is based on frequent misalignment and misfit: the technology being accumulated is greater, or different in its potential, from current internal and external needs. The ensuing paradoxical prescription for the firm is to overextend: cultivation is about destabilizing current strategy and 'creating imbalances' with the current level of technology. One example is a strategy of coexistence of multiple projects in different stages of technological evolution as opportunities to create new knowledge (Clark and Fujimoto 1991): the resulting tension, misfit, and coping will stimulate learning and possibly the building-up of new solutions.

For Dahlbom and Janlert (1996), cultivation is a way of shaping technology that is fundamentally different from rational planning and constructing a technical system. While constructing and aligning are about selecting and putting together objects (systems) to form a coherent system, cultivation is about interference with and support for a material that is in itself dynamic and possesses its own logic of growth, like helping a wound to heal.

Besides evoking misfits, breakdowns, and resistance, as the stuff which 'alignment-in-action is made of', the concept of cultivation invites us to reconsider the role played by the object of alignment—technology.

Technology tends to drift when put to use. Thus, the idea emerges of technology with a certain degree of autonomy and inner dynamics; of technology both as a drifting system and as an organism to be cultivated (see Chapter 5).

The traditional conception of technology, which originated with Aristotle (Hood 1983), is that technology is a human development or arrangement of tools, machines, materials, and methods to serve the attainment of human purposes. In other words, technology is a 'passive' and neutral set of means to achieve some ends. This perspective lies implicitly at the core of most management and economic literature in good currency.

As a logical system (a set of beliefs about cause–effect relationships (Thompson 1967)), technology possesses its own tendency towards perfection and systematization. On the other hand, recall the definition of infrastructure given by the science studies scholars (Star and Ruhleder 1996):

- it operates through standardization and extension of linkages;
- it is sunk into other social arrangements, institutions, or technologies;
- it is invisible and transparent in supporting the execution of tasks;
- it is embedded in a set of conventions of practice;
- it is an installed base: infrastructure does not grow *de novo*; it wrestles with the inertia of the installed base and inherits strengths and limitations from that base.

A closer look at the *internal* dynamics of IT infrastructure would show that:

- many actors are involved in its establishment or development, so that it cannot be controlled by only one actor;
- the issue of standards becomes paramount; battles of standards involve the setting-up and management of complex coalitions of actors and technologies (David 1987);
- history, path dependency, unique events punctuate the development of infrastructure and have an irreversible influence on its configuration at any given moment.

Such phenomena can be observed, for example, when looking at the dynamics of the 'installed base' (see Chapter 4). As a consequence, a totally new idea about what alignment is can emerge: it is an alliance between humans and non-humans, where non-humans (the architectures, the operating systems, the standards) seem to have a say as important as the humans (Latour 1999). Specifically, alignment would correspond to the successful translation of the interests of one actor into the behaviour of another actor, within a complex network of actors and intermediaries (Callon 1991; see also Chapters 5 and 9).

The idea of the information-technology portfolio

We have seen above the close parallel instituted by the recent management literature between an ordinary financial portfolio, even an individual one, and the corporate IT portfolio. The new definition of infrastructure, in particular its installed-base dimension (see Chapter 4), suggests a different scenario. The portfolio analogy invites the idea that the assets involved are easy to acquire or to dispose of, according to the evolving strategic goals, and the necessity of constant fine-tuning of IT strategic alignment. The governance of IT would, then, resemble a 'holding organization' (Williamson 1975), exiting and entering businesses according to their respective returns. The current corporate landscape offers, however, a more complex picture than the one of a frictionless investment environment. There are signs of this 'holding-organization' approach in managing an infrastructure portfolio—for example, in the process of outsourcing IT services. But the very 'politics' of outsourcing (Willcocks and Lacity 1997) also shows that some outsourcing decisions are much more complicated than expected, have to be reversed, and in some cases lead to failure. In one word, externalizing IT does not prove to be as smooth as promised: after all, assets are *not* easily transferable. There are transaction costs. The analogy with a personal portfolio, composed of stocks, obligations, cash, and so on, assumes a context with very low—at the limit zero—switching costs. Consider again the IT portfolio, and in particular its main infrastructural component. Look at infrastructure-in-use as a set of *shared* resources, where *synergy* is paramount, and consider its aspect of sunk and sticky investment (the installed base). These assets have all the characteristics of idiosyncratic, transaction-specific investments that generate switching costs. Hence, the holding organization model cannot be applied in this case where transaction costs are high. The litigations that often punctuate outsourcing decisions and the other phenomena of slow-moving infrastructures, or even infrastructures impeding business redesign exercises because of their stickiness and lock-in effects (see the IBM case, Chapter 7), seem to confirm the latter perspective. The portfolio idea gives management the illusion of being able to plan and decide how to pick or drop the more revenue-generating applications or systems. But this freedom is simply not there. There are constraints, instead, or actions performed by the technology itself (see Chapter 5), that limit severely such easiness to revise investment initiatives on an ongoing basis. Switching costs may dictate that management accepts compromises and lives with a suboptimal infrastructure, being allowed to modify its components only incrementally and slowly. Existing infrastructures are far from being liquid assets. This does not rule out different possibilities for the future (see Chapter 12). Indeed, an infrastructure could be treated in the same way as a personal investment portfolio, if its components, standards, and applications could be easily (with low transaction costs) dropped, as one can get rid of falling stock to increase the value of a portfolio. But such a scenario would hardly justify the need for books or case studies on infrastructure management. It would be Legoland: components of an infrastructure could be rejected or added on swiftly as building blocks equipped with standardized interfaces. The invisible hand of the market would be the main governance mechanism needed for the 'management' of such a modular infrastructure. And, above all, there would be no need to represent an infrastructure in a hierarchical way.

But at the time of writing companies are struggling with a very different problem: complexities in outsourcing, and the panic and huge investments to avoid the problem of the year 2000, testify that the corporate world is far from operating in such a Legoland infrastructure environment. They are living in a world where infrastructure tends to be a *non-separable* technology: replacing, modifying, or splitting it involves high switching costs and sticky assets. Effective governance must deal with these issues (Shapiro and Varian 1999). The cases in this volume bring further evidence of how attempts at governance are made in action: they all seem to be distant from the portfolio approach. In the only case where a whole infrastructure was dropped (actually its upper, more volatile applications layers), it took eight years to make this decision, given the symbolic as well as the material investments that had been made in it by managers and systems developers (see the Roche case, Chapter 11).

Last, but not least, the IT investment portfolio idea does not seem to capture one key aspect of infrastructure: its being above all a 'relation' (recall our second definition). A fundamental economic dimension of 'infrastructure as relation' is to be able to enjoy the positive feedback effects of the economics of networks, as opposed to the economies of scale (Shapiro and Varian 1999). A successful infrastructure is able to 'tip' the user community (and the market) in its favour, by exploiting the fact that the value of connecting to and using the infrastructure depends on the number of the extant user base. As a consequence, the value of the IT portfolio depends upon demand-side economies of scale—in other words, on the size and dynamics of the virtual network of users. The value of the IT portfolio depends, then, upon a factor that lies outside the 'pyramid' of high- or low-risk items that compose the information infrastructure: the networking of users and the positive externalities it may bring.

From knowledge to action

While the management agendas are very effective in guiding the *formulation* of an infrastructure plan, they do not give any special advice on the *implementation* and adaptation side. They provide only wise words of caution: the business world out there is complex, varied, and changing; any of the models on which the management agenda is based should be used with a grain of salt, and so on.

However, these obvious caveats and words of caution may make the management agenda largely irrelevant for action, since it does not deal with the key transition between having a nice vision and producing that vision (Argyris and Schön 1996). Management agendas are obvious, sound, and look pragmatic. In reality, they are deceivingly persuasive. They are not actionable, first, because they are highly simplified and based on sweeping generalizations and abstractions (such as 'strategy', 'utility', 'infrastructure') as discussed in the previous sections, and, secondly, because they do not take into account the counter-productive effects of self-defensive routines in organizations pointed out by the organizational learning literature. Let us look at the latter point in more detail.

Introducing a new infrastructure, or—as the advocates of strategic alignment proclaim—the design and implementation of new business platforms (Venkatraman and Henderson 1999), implies the management of broad and sweeping changes across the organization (see, for example, the IBM case study, Chapter 7). What course of action should management follow? As Fig. 2.2 suggests, it depends

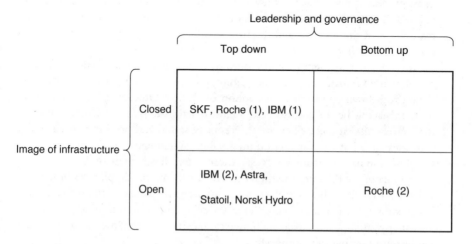

FIG. 2.2. Approaches to infrastructure governance

upon the match between the scope of the infrastructure *definition* (a closed, controllable system versus an open and embedded network) and the style of management *intervention* (top-down, control oriented versus tactics or deals or 'releasement' oriented). The strategic, top-down approach works when the infrastructure can be planned and controlled in all its main features. In the cases reported in this volume, only SKF conforms to this approach. The infrastructure of the Swedish multinational could be developed according to the control model given the particular circumstances of a firm that was enjoying stability, growth, and market dominance over time, while its products were not subject to radical innovations. The result is a uniform, but rather 'old' infrastructure that serves the business well (good alignment), but with a question mark: how long will it last? Will the extant infrastructure adapt to the dramatic changes that might affect the industry in the future, or will it prove to be too rigid?

All the other cases in the figure are characterized by ineffective or effective ways of dealing with large, amorphous infrastructures. In particular, the attempts made by Astra, IBM (in an earlier phase of CRM deployment), and Roche (in a first phase with their corporate network, MedNet), are biased towards the idea that infra-structure can be designed and implemented top down in a controlled way. All such attempts backfired, led to more or less explicit failures, and were subsequently abandoned, in favour of various ad hoc tactics, if not the complete releasement of central control, as in the Roche case (second phase), in order to foster the devel-opment of the Internet and Intranet platforms (see Chapter 11).

Thus, the cases in this volume point to the fact that, while, at the start of their infrastructure projects, the firms studied would split in a fifty–fifty percentage, in a similar fashion to that reported by Weill and Broadbent (1998), over time manage-ment by deals emerged as the prevailing approach in all but one. And, as already pointed out, the conservative success of SKF may be due more to the special cir-cumstances of the industry and the firm that has dominated it for decades, rather than to the validity of the top-down approach itself.

Now, the management literature portrays all this as a matter of will. If top man-agement and IT management *favour* a joint, comprehensive view of infrastructure, then a top-down approach is the option of choice. Otherwise, management by deals appears to be the second-best, almost default, alternative: 'Good infrastruc-tures rarely just emerge. They are the result of sound and proactive management processes aimed at maximizing business value' (Weill and Broadbent 1998: 173). Our longitudinal case studies suggest a more deterministic view of the matter. It is the very nature of the infrastructure, captured by the more complex definition pro-vided by science studies (see above), that dictates the failure of the management-by-maxims approach, and favours a variety of ad hoc, partial moves. Conversely, almost any attempt to manage a complex infrastructure top down is voted to fail. Let us see a number of reasons why.

Separation between formulation and implementation.   The management-by-maxims approach is just the latest form of strategy model that focuses on getting the 'right' strategic formula (here concerning infrastructure and its links to the business), by identifying the abstract characteristics of the context and the technology. As Mintzberg (1980) has suggested in general, and Ciborra (1994) in the case of Strategic Information Systems, it is dangerous to assume a divide between formu-lation and implementation, in the sense that what may appear valid and seductive on paper cannot be achieved during implementation. Strategy should not be looked at as an analytical document to be handed over to the organization in order to be executed. Strategy is what emerges from the actual implementation process, which may be characterized by deviations, surprises, and conflicts. No initial 'ana-lytical formula' will be able to address beforehand all such events occurring during implementation. Only special circumstances—long planning horizon, continuous care, and relative immunity from market or technology pressures—can guarantee enough leeway for the detailed implementation of a plan into its concrete realiza-tion. Today, most firms operate in a much more volatile and unpredictable con-text to be able to ensure such an orderly implementation process. Furthermore, the very nature of the infrastructure itself, given its ramifications, internal dynamics, and almost boundary-less character, is a relevant source of unpredictability, side effects, and surprises (see Chapter 3), as most of our cases show with due detail.

Espoused theory versus theory in use.   Our cases also suggest something more fundamental that connotes all the management agendas provided so far in the area of IS and infrastructure management. Such approaches are formulated in forms of 'advice' to senior and IT management. They list all the governance aspects to be considered, from the strategic issues up to the information politics. They then point to implementation approaches, such as 'start with low profile, transactional applications', 'set up user committees', and so on. What our cases show is that senior and IT management are well aware of these 'leadership principles' in one form or another, but adhering to these principles does not imply success or the avoidance of having to 'muddle through'. One of the main reasons for such a deviation is that the advice given and followed concerns only the espoused, expressed theories and visions that actors claim will orient their actions, not those theories that actually lead action (theories-in-use) (Argyris and Schön 1996). So, in some of the cases it emerges that the vision might be one of user-led development, while the practice is of centralization. Or, the new organization might put a premium on teamwork, but the technology inscribes a centralization of the data flows. Or, processes and the tools that support them are launched to streamline the company, but their accompanying procedures are extremely bureaucratic (that is, new red tape). And so on. The result is that the management literature may indeed convey all that 'the world needs to know' about infrastructures and their deployment, but this knowledge is not directly *actionable*—that is, the advice does not prevent it shifting, or being biased by the extant circumstances, when it is put into practice. And the more infrastructure is 'embedded', the more the web of local and global circumstances will have an impact on the implementation of any advice, no matter how sound it may be.

Single-loop learning.   The managerial literature urges senior management to learn from experience, too. One of Weill and Broadbent's (1998) leadership principles is to make a systematic evaluation of infrastructure projects in the spirit of organizational learning for future design and implementation efforts, taking care to avoid any witch hunt. However, we submit that there might be a mismatch between the learning requirements of an infrastructure project and those advocated by the literature. The latter are inspired by the governing values of single-loop learning: be in (unilateral and top-down) control, be rational, win (over resisting forces), and do not lose. The implementation advice also is consistent with such governing values: start with 'easing-in' approaches, plan to avoid information politics so as to preempt destructive behaviour during implementation, and so on. Our cases report instances where these approaches have proved to be lacking, leading to situations characterized by the very same features that they were supposed to eliminate. We submit that, to the extent that infrastructure projects may require a deep change in the way of running business, easing-in approaches may have a short lifespan; also that information politics might flourish in new, unexpected ways, and so on. It is not so much a matter of finding new 'leadership principles' as of revising the very governing values that mould the articulation of those principles and ensuing practices. Roche, in its deployment of the Internet and Intranet, offers an example where such governing principles were deeply revised (in particular the principles of unilateral, central control). But this instance of double-loop learning (Argyris and Schön 1996) is still rare, and in any case difficult, and costly to achieve. The management literature is not helpful in this respect. On the contrary, it muddies the waters by reinforcing the illusion that extant management values and single-loop learning can govern the deployment of large, only partially predictable infrastructures.

Separation between management politics and the politics of non-human components. Another reason why the leadership principles and ensuing advice of the current literature may prove of only modest impact is the implicit, but fatal, assumption it makes about the nature of the infrastructure and technology in general. In its basically closed, pyramidal view of organizations and infrastructures, technology is a tool that has to be planned for and constructed. On the other (separate) side of the fence there is the managerial information and resources politics to be addressed. We submit instead that the take-off of an infrastructure is due to the 'alignment' of a complex, varying alliance between human and non-human components (see Chapter 5). At each point in time and for any organization one can identify competing complexes of people and technologies. Infrastructure as an installed base is a powerful actor in itself, driven by its own logic, seeking allies and fighting battles in order to survive (see the Norsk Hydro case, Chapter 8). The 'angry orphans' created by the new standards are most probably its first allies. Given the embeddedness of the infrastructure (highlighted by our second definition), separating a priori human actors and non-human tools creates difficulties in understanding and intervening in the implementation of infrastructure. Black-boxing an infrastructure into a pyramid hides the multiple, tortuous processes, interventions, and side effects that punctuate the process by which those diagrams can be painfully drawn. A well-run infrastructure is the outcome of a successful alliance between human and non-human actors. In most of the cases we have studied such an alliance is emerging, temporarily, and often steered, to the dismay of the strategic-alignment advocates, by non-human actors (for example, the expanding and inertial installed base).

A more 'symmetrical' approach to the whole issue (see Latour 1999) would lead us away from the naive assumptions and 'cowboy-like' managerial models based on the unilateral control strategies of humans over non-humans, plagued by uncontrollable surprises.

Conclusion: The Control Idea

Our critical review so far has pointed to the fact that the literature on infrastructure is moulded by the basic tenets of management literature in general, one of which is the *centrality of control*. Although it is acknowledged that today's firms operate in fast-moving, global, and volatile business environments, when it comes to dealing with large IT assets that have a long life, investment must be managed 'judiciously'. Infrastructures that are 'undermanaged' can become a liability instead of an asset. 'The thousands of small information-technology investment decisions that are made every day in a large corporation are even harder to manage and co-ordinate. But if they aren't co-ordinated and managed, information technology can become a barrier, not an enabler' (Weill and Broadbent 1998: 10). Given its increasing size, information technology as corporate infrastructure runs the risk of being 'undermanaged'. Hence, the need seriously to rethink IT investments, and the way a firm manages and governs them. But along which lines should such a rethinking unfold? In the management-infrastructure literature the answer is quite clear: along a line of *increased control* (see Peppard 1999). For example, in the diagnostic questionnaire put forward by Weill and Broadbent (1998) to check the level of alignment between business strategy and infrastructure, and hence the level of urgency required for top-management intervention, seven out of the ten items are related to some form of control over IT resources, or the policies relevant to their deployment. Earl (1996) and Peppard (1999), on the other hand, suggest alternative ways of combining different strategies for the decentralization and centralization of control over IT resources. Their aim is to devise rules setting out the parameters and mechanisms for deciding how to divide activities, resources, and responsibilities between the centre and the peripheral units of the organization. In sum, what gets proposed as an effective means to manage these new degrees of complexity is a 'more elaborated control structure', such as 'an organizational body which will oversee changes and additions to the suprastructure [the set of infrastructure as well the policies and mechanisms for its governance] addressing any disputes which may emerge: a meta-decision making forum' (Peppard 1999: 89). Eventually, a single-loop learning approach will 'seal' the process of managing the infrastructure: learning about mistakes and deviations will be governed by principles that confirm and further sustain the idea of control.

We believe, instead, that our cases show that the control approach does not always work, and, surprisingly, works only if it is radically denied. Hence, the need to explore alternatives, challenging the very idea that the main risk for infrastructure, given its size and complexity, is undermanagement, and that the default alternative can only be ad hoc deals and a fragmented platform. What if size and complexity make the single-loop control approach impractical and ineffective, giving only the illusion of governance, for something that cannot be fully controlled? What if the infinite shifts and deviations of infrastructure are sources of innovations in use that may contain seeds for new, strategic ways of running the business (Ciborra 1994), and learning new things about a complex we do not know much about? What if our power to bring to life sophisticated and evolving infrastructures must be associated with the acceptance of the idea that we are bound to lose control? And that any attempt to regain top-down control will backfire, lead to further centrifugal drifts, and eventually impede our making sense and learning about how to effectively take care of the infrastructure? Instead of worrying about under-management, and trying to regain control through approaches that prove from the outset to be too simplified, why not play with the idea of a different partition between the limited scope for our management of the infrastructure and the scope for the infrastructure itself to manage us?

3

Globalization and 'Risk Society'

OLE HANSETH AND KRISTIN BRAA

Globalization is widely acknowledged to be an important contemporary phenomenon. Globalization and technology are mutually reinforcing drivers of change. The role of IT as a key factor to bring about this change is often thought of as an opportunity to enhance control and coordination, while opening access to new global markets and businesses (Ives and Jarvenpaa 1991). Bartlett and Ghoshal (1998) claim that firms operating in these global markets will be at a serious strategic disadvantage if they are unable firmly to control their worldwide operations and manage them in a globally coordinated manner. According to their model, corporations are focusing on closer coordination of increasingly more complex and global processes. At the same time, we are aware that all globalization is creating an increasingly changeable, dynamic, and unpredictable world. These issues are in contradiction. Models for tight control and coordination presume stability. Such models require the different elements in the processes to be coordinated—the cogwheels in the machine—to be known and well specified. In a global system they need to be standardized. As the complexity of the 'machine' grows, the more time it takes to change it. And a global 'machine' made up of standardized components requires stability.

The companies studied in this volume are all struggling with this contradiction. They are all trying to implement more powerful control structures and improve global coordination while it seems as if their ability actually to control their business processes is decreasing.

In this chapter we look into this contradiction. We discuss models proposed for managing global organizations. These models are presented in the light of the more general management models proposed during the 1990s. We focus in particular on the issue of *control* in global organization: the issue of whether firms can control their worldwide operations, whether IT infrastructures can facilitate such control, and whether IT infrastructures themselves can be controlled. We look into these issues by following the thinking of Anthony Giddens and Ulrich Beck.

Organizational Models and Business Strategies

General organizational models and strategies

Organizational change in the modern era means increased rationalization, as described by Max Weber. This means seeing organizations as machines, and then making new and improved organizations like bigger and better machines. Better here means leaner and faster—that is, more efficient and productive. Weber described this process as bureacratization, seeing bureaucracies as ideal models of rational organizations.

Bureacratization has taken many forms: vertical integration, the multi-divisional organization, and so on. This evolution of organizational forms can be looked at as the result of the development of more powerful control systems, to harness complex processes in nature and society (Beniger 1986; Yates 1989).

More recent approaches to organizational change, like Business Process Re-engineering (BPR), are in perfect line with this development. The basic idea behind BPR is that, by designing organizations and IT solutions at the same time, one can engineer organizations that are radically more efficient and powerful than existing ones (Hammer and Champy 1993). The same is true for models like 'just-in-time' and 'lean production' (Womack *et al.* 1991). The basic assumptions underlying these organizational models are that increased productivity and a more efficient organization are obtained not just by redesigning the processes going on inside one organization, but rather by redesigning the processes going on inside and across all organizations as a whole. Through tight integration and just-in-time delivery of all components, the need for storage of components disappears, the need for employees involved in the management of the stock of components is reduced, and investing capital in these components and their warehouses is unnecessary. The idea behind these models is also closely related to Michael Porter's proposal of focusing on the 'value chain'. All these strategies are strategies for increased integration within, but first of all between, organizations.

Since about 1980, however, organizational models that are not just proposals for how to change organizations by making bigger and better machines have been put forward. These are models stressing the need for increased *flexibility*. Many of these models have been developed as a response to problems experienced by US corporations in the 1980s. These problems were to a large extent seen as being caused by increased competition, from Japanese corporations ('the yellow peril') in particular. But they were also seen as caused by *global* competition in general. The responses were designed partly to learn from and copy the organizational models implemented in Japanese corporations, partly to develop models better suited for the new focus on competition in general. These two different starting positions led to the same result: more flexible organizational forms. Looking at the successful Japanese organizations, it emerged that their ability to catch up with US companies so fast could to a large extent be explained by their flexible, network-like organizational structures, which enabled a focus on learning and flexibility, leading to a rapid improvement of performance. Looking at the new global competition, it was clear that more rapid and continuous improvements of products and services were required, which led to more flexible and learning-focused organizational structures. These new models were presented in books with fancy titles such as *In Search of Excellence* (Peters and Waterman 1982), *Thriving on Chaos* (Peters 1989), *and Liberation Management: Necessary Disorganization for the Nanosecond Nineties* (Peters 1992). In the more research-focused literature, various forms of network organizations were proposed and analysed (see e.g. Itami 1988; Powell 1990).

Other models tried to combine the traditional modernization strategies in terms of mass production and specialization (Boyton *et al.* 1993), on the one hand, and flexibility and customization, on the other. Examples of such models are found behind the slogan-like concepts 'flexible specialization' (Piore and Sabel 1984) and 'mass customization' (Davis 1982).

When globalization is emerging as an important challenge, we see that issue of control is reframed. However, none of the models seems to have found a new 'silver bullet' to solve the 'control problem' in a globalized world.

Strategies for managing global organizations

In the managerial literature, the global business strategy models of Bartlett and Ghoshal (1998) are widely referred to. They tie business strategy to a set of organizational forces faced by the corporation.

They identify four strategies among which a multinational corporation may choose. In the process of becoming increasingly global, firms are supposed to follow a sequential path through these strategies: from multinational to international, to global, and finally to transnational.

The company pursuing a *multinational strategy* operates its foreign subsidiaries nearly autonomously or in a loose federation so as quickly to sense and respond to diverse local needs and national opportunities. Under this model the value chains are duplicated across countries, and the local units have a strong degree of autonomy. The resulting configuration of distributed resources and delegated responsibilities is described as decentralized federation. The requirement for local responsiveness is the driving organizational force. This was the classic organizational pattern adopted by companies expanding in the pre-war period. The multinational organization is defined by a decentralized federation of assets and responsibilities, a management process defined by simple financial control systems overlaid on informal personal coordination, and a dominant strategic mentality that views the company's worldwide operations as a portfolio of national businesses.

The company pursuing an *international strategy* exploits parent company knowledge through worldwide diffusion and adaptation. Rapid deployment of innovation is the prime operating principle. This organizational structure became predominant in the early post-war decades. The key task for companies that internationalized then was to transfer knowledge and expertise to overseas environments that were less advanced in technology or market development. The structural configuration is described as coordinated federation. The subsidiaries are then dependent on the centre for the transfer of knowledge and information. The parent company makes greater use of formal systems and controls in the headquarters–subsidiary connection than in the multinational company.

The company pursuing a *global strategy* closely coordinates worldwide activities through central control from headquarters gaining benefit from a standard product design, global scale manufacturing, and centralized control of worldwide operations. In this strategy, the firm is based on a centralization of assets, resources, and responsibilities. The decisions are still decentralized but controlled by the headquarters and organized to achieve global efficiencies. Here, the new strategy is characterized by increasing geographic scope for integration of activities and policies. The national subsidiaries have little independence, and the global managers have less understanding of local environmental differences. The dominant management perspective is that the world could, and should, be treated as a single integrated market in which similarities are more important than differences.

All these models and strategies focus on integration and control. Each strategy (except the first) tries to go one step further along these dimensions than the previous one. These three models are also based on the assumption that increased globalization means increased homogenization in the sense that the same products can be sold everywhere. Local needs are disappearing.

Despite their very different starting point, Bartlett and Ghoshal's thesis was that companies in the 1980s and 1990s tended to converge towards a common configuration because of the complex environment, technological change, and creation of large integrated markets. The organizational solution was to move towards what they call the *transnational model*. This model tries to combine the needs for integration and control, on the one hand, and flexibility and sensitivity towards local needs, on the other.

The firm following a transnational strategy coordinates a number of national operations in a way that preserves its ability to respond to national interests and preferences. National subsidiaries are viewed, not only as implementers of centrally developed strategies, but also as sources of ideas, skills, capabilities, and knowledge that can benefit the company as a whole. Under this network organizational structure, top managers are responsible for coordinating the development of strategic objectives and operating policies, logistics between operating divisions, and the flow of information among divisions. During the 1980s, global competition forced global firms to become more responsive nationally. In the following decade, according to Konsynski and Karimi (1993), these firms faced a growing need for worldwide coordination and integration of activities upstream in the value chain, and greater national differentiation and responsiveness downstream.

The new overarching principles would be dispersal of assets and resources to capitalize on local strength and minimize political risk. Other principles are specialization of tasks to achieve economies of scale when necessary, in addition to interdependence between organizational units to foster information sharing and organizational learning.

The firm pursuing a transnational strategy should adopt an organizational structure that facilitates the simultaneous achievement of three objectives: global
efficiency, national responsiveness, and the ability to develop and access knowledge
on a worldwide basis. It should seek to retain local flexibility while simultaneously
aiming at global integration and efficiencies as well as worldwide diffusion of innovations. Dynamic interdependence is the basis of a transnational company, one that
can think globally and act locally (Bartlett and Ghoshal 1998).

At the end of the decade, the transnational model of a corporation had become
the orthodox ambition to which an ideal organization should aspire to become
global. This model seems to follow the same trend of increasing control. At the
same time, this doctrine indicates moving one (or two—or may be even three)
steps 'backwards' in terms of flexibility and local responsiveness. The question then
is: is this possible? Turner and Henry (1994) found that, for most international
companies, the transnational model is an aspiration rather than a reality. They claim
that not all companies need the degree of cross-national interdependence posed by
the transnational model or possess the necessary skills to make it work. Where success in overseas markets is dependent upon the transfer of resources or expertise
from the home base and where the national culture, location, and administrative
heritage have produced an organizational culture that is conducive to integrating
diversity, then the transnational integrating mechanisms such as centres of excellence and international product teams are highly desirable. On the other hand, if
firms do not have a history of exposure to cross-border activities and their home
market is still dominant, then they will often find it easier to replicate systems and
recipes from their domestic market.

We will look deeper into the nature of globalization processes in order to get a
better grasp of the nature of the ongoing integration processes, what kind of
dynamics they generate, and to what extent increased control can be combined
with increased integration as well as increased flexibility—as the transnational
model presumes. We will do this on the basis of Giddens's and Beck's theories of
modernization and globalization.

A Broader View of Globalization

Giddens sees globalization as an inherent aspect and consequence of modernity.
Globalization, he says, causes 'the sense many of us have of being caught up in a
universe of events we do not fully understand, and which seems in larger part outside our control. To analyse how this has come to be the case . . . we have to look
at the nature of modernity itself' (Giddens 1991: 2–3).

Giddens identifies modernity as the modes of social life or organization that
emerged in Europe from about the seventeenth century onwards. Modernity has
been about the development of knowledge and technologies to enable more
efficient control of increasingly more complex processes (production, transport,
and so on)—an enhanced control over nature and social life, a process that Beniger
(1986) describes as the control revolution.

Giddens relates his way of seeing modernity with that of Marx, Durkheim, and Weber. These three authors saw, according to Giddens, modernity as capitalism (Marx), industrialism (Durkheim), and rationalization and bureaucratization (Weber) respectively. These are all parts of, or closely related to, the institutions of modernity, but, according to Giddens, modernity cannot be reduced to just one institution. He sees modernity as multidimensional on the institutional level, defining the institutions of modernity as capitalism, surveillance institutions, industrialism, and military power. But to get a proper grasp of modernity, we have to go beyond this level.

The essential dynamics of modernity

Giddens distinguishes between three dominant sources of the dynamism of modernity, each connected with the others.

The separation of time and space.   This is the condition of time–space distantiation of indefinite scope; it provides the means of precise temporal and spatial zoning.

The separation of time and space has in particular been possible through the invention of various technologies such as the clock, the standardization of time zones, calendars, and so on. These tools are absolutely essential to the coordination of activities across time and space. (See e.g. Yates 1989 on the importance of standardization of time (zones) and the invention of timetables for the development of railroad traffic.) Powerful 'tools' for coordination across time and space are preconditions for the rationalization of organizations and society (which modernity is all about, according to Weber) and the development of more powerful control technologies (Beniger 1986).

The development of disembedding mechanisms.   These mechanisms enable the 'lifting-out' of social activity from localized contexts and the reorganization of social relations across large time–space distances.

Giddens distinguishes between two disembedding mechanisms: symbolic tokens and expert systems. He does not give an explicit definition of symbolic tokens, he just presents a paradigm example: money. Other symbolic tokens we can think of are 'other forms of money'—stocks, bonds, funds, derivatives, futures, and so on. 'Symbolic tokens' can also be interpreted as various forms of *formalized information*. As notes and coins are disappearing, money can be seen as just one form of formalized information.

'Expert systems', in Giddens' terms, mean systems of (experts and) expert knowledge (and not 'experts in silicon', as envisioned in the Artificial Intelligence era of the late 1980s). Expert knowledge—under modernity—is developed under regimes underlining universality and objectivity. Expert—including scientific—knowledge should be built up of facts, theories, and laws that are universal and not linked to specific contexts or subjective judgements. The fact that expert knowledge is free of context implies, of course, that it can be transported anywhere and applied to anything.

Both forms of disembedding mechanisms presume as well as foster time–space distantiation.

The reflexive appropriation of knowledge. The production of systematic knowledge about social life becomes integral to systems reproduction, rolling social life away from the fixities of tradition.

Giddens says that modernity is constituted in and through reflexively applied knowledge. The reflexivity of modern social life consists in the fact that social practices are constantly examined and re-examined in the light of incoming information about those very practices, thus constitutively altering their character. Reflexivity is introduced into the very basis of system reproduction, such that thought and action are constantly refracted back upon one another.

Knowledge claimed by expert observers rejoins its subject matter, thus altering it. The chronic revision of social practices in the light of knowledge about those practices is part of the very tissue of modern institutions.

To illustrate the reflexivity of modern institutions Giddens uses marriage and divorce practices as an example. Expert knowledge about divorce rates and causes and effects of divorce is adopted by members of our societies and changes our practices concerning when we marry and how we organize marriage, which further alters the divorce rates and makes existing knowledge obsolete.

Globalization and modernity

For Giddens modernization and globalization are closely connected. Globalization is the most visible form modernization is taking. And, as a part of this, modernity itself is inherently globalizing. Giddens describes globalization as a consequence of modernity as follows.

The conceptual framework of time–space distantiation directs our attention to the complex relations between local involvements and interaction across distance. Globalization refers essentially to that stretching process, in so far as modes of connection between different social contexts or regions become networked across the earth's surface as a whole. Globalization further involves an intensification of worldwide social relations that link distant localities in such a way that local happenings are shaped by events occurring many miles away and vice versa. This is a dialectical process, because such local happenings may move in a different direction from the very distantiated relations that shape them. Local transformation is as much a part of globalization as the lateral extension of social connections across time and space.

During this globalization process, place becomes, in Giddens' terms, 'increasingly phantasmagoric'—that is to say, locales are thoroughly penetrated by and shaped in terms of social influences quite distant from them. What structures the locale is not simply that which is present on the scene; the 'visible form' of the locale conceals the distantiated relations that determine its nature.

Certainly, Giddens says that one of the most important effects of industrialism has been the transformation of technologies of communication, and that technologies of communication have dramatically influenced all aspects of globalization since the first introduction of mechanical printing into Europe.

Consequences of Globalization and Modernization: Risk Society

So far, reference to Giddens' work has allowed us to get to the broader 'essence' of globalization. But what are the consequences of modernity that may affect businesses?

A first general consequence of modernization and globalization is the emergence of what Beck (1992) calls 'risk society'. Beck uses this term to argue that most characteristic of our contemporary society is the unpredictability of events and the increased number of *risks* with which we are confronted. Giddens (1991) has described what he calls the risk profile of modernity. This includes, among others, the following points:

- the globalization of risk in the sense of intensity—for example, the threat of nuclear war to the survival of humanity;
- globalization of risk in the sense of the expanding number of contingent events that affect everyone or at least large numbers of people on the planet—for example, changes in the global division of labour;
- risk stemming from the created environment, or socialized nature: the infusion of human knowledge into the material environment;
- the development of institutionalized risk environments affecting the life chances of millions—for example, investment markets;
- awareness of the limitations of expertise: no expert system can be wholly expert in the consequences of the adoption of expert principles.

Obviously, all these risks affect global corporations. But most relevant in this context is the second one—the risks created in terms of a growing number of contingent events affecting more or less everybody. Such events include those taking place in one local context inside a corporation that affect 'everybody' inside that corporation. The more a global company is integrated into one global unit, the more this kind of risk arises. But modern corporations also get more integrated with their environment—customers, suppliers, partners in strategic alliances, and so on. This means that such companies are more affected by events taking place further away in their environment.

Increasing risk means decreasing control. Both Giddens and Beck see current modernization and globalization processes as a break from earlier modernization. Traditionally, modernization implied more sophisticated control according to the tenets of the 'control revolution' (Beniger 1986). More knowledge and better technology implied sharper and wider control. In the age of high modernity and globalization, however, more knowledge may just as well lead to *more unpredictability, more uncertainty*, and *less controllability*. This is what Beck and Giddens see as the hard core of the reflexivity argument. Here, the theory of reflexive modernization contradicts the instrumental optimism regarding the predetermined controllability of uncontrollable things: 'the thesis that more knowledge about social life . . . equals greater control over our fate is false' (Giddens 1991: 43), and 'the expansion and heightening of the intention of control ultimately ends up producing the opposite' (Beck *et al.* 1994: 9).

This shift, which may appear contradictory, can be explained by the *ubiquitous role of side effects*. Modernization means integration. At the same time, all change—new technologies introduced, organizational structures and work procedures implemented, and so on—has unintended side effects. Any change may affect those interacting with processes that are involved in the change. Side effects of local events often have global consequences. And, the more integrated the world becomes, the longer and faster side effects travel and the heavier their consequences. Globalization also means globalization of side effects. In Beck's (Beck *et al.* 1994: 175, 181) own words: 'it is not knowledge but rather non-knowledge that is the medium of reflexive modernisation . . . we are living in the age of side effects . . . The side effect, not instrumental rationality, is becoming the motor of social change.'

For Beck, the paradigm example of this phenomenon is the ecological crisis. Another well-known example is 'Black Monday'. For companies, important types of risks are those concerning the future markets and opportunities; for individuals, important types of risks are those concerning future job opportunities, and so on.

Modernity is in contrast to tradition. Risks are caused by the inherent striving to change traditions. If we all stick to traditions, if everybody does just what we have always done, we know the effects of our action and there is little or no risk.

The fact that even new knowledge may decrease control might be a bit counter-intuitive. Giddens says that this happens because knowledge reflexively applied to social activity is filtered by four sets of factors:

- *Differential power.* The appropriation of specialist knowledge does not happen in a homogeneous fashion, but is often differentially available to those in power positions who are able to place it in the service of sectorial interests.
- *The role of values.* Changes in value orders are not independent of innovations in cognitive orientation created by shifting perspectives on the social world. If new knowledge could be brought to bear upon a transcendental rational basis of values, this situation would not apply. But there is no such rational basis of values, and shifts in outlook deriving from inputs of knowledge have a mobile relation to changes in value orientations. Values and empirical knowledge are connected in a network of mutual influence. This implies, for instance, that different pieces of knowledge about how to solve a specific problem may be inconsistent and even contradictory because of the different 'value systems' they are based upon. As globalization unfolds, more problems become shared by 'all' of us—like typically environmental problems. And, as long as we believe in different value systems, we will generate different knowledge about such problems, which may—and often certainly will—further lead to conflicting strategies for solving the problems, which again may make the problem more serious and difficult.

- *The impact of unintended consequences.* No amount of accumulated knowledge about social life could encompass all circumstances of its implementation. Knowledge about social life transcends the intentions of those who apply it to transformative ends.
- *The circulating of social knowledge in the double hermeneutic.* Knowledge claimed by expert observers rejoins the subject matter, and accordingly changes it. This may further invalidate the specific knowledge generated as well as other stocks of knowledge.

Taken together, the three features of modern institutions (time–space distantiation, the development of disembedding mechanisms, and the reflexive appropriation of knowledge) explain why living in the modern world is more like being aboard a careering juggernaut than being in a carefully controlled and well-driven motor car. Giddens uses the juggernaut as an image to illustrate modernity as a runaway engine of enormous power that, collectively as human beings, we can drive to some extent but that also threatens to rush out of our control and that could rend itself asunder. The juggernaut crushes those who resist it and, while it sometimes seems to have a steady path, there are times when it veers away erratically in directions we cannot foresee. The juggernaut of modernity is, in Giddens' perspective, not all of one piece. It is not an engine made up of integrated machinery, but one in which there is a push-and-pull of tensions, contradictions, and different influences.

Reflexivity and Management Models

Having presented reflexivity as the key characteristic of modernization (and globalization), we will now look briefly at how this issue is considered by the management models presented above.

Certainly, the need for more flexible organizational forms is caused by the reflexivity of modernization. It is an attempt to find a response to 'risk society'. As corporations become more global, they become more integrated with each other and with distant local contexts. This integration, of course, increases the reach of side effects of local events and the unpredictability of the world as experienced by the corporations. And the degree of globalization, integration, and accordingly side effects, unpredictability, and risks increase as a consequence of the strategies chosen to meet globalization. Corporations meet the challenges of globalization by becoming more global, which adds to the challenges they meet in the future.

Higher flexibility means more sophisticated capabilities in adapting to changes in the environment. But it also means higher capabilities in adapting products and services to specific customers' needs. One important globalization strategy is to standardize goods and services and sell them in a larger—that is, global—market. This is the orthodox globalization strategy advocated by Levitt (1983). But, if a company is selling standardized products, the only way it can compete with others selling products following the same standard is by offering the products for a cheaper price. In such a market, profit margins will shrink. To avoid this trap, companies have to provide something extra, something adding value to the product—as seen by the customer—beyond the standard. To make money, a company should offer something that is unique in terms of functionality and quality to every customer. And what kind of functions and qualities a customer prefers is unique—more or less— for each individual customer. Reich (1991), among others, has presented a careful analysis and description of this process, where, as he sees it, every company has to turn itself into a service organization to survive.

The essence of service orientation is a focus on customer needs, which again requires close customer interaction (Normann and Ramirez 1994). Service orientation can, then, be looked at as a 'reflexive' strategy. It is a strategy for becoming competitive in a more dynamic and unpredictable world. But closer customer interaction means closer customer *integration*. This makes the companies following this strategy more exposed to customer actions—also including the side effects of actions that in principle are completely irrelevant for the supplier.

Similar reflexive effects are inherent parts of the other strategies for implementing competitive global organizations and for dealing with the consequences of globalization. When companies are establishing strategic alliances, implementing just-in-time, lean production models, and so on, they also become closely integrated with strategic partners, suppliers, customers, and so on. This integration implies that a company is strongly affected by events taking place in other organizations. As a consequence of implementing any of these strategies, the role of side effects, unpredictability, and risks rises.

We can see that most organizational and strategic models for 'modern' corporations try to address the consequences of modernization and globalization Giddens and Beck describe. But their understanding of the reflexive character of modernity seems limited. Paradoxically, all models seem to be based on what we could call a non-global perspective on globalization. They propose solutions intended to increase managerial control, but at the same time they advocate increased integration with externals. This makes the companies following these strategies more exposed to changes outside the corporation, and at the same time the side effects of their own actions will more strongly affect those to whom they link themselves.

IT, Modernization, and Globalization

Let us now turn to how the information-systems literature looks at the link between IT and globalization. In their study of managing IT in global companies, Ives and Jarvenpaa (1991) found four generic patterns, which they see as aligned with the four strategies proposed by Bartlett and Ghoshal. At the time of their study, however, few firms were able to state their overall strategy for managing global information technology.

One pattern is the independent global IT operation, where the subsidiaries pursue independent systems initiative and common systems were the exception. Technology choices reflect the influence of local vendors and prevailing national communication standards, resulting in a lack of integration in both hardware and software. This pattern most closely relates to the multinational strategy, with the focus on local responsiveness and the application portfolio strongly oriented toward local requirements.

Another pattern is the headquarters-driven global IT, where the firm imposes corporate-wide IT solutions on subsidiaries. The compelling business need and the opportunity to harvest worldwide economies of scale force the firm towards a global systems solution. This approach is aligned with the global strategy. Ives and Jarvenpaa found that, without a strong global business need, the headquarters-driven global IT approach runs into problems.

Some firms establish strong links between home office and foreign subsidiaries based on cooperation and mutual assistance rather than on management authorization. This intellectual cooperation in global IT fits with the international strategy of Bartlett and Ghoshal. The intention is rapidly to disseminate corporate innovation while continuing to provide the flexibility required to be responsive to local business entities. Ives and Jarvenpaa did not find examples of the transnational strategy, which they denote as integrated global IT. But several firms have recognized the need to move towards the cooperative development of globally integrated applications.

When the focus is on linking IT more tightly to the firm's global business strategy, the most common approach to overcome problems in development and implementation of global systems is to transform the home-office or 'best-of-firms' application into a global system. For the rest, the classic variables of 'strategy', 'organizational structure', 'culture', or 'people' encompass the most important combinations of possibilities of how to 'globalize' IT. Globalization is read only through management 'lenses'.

In contast to such a literature, we will now look a bit deeper into the relationships between IT infrastructure and modernization, in particular the reflexivity issue.

Control technology

As seen above, technological development is a crucial part of modernization. And the development of information and communication technologies is a crucial part of globalization. Specifically, the role of IT can be explained by the way it supports and enables time–space distantiation and supports the development and use of 'symbolic tokens'.

As argued by Beniger (1986), a most important part of technological development has been the development of enhanced control technologies. The same applies for IT. IT is a very important tool, which enables and is developed to support integrated production processes that are distributed more or less globally. Control of global logistics processes such as global JIT is a typical example. IT enables organizations to be distributed globally while at the same time being tied together into one organization; business processes are coordinated globally by means of IT, and so on. A typical example of 'modern' IT-based control technologies would be a shared SAP installation in a global corporation (see, for example, the Norsk Hydro case, Chapter 8).

Reflexivity and flexibility

If IT is so closely related to modernity, how does it interact with the 'consequences of modernity'? One answer would be for IT systems to support flexible organizational forms—that is, various loosely organized networks and market transactions—rather than just the flow of control information in hierarchies. This means—to a large extent—that we should use IT as a communication technology rather than a control technology. Communication technology in this context means a technology supporting informal personal communication (Ciborra 1998).

And what about the role of IT in organizational models such as 'mass customization' and 'flexible specialization'? These models can be seen as the ultimate modern organizations, often called neo-Fordist, because they are based on more advanced control technologies than traditional manufacturing organizations, as they should be able to produce a larger number of different products in smaller series. But they can be seen as alternative, more flexible forms of organizations, i.e. as post-Fordist. Independently of the interpretation chosen, IT is crucial in making these forms possible. In the first interpretation, IT makes it possible to set up production facilities that can produce a wider range of products than earlier because different aspects of the products may be parameterized in the production control system and it may be easy to determine which product to produce in terms of input to the system. This is so because a larger part of the production (control) system is implemented in software.

If the latter interpretation of the models is chosen, IT is also playing an equally important role. In this case, the production technology is assumed to be more easily adapted to new needs, as software is believed to be easier to change than the physical production equipment.

Flexible material or autonomous agent? The reflexivity of IT infrastructures

Software and IT play vital roles in making more flexible organizational forms possible. But it is an illusion to believe that IT systems in general are flexible. Software is often seen as an extremely plastic material because you can change your software just by pushing a few buttons on the keyboard of your PC. But changing large software systems from one working and useful version to a different version, which is also working and useful, is often extremely difficult. Software and other forms of IT systems may be just as inflexible as any other production or control systems.

However, some systems may be more flexible than others. And, like any technology, an IT system can be flexible in use in the sense that it can be used in many different ways without the technology having to be changed at all. E-mail systems are examples of such systems. They can support almost any kind of collaborative process (obviously within certain medium-dictated constraints). Such technologies are flexible because the information processed (exchanged) is not required to be formalized. You can exchange free format text as well as more formalized structures like EDI messages: the less formal the information, the more flexible the technology in use. On the other hand, advanced support of specialized functions and complex and efficient control systems require highly formalized information, which makes such systems less flexible.

Seeing technology as a flexible tool that can be used in many different ways depending on the users' needs and as a malleable material to be changed as the users' needs change is only one perspective on technology. Another perspective is to see technology and technological development as autonomous (Winner 1977). In this perspective it is the technology that is 'controlling' the users and the designers. Giddens is closer to this perspective when he says that 'the constant revolutionizing of technology . . . has a dynamism of its own' and points (by referring to Jacques Ellul) to the fact that all new technology generates 'needs' and solutions to 'problems' we never knew we had.

Large systems, like the Internet and other IT infrastructures, are built by many independent actors over time. Such systems often appear as independent living actors because:

- the number of actors shaping the system/network is so high that it is impossible for any of them to overlook the actions of others; this makes the network change in unpredictable ways;
- side effects of known as well as unknown actions make the network change in unpredictable ways;
- one change—including the side effects of the change—triggers new changes.

Giddens' image of modernity (and of what it means to live in the age of globalization) as riding a juggernaut evokes this situation. In the area of high—or reflexive—modernity, technology not only helps us build enhanced or more flexible control systems; it also creates risks and unpredictable side effects. And, as we are building more interconnected systems, the risks and unpredictability increase, because the high interconnectivity causes side effects to transfer faster and wider.

Infrastructures—at least from a theoretical point of view—are indeed the technology that creates risks, because the essence of infrastructures is—to a large extent—to interconnect. And infrastructures are themselves reflexive: they generate globalization, which demands more powerful and extensive infrastructures, and so on. This dynamic is well illustrated by the Internet. The Internet is widely held to be a crucial driving force behind ongoing globalization processes. An important element in the corporate strategies chosen to meet this challenge (for instance, one of those presented above) is the advanced use of the Internet. This again leads, of course, to a further growth of the Internet and the development of new solutions and technologies, which again generates requirements for improving the existing Internet technology. The Internet drives globalization, which again drives the development of the Internet. This makes one question particularly relevant: who is in control?

4

The Economics of Standards

OLE HANSETH

Weill and Broadbent (1998: 7) see an organization's collection of hardware, software, devices, data, and IT-related personnel as its IT infrastructure. They describe this as an IT portfolio, which should be regarded as any other investment portfolio. This investment-portfolio metaphor can certainly be useful for understanding some aspects of IT infrastructures. But it is a metaphor that can also be very misleading (see Chapter 2).

Investment portfolios are usually very flexible and easy to change, manage, and control. Elements of such portfolios may be sold at almost any time, and individual elements might be sold or bought independently (although portfolios should be balanced to minimize risks, and so on). Infrastructures are different. The individual elements are very interdependent, and their size and complexity may make them extremely difficult to control and manage. In this chapter we will present basic findings and concepts from economic studies of infrastructures and standards. These studies are focused on public standards and infrastructures. But, as we will argue below, the results are equally valid for corporate IT infrastructures.

Here we see another deficiency of the management literature. On the one hand, it argues for the importance of *corporate* information infrastructure by making reference to the vital role played by *public* infrastructures at national and international levels. But, on the other hand, it stays clear of all the intricacies and dilemmas that the development and management of such public infrastructures imply, and that the economic studies reported below try to discuss.

Infrastructure and Standards

We will here identify a few key characteristics of infrastructures. These are aspects that we see as essentials of traditional, public infrastructures, and at the same time characteristics that make IT infrastructures different from traditional information systems.

In Webster's *Dictionary* infrastructure is defined as 'a sub-structure or underlying foundation; esp., the basic installations and facilities on which the continuance and growth of a community, state, etc. depend as roads, schools, power plants, transportation and communication systems, etc.' (Guralnik 1970).

One aspect of infrastructures that we can extract out of this definition is that they have a supporting or *enabling* function. An infrastructure is designed to support a wide range of activities; it is not especially tailored to one. It is enabling in the sense that it is a technology intended to open up a field of new activities, not just to improve or automate something that already exists. This is opposed to being designed especially to support one way of working within a specific application field. The enabling feature of infrastructures plays an important role in policy documents, such as the Clinton–Gore and Bangemann *et al.* (1994) reports on national and European information infrastructures respectively.

Although infrastructures are considered to be enabling, they are, of course, designed to provide certain supporting functions. The interdependencies between the specific *design* of infrastructural services and their *use* is often overlooked. Joerges (1988) has pointed to the fact that infrastructures are subject to 'deep ecological penetration'. This penetration takes place very gradually and over a long time, which to a large extent may make us blind to its existence as well as its implications.

A second aspect we can extract from Webster's definition is the fact that an infrastructure is *shared* by a larger community (or collection of users and user groups). An infrastructure is shared by the members of a community in the sense that it is the same single object used by all of them (although it may appear differently). In this way infrastructures should be seen as irreducible; they cannot be split into separate parts to be used independently by different groups. An e-mail infrastructure is one such shared irreducible unit. An example of the opposite is the various installations of a word processor that may be used completely independently of each other. However, an infrastructure may, of course, be broken down into separate units for analytical or design purposes.

The different elements of an infrastructure are integrated through *standardized interfaces*. Often it is argued that such standards are important, because the alternative—bilateral—arrangements are all too expensive. This is certainly true. However, standards are not only economically important but also a necessary constituting element. If an 'infrastructure' is built on the bases of bilateral arrangements only, this is not a real infrastructure, but just a collection of independent connections.

The shared and enabling aspects of infrastructures have made the concept increasingly popular over recent years. Just as in the case of information infrastructures, the role of infrastructures is believed to be important, as its enabling character points to what may be kept as a stable basis in an increasingly more complex and dynamic world. Håkon With-Andersen (1997) documents how the Norwegian shipbuilding sector has stayed competitive through major changes from sailing ships, through steamboats and tankers, to offshore oil drilling supply boats, because of the crucial role of an infrastructure of competence centres and supporting institutions such as shipbuilding research centres, a ship classification company, and specialized financial institutions. In the same way, Ed. Steinmueller (1996) illustrates how the shared character of infrastructures is used to help understand the growing importance of knowledge as public good and infrastructure in societies where innovation and technological development are crucial for the economy.

The third aspect of infrastructures we will emphasize is their *openness*. They are open in the sense that there are no limits to the number of users, stakeholders, and vendors involved, nodes in the network and other technological components, application areas, network operators, and so on. This defining characteristic does not necessarily imply the extreme position that absolutely everything is included in every information infrastructure. However, it does imply that one cannot draw a strict border saying that there is one infrastructure for what is on one side of the border and others for the other side and that these infrastructures are independent.

Whatever the numbers of an infrastructure's user groups, application areas, designers and manufacturers, network operators, service providers, and so on, there will always be someone or something outside that should be involved or to which the infrastructure should be connected.

Unlimited numbers of users, developers, stakeholders, components, and use areas imply:

- several activities with varying relations over time;
- varying constellations and alliances;
- changing conditions for development;
- changing requirements.

In sum, all this leads to heterogeneity.

In the Clinton–Gore report, the envisioned NII (or 'electronic superhighway') is meant to include more than just the physical facilities used to transmit, store, process, and display voice, data, and images. It is considered to encompass the following.

- A wide and ever-expanding range of *equipment*, including cameras, scanners, keyboards, telephones, fax machines, computers, switches, compact disks, video and audio tape, cable, wire, satellites, optical fibre transmission lines, microwave nets, switches, televisions, monitors, printers, and much more.
- The *information* itself, which may be in the form of video programming, scientific or business databases, images, sound recordings, library archives, other media, and so on
- *Applications* and *software* that allow users to access, manipulate, organize, and digest the proliferating mass of information that the NII's facilities will put at their fingertips.
- The network *standards* and transmission codes that facilitate interconnection and interoperation between networks.
- The *people* who create the information, develop applications and services, construct the facilities, and train others to tap its potential.

The report says that every component of the information infrastructure must be developed and integrated if the USA is to capture the promise of the Information Age.

This definition also sees infrastructures as enabling, shared, and open. Further, it points to some other crucial features we now will turn to. Infrastructures are *heterogeneous* phenomena. They are so in at least two ways.

First, information infrastructures are more than 'pure' technology; they are rather *socio-technical networks*. Infrastructures are heterogeneous concerning the qualities of their constituencies. They include technological components, humans, organizations, institutions, and so on. This fact is most clearly expressed in the last point in the list above. It is true for information technologies in general, as they will not work without support staff. Nor will an information system work if the users are not using it properly. For instance, flight-booking systems do not work unless all booked seats are registered in the systems.

Secondly, infrastructures are connected and interrelated, constituting *ecologies of infrastructures*. One infrastructure is composed of ecologies of (sub)infrastructures by

- building one infrastructure as a layer on top of another;
- linking logical related networks;
- integrating independent components, making them interdependent.

Infrastructures are layered upon each other just as software components are layered upon each other in all kinds of information systems. This is an important aspect of infrastructures, but one that is easily grasped as it is so well known. An example is the World Wide Web as a global infrastructure built on top of the Internet's global TCP/IP infrastructure.

Infrastructures are also heterogeneous in the sense that the same logical function might be implemented in several different ways. Larger infrastructures will often be developed by interconnecting two existing different ones, as has typically happened when networks such as America Online and Prodigy have been connected to the Internet through gateways. In principle the same happens when one standardized part (protocol) of an infrastructure is being replaced over time by a new one. In such transition periods, an infrastructure will consist of two interconnected networks running different versions. A paradigm example of this phenomenon is the transition of the Internet from IPv4 to IPv6 (Hanseth *et al.* 1996; Monteiro 1998).

Infrastructures are also heterogeneous in the sense that larger components or infrastructures are built based on existing smaller, independent components. When these components are brought together into a larger unit, they become interdependent. When one of them is changed, for whatever reason, the others will often need to be changed as well. Examples of this phenomenon are the various formats for representing text, video, sound, image, and graphical representations that are brought together and put into MIME to enable transfer of multimedia information on the Web/Internet. At the time of writing, the Internet integrates a vast range of standardized formats and protocols, in total more that 200 standards (RFC 1994). The latest version of IP, IPv6, contains only modest changes to the former. However, it requires fifty-one other Internet standards to be changed.

Building large infrastructures takes *time*. All elements are connected. As time passes, new requirements appear to which the infrastructure has to adapt. The whole infrastructure cannot be changed instantly—the new has to be connected to the old. The new version must be designed in such a way as to make the old and the new interlinked and 'inter-operable' in one way or another. In this way the old—the installed base—heavily influences how the new can be designed. This leads us to the last aspect of infrastructures that we want to point out: they develop through extending and improving the *installed base*.

The focus on infrastructure as an 'installed base' implies that infrastructures are always considered as existing already; they are NEVER developed from scratch. When 'designing' a 'new' infrastructure, it will always be integrated into or replace part of an existing one. This has been the case in the building of all transport infrastructures. Every single road—even the first one, if it makes sense to speak of such a thing—has been built in this way; when air-traffic infrastructures have been developed, they have been tightly interwoven with road and railway networks—for these are needed for travel between airports and travellers' destinations. Moreover, air-traffic infrastructures can be used for only one part of a journey, and isolated air-traffic infrastructures, without the support of other infrastructures, would be useless.

The notion of an installed base does to a large extent include all the aspects of infrastructure mentioned above: an *infrastructure is an evolving shared, open, and heterogeneous installed base.*

Public versus Corporate Infrastructures

The aspects of infrastructures pointed out above are derived from how we see traditional public infrastructures. Are public and corporate infrastructures essentially of the same nature, so that these aspects are also the most important ones for corporate information infrastructures? We believe so.

Of the aspects mentioned, openness is the most crucial one in this respect. In general we can say that (public) infrastructures are shared by open communities, while (information) systems (in particular as presented in IS development methodology and strategy textbooks) are used by closed organizations. This is important with regard to the size and complexity of infrastructures, but above all with regard to their governance—that is, what makes the control of the design and use of infrastructures different from that of information systems.

Infrastructures are primarily designed through the standardization of interfaces and protocols and through the diffusion of the various standardized components. The actual infrastructure can be said to be designed through the latter processes. The Internet, for instance, is designed (as a network) as the individual users and Internet Service Providers install Internet software on their computers and link them to the existing network. Both the standardization and infrastructure building activities are carried out by a huge number of independent actors. Some institutions, like standardization bodies, are set up in order to try to coordinate such processes. But these institutions have hardly any authority or power to enforce any kind of behaviour on the individual actors. This is the opposite of the picture usually drawn of organizations. The hierarchical structure was invented to control and coordinate processes. Any manager has the authority to make decisions and instruct his or her subordinates what to do. But this is an ideal picture and not the reality.

Modern global corporations are more like an open community than a closed organization—at least as far as their information infrastructures are concerned. The size, variety, and complexity of global organizations such as those presented in this volume make them difficult to manage as one coherent unit. This is possible only for a few issues to which top management dedicate their resources. The character of global corporations as a collection of a large number of independent units is also a result of their dynamics and modern management models emphasizing fast decision-making, flexibility, and accordingly local autonomy (see Chapter 3). Such models become more important as the company grows and its level of competence and knowledge intensity increase. Further, the technological development that all IT activities in a corporation depend on is external. It is controlled externally and not by the corporation. In addition, the companies are becoming less manageable as they become more deeply embedded in their environment—for instance, through closer collaboration with suppliers, customers, and other strategic partners. The last point is of particular relevance for the governance of infrastructures. This implies that the information infrastructures of modern organizations are to a large extent shared with collaborating organizations; they are becoming public infrastructures. All these aspects are, as shown in the previous chapter, becoming more important, as organizations are becoming increasingly more modern and global.

A crucial aspect of infrastructure development is the design and diffusion of *standards*. This is also valid for corporate IT infrastructures. Weill and Broadbent (1998: 266) say that, to succeed in the establishment of IT infrastructures, a corporation should 'enforce IT architecture and standards'. This statement is presented without any explanation, justification, or arguments, which makes one believe that the authors see this as an obvious truth and a plain and simple guideline to follow in practice. We believe that the opposite is the case. Below we will enquire into the nature of standardization definition and implementation processes by presenting the basic lessons learned by economists who have studied standardization processes.

Economics of Standards

The main concepts within the 'economics of standards' that should attract our attnetion are: increasing returns and positive feedback, network externalities, path dependency, and installed base.

Increasing returns and positive feedback

Increasing returns mean that, the more a particular product is produced, sold, or used, the more valuable or profitable it becomes. Infrastructure standards are paradigm examples of products having this characteristic. The development and diffusion of 'infrastructural' technologies are determined by 'the overriding importance of standards and the installed base compared to conventional strategies concentrating on programme quality and other promotional efforts' (Grindley 1995: 7).

A communication standard's value is to a large extent determined by the number of users—that is, the number of users you can communicate with if you adopt the standard. This phenomenon is illustrated by well-known examples such as Microsoft Windows and the rapid diffusion of the Internet in recent years. Earlier examples are the sustainability of FORTRAN and COBOL far beyond the time when they had become technologically outdated.

The basic mechanism is that the large installed base attracts complementary products and makes the standard cumulative more attractive. A larger base with more complementary products also increases the credibility of the standard. Together these make a standard more attractive to new users. This brings in more adoptions, which further increases the size of the installed base, and so on, as illustrated by Fig. 4.1 (Grindley 1995: 27).

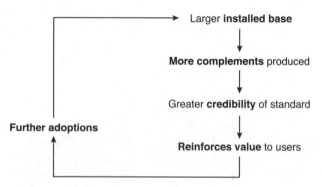

FIG. 4.1. Standards reinforcements mechanism
Source: Grindley (1995).

The phenomenon of positive feedback has been focused and theorized over recent years in studies of standards. The concept is opposed to basic assumptions of classical economics. Classical economics is centred on the notion of negative feedback or decreasing returns. These processes hold for economies based on natural resources such as agriculture and mining, which are subject to diminishing returns caused by limited amounts of fertile land or high-quality ore deposits. In such cases, the most fertile and easily available land and the most easily available oilfields are utilized first. As more agricultural products or oil are produced, so the land that is more difficult to access, or the more marginal resources, have to be used, and production becomes more expensive (Arthur 1994).

Increasing returns stem from more than one source. The most widely known one is the fact that larger firms tend to have smaller unit costs. This source of positive feedback is known as scale economies—or, more precisely, economies of scale in production (Shapiro and Varian 1999).

Economies of scale, again, have several causes. Large-scale production machinery produces units at lower cost. But, in some sectors, the costs of developing new products are large, while making copies of the product is cheap. This phenomenon is particularly important in high-tech and research-intensive industries, and in the software and information sector more than in any other, as the unit costs of making software and information products (like a digital encyclopedia) are close to zero, while the product development costs can be extremely high.

Further, there is a strong connection between increasing-returns mechanisms and *learning* processes. Increased production brings additional benefits: producing more units means gaining more experience in the manufacturing process, achieving greater understanding of how to produce additional products even more cheaply. Moreover, *experience* gained with one product or technology can make it easier to produce new products incorporating similar or related technologies.

What is most focused in the economics of standards, however, is rather demand-side increasing returns and demand-side economies of scale. Demand-side economies of scale are partly created by learning effects. The transmission of information based on experience may serve as a reinforcement for early leading positions and so act in a manner parallel to more standard forms of increasing returns. A similar phenomenon is individual learning, where again success reinforces some courses of action and inhibits others, thereby causing the first to be sampled more intensively, and so forth (Arrow 1994).

Where learning takes place, beliefs can become self-reinforcing (Arthur 1994), and, accordingly, the product that is expected to become the standard will become the standard. Self-fulfilling expectations are one manifestation of positive-feedback economics and bandwagon effects. If customers expect your product to become popular, a bandwagon will form, a virtuous cycle will begin, and customers' expectations will prove correct. Success and failure are driven as much by expectations and luck as by the underlying value of the product (Shapiro and Varian 1999).

Although the concept of increasing returns has attracted the focus of many economists, it is not a new one. It has had a long but uneasy presence in economic analysis. The opening chapters of Adam Smith's Wealth of Nations put great emphasis on increasing returns to explain both specialization and economic growth. But this tradition acts like an underground river, springing to the surface every few decades (Arrow 1994). Increasing returns have been identified within traditional economies too. Manufacturing, for instance, enjoyed increasing returns because large plants allowed improved organization and created economies of scale. But the theory of 'increasing returns' is argued in particular to be the appropriate theory for understanding modern high-technology economies (Arthur 1994) and the modern emerging information economy (Shapiro and Varian 1999). For instance, Arthur (1994) argues that the economic circumstances under which a new, superior technology might replace an old inferior one, and how long this time might take, is well explained by the theory. This 'competing technologies problem' is one of increasing returns par excellence.

According to Arthur (1994), positive feedback mechanisms are now central to modern theorizing in international trade theory, growth theory, the economics of technology, industrial organization, macroeconomics, regional economics, economic development, and political economy. Further, the part of the economy that is knowledge-based is largely subject to increasing returns. Products such as computers, pharmaceuticals, aircraft, software, and so on are complicated to design and to manufacture. They require large initial investments in research and development and tooling but, once sales begin, incremental production is relatively cheap (Arthur 1994).

Shapiro and Varian (1999) see positive feedback as the central element in the information economy, defining information as anything that may be digitized. An information good involves high fixed costs but low marginal costs. The cost of producing the first copy of an information good may be substantial, but the cost of producing (or reproducing) additional copies is negligible. They argue that the key concept in the network economy is positive feedback. The case of Microsoft is a good illustration of this. Demand-side economies of scale are the norm in information industries.

Network effects, network externalities

Whether real or virtual, networks have a fundamental economic characteristic: the value of connecting to a network depends on the number of other people already connected to it. This fundamental value proposition goes under many names: network effects, network externalities, demand-side economies of scale. They all refer to essentially the same point: other things being equal, it is better to be connected to a bigger network than a smaller one (Shapiro and Varian 1999.)

Externalities arise when one market participant affects others without compensation being paid. In general, network externalities may cause negative as well as positive effects. The classic example of negative externalities is pollution: my sewage ruins your swimming or drinking water. Positive externalities give rise to positive feedback (Shapiro and Varian 1999).

Path dependency

Network externalities and positive feedback give rise to a number of more specific effects. One such is *path dependence*. Path dependence means that past events will have large impacts on future development, and in principle irrelevant events may turn out to have tremendous effects (David 1986). For instance, a standard that builds up an installed base ahead of its competitors becomes cumulatively more attractive, making the choice of standards 'path dependent' and highly influenced by a small advantage gained in the early stages (Grindley 1995: 2). The classical and widely known example illustrating this phenomenon is the development and evolution of keyboard layouts, leading to the development and *de facto* standardization of QWERTY (David 1986).

We can distinguish between two forms of path dependence.

- Early advantage in terms of numbers of users leads to victory.
- Early decisions concerning the design of the technology will influence future design decisions.

The first one has already been mentioned above. When two technologies of a kind where standards are important—such as communication protocols or operating systems—are competing, the one getting an early lead in terms of number of users becomes more valuable for the users. This may attract more users to this technology and it may win the competition and become a *de facto* standard. The establishment of Microsoft Windows as the standard operating system for PCs followed this pattern. The same pattern was also followed by the Internet protocols during the period they were competing with OSI protocols.

The second form of path dependence concerns the technical design of a technology. When, for instance, a technology is established as a standard, new versions of the technology must be designed in a way that is compatible (in one way or another) with the existing installed base. This implies that design decisions made early in the history of a technology will often live with the technology as long as it exists. Typical examples of this are various technologies struggling with the backward compatibility problem. Well-known examples in this respect are the different generations of Intel's microprocessors, where all later versions are compatible with the 8086 processor, which was introduced into the market around 1982.

Early decisions about the design of the Internet technology, for instance, have had a considerable impact on the design of new solutions both to improve existing services and to add new ones to the Internet. For instance, the design of the TCP/IP protocol constrains how improved solutions concerning real-time multimedia transfer can be designed and how security and accounting services can be added to the current Internet.

Lock-in: switching costs and coordination problems

Increasing return may lead to yet another effect: *lock-in*. Lock-in means that, when a technology has been adopted, it will be very hard or impossible to develop competing technologies. 'Once random economic events select a particular path, the choice becomes locked-in regardless of the advantages of alternatives' (Arthur 1990). In general, lock-in arises whenever users invest in multiple complementary and durable assets specific to a particular technology. We can identify different types of lock-in: contractual commitments, durable purchases, brand-specific training, information and databases, specialized suppliers, search costs, and loyalty programmes (Shapiro and Varian 1999). We can also say that lock-ins are caused by the huge switching costs or by coordination problems (or a combination of these) that would be incurred when switching from one standardized technology to another.

Switching costs and lock-ins are ubiquitous in information systems, and managing these costs is very tricky both for sellers and buyers. For most of the history of computers, customers have been in a position where they could not avoid buying (more or less) all their equipment and software from the same vendor. The switching costs of changing computer systems could have been astronomical—and certainly so high that no organization did. To change from one manufacturer (standard) to another would imply changing all equipment and applications at the same time. This would be very expensive—far beyond what anybody could afford. But it would also be an enormous waste of resources, because the investments made have differing economic lifetimes, so there is no easy time to start using a new, incompatible system. As a result, buyers face switching costs, which effectively lock them into their current system or brand (Shapiro and Varian 1999).

Switching costs also go beyond the amount of money an organization has to pay to acquire a new technology and install it. Since many software systems are mission critical, the risks in using a new vendor, especially an unproven one, are substantial. Switching costs for customers include the risk of a severe disruption in operations.

Lock-in is not only created by hardware and software. Information itself—its structures in databases as well as the semantics of the individual data elements—is linked together into huge and complex networks that create lock-ins. One of the distinct features of information-based lock-in is that it proves to be so durable: equipment wears out, reducing switching costs, but specialized databases live on and grow, increasing lock-in over time (Shapiro and Varian 1999).

The examples of lock-ins and switching costs mentioned so far are all related to infrastructures that are seen as local to one organization. As infrastructures and standards are shared across organizations, lock-in problems become even more challenging.

Network externalities make it virtually impossible for a small network to thrive. But every network has to start from scratch. The challenge to companies introducing new but incompatible technology into the market is to build a network size that overcomes the collective switching costs—that is, the combined switching costs of all users. In many information industries, collective switching costs are the biggest single force working in favour of incumbents. Worse yet for would-be entrants and innovators, switching costs work in a non-linear way: convincing ten people connected in a network to switch to your technology is more than ten times as hard as getting one customer to switch. But you need all ten, or most of them: no one will want to be the first to give up the network externalities and risk being stranded. Precisely because various users find it so difficult to coordinate a switch to an incompatible technology, control over a large installed base of users can be the greatest asset you can have.

But lock-in is more than cost. As the community using the same technology or standard grows, switching to a new technology or standard becomes an increasingly larger *coordination* challenge. The lock-in represented by QWERTY, for instance, is most of all a coordination issue. It is shown that the individual costs of switching are marginal (David 1986), but, as long as we expect others to stick to the standard, it is best that we do so ourselves as well. There are too many users (everybody using a typewriter or PC/computer). It is impossible to bring them together so that they could agree on a new standard and commit themselves to switch.

Many lock-in situations are of such a character that to get out of them requires both huge switching costs and coordination tasks. A typical example of such a lock-in situation is again Microsoft Windows. It is hard to imagine, at the time of writing, that any operating system can compete with Windows in the PC market, however fantastic it might be. The Linux operating systems might possibly be a competitor. But this system is developed under quite extraordinary conditions—by a huge group of enthusiastic individuals who are working without getting paid. The Internet is another example. (For more on this aspect, see Hanseth *et al.* 1996; Monteiro 1998.) It has been widely acknowledged for a long time that the TCP/IP protocol is becoming outdated. At the end of the 1990s its address space was running out, and it lacked appropriate support for wireless and mobile networks, real-time multimedia, the accounting that was required by commercial service providers, security, and so on. For these reasons, the development of a new protocol had already been launched in 1990. As the design work proceeded, the fact that the new version had to be compatible with the existing one emerged as the single most important requirement. As a consequence, other issues, except increased address space, were given up. A new protocol has been defined, but it remains to be seen whether it will be adopted by users of the Internet. The Internet example also illustrates that getting out of the lock-in trap also involves a third challenge. To avoid a lock-in, the new technological solutions must support the transition from the old to the new.

We have so far illustrated the coordination problems related to public standards and infrastructures. But there may also be huge coordination problems related to the change of corporate infrastructures. The hierarchical structure of organizations is developed for making decisions and coordination processes across the organization. Accordingly, this hierarchical structure should take care of the coordination required for changing IT infrastructures. But this will not always be possible. There will often be too many complex issues involved, too many actors and units, and the infrastructure may also be embedded in local contexts (see Chapter 5). Indeed, corporate infrastructures may be locked-in in just the same way as are public ones.

Inefficiency

The last consequence of positive feedback we mention is what is called *possible inefficiency*. This means that the best solution will not necessarily win. An illustrative and well-known example of this phenomenon is the competition between the Microsoft Windows operating system and Macintosh. Macintosh was widely held to be the best technology—in particular from a user point of view—but Windows won because it had early succeeded in building a large installed base.

Strategies

David (1987) points out three strategy dilemmas that one would usually face when developing networking technologies and that are caused by the phoneomena of network externalities and increasing returns.

- *Narrow policy window.* There may be only brief and uncertain 'windows in time' during which effective public policy interventions can be made at moderate resource costs.
- *Blind giants.* Governmental agencies are likely to have the greatest power to influence the future trajectories of network technologies just when the suitable informational basis on which to make socially optimal choices among alternatives is most lacking. The actors in question, then, resemble 'blind giants'—whose vision we would wish to improve before their power dissipates. Corporate headquarters will typically be in the same position when defining corporate standards.
- *Angry orphans.* Some groups of users will be left 'orphaned'; they will have sunk investments in systems whose maintenance and further elaboration are going to be discontinued. Encouraging the development of gateway devices linking otherwise incompatible systems can help to minimize the static economic losses incurred by orphans.

There are, in principle, two strategies to choose between to get out of a lock-in and to help avoid the dilemmas: an evolution strategy of backward compatibility or a revolution strategy of compelling performance. These strategies reflect an underlying tension when the forces of innovation meet up with network externalities: is it better to wipe the slate clean and come up with the best product possible (revolution) or to give up some performance to ensure compatibility and thus ease consumer adoption (evolution) (Shapiro and Varian 1999)?

The evolution strategy, which offers users an easy migration path, centres on reducing switching costs so that users can try your new technology gradually. In virtual networks, the evolution strategy of offering users a migration path requires an ability to achieve compatibility with existing products. In real networks, the evolution strategy requires physical interconnection to existing networks. In either case, interfaces are critical. The key to the evolution strategy is to build a new network by linking it first to the old one. The technical obstacles faced have to do with the need to develop a technology that is at the same time compatible with, and yet superior to, existing products.

The revolution strategy is inherently risky. It cannot work on a small scale and usually requires powerful allies. Worse yet, it is devilishly difficult to tell early on whether your technology will take off or crash and burn. Even successful technologies start off slowly and accelerate from there.

Radical changes are often advocated—for instance, within the business process re-engineering (BPR) literature. Empirically, however, such radical changes of larger networks are rather rare. Hughes (1987) concluded that large networks change only in the chaos of dramatic crises (such as the oil crises in the early 1970s) or in the case of some external shock.

Gateways

We can distinguish between two variants of the evolutionary strategy—slow evolution based on *backward compatibility* and fast evolution based on *gateways* linking the new and the old networks.

The term 'gateway' has a strong connotation. It has traditionally been used in a technical context to denote an artefact that is able to translate back and forth between two different communication networks. A gateway in this sense is also called a 'converter' and operates by inputting data in one format and converting them to another. In this way a gateway may translate between two, different communication protocols that would otherwise be incompatible, as a protocol converter accepts messages from either protocol, interprets them, and delivers appropriate messages to the other protocol.

A well-known and important example of gateways, which is also analysed in the economics of standards literature, is the alternating/direct current (AC/DC) adapter (David and Bunn 1988; Hughes 1983). At the beginning of the twentieth century, it was still an open and controversial issue whether electricity supply should be based on AC or DC. The two alternatives were incompatible and a 'battle of systems' unfolded. As a user of electrical lighting, you would have had to choose between the two. There were strong proponents and interests behind both. Both had their distinct technical virtues. AC was more cost effective for long-distance transportation (because the voltage level could be higher) whereas a DC-based electrical motor preceded the AC-based one by many years. As described by Hughes (1983) and emphasized by David and Bunn (1988), the introduction of the converter made it possible to couple the two networks. It accordingly became feasible to combine the two networks and hence draw upon their respective virtues.

Other scholars have developed notions related to this notion of a gateway. Star and Griesemer's (1989) concept of *boundary objects* may also be seen as a gateway enabling communication between different communities of practices. The same is the case for Cussins' (1998) objectification strategies. These strategies may be seen as constituting different networks, each of them being connected to the networks built by the different practices through gateways translating the relevant information according to the needs of the 'objectification networks'.

Gateways fill important roles in a number of situations during all phases of an information infrastructure development. The key effect of traditional converters is that they sidestep—either by postponing or by altogether avoiding—a confrontation. The AC/DC adapter is a classic example. The adapter bought time so that the battle between AC and DC could be postponed. Hence, the adapter avoided a premature decision. Instead, the two alternatives were able to coexist and the decision to be delayed until more experience had been acquired.

Sidestepping a confrontation is particularly important during the early phases of an infrastructure development as there is still a considerable amount of uncertainty about how the infrastructure will evolve. And this uncertainty cannot be settled up front; it has to unfold gradually. Gateways may prevent those in the position of making decisions from acting like 'blind giants'.

But it is not only during the early phases that sidestepping confrontation is vital. It is also important in a situation where there are already a number of alternatives, none of which is strong enough to 'conquer' the others. In the case of e-mail systems, for instance, many different proprietary systems and protocols were developed before the Internet or other standards were available. On this basis, it has been considered more convenient to develop the different protocols separately and link the networks together through gateways.

A more neglected role of gateways is the way they support modularization. The modularization of an information infrastructure is intimately linked to its heterogeneous character. The impossibility of developing an information infrastructure monolithically forces a more patchlike and dynamic approach. In terms of actual design, this entails decomposition and modularization. The role of a gateway, then, is to encourage this required decomposition by decoupling the efforts to develop the different elements of the infrastructure and coupling them tightly only at the end. This allows a maximum of independence and autonomy.

Modularization, primarily through black-boxing and interface specification, is, of course, an old and acknowledged design virtue for all kinds of information systems, including information infrastructures. But the modularization of an information infrastructure supported by gateways has another, essential driving force that is less obvious. As the development is more likely to take ten years than one, the contents are bound to evolve or 'drift'. As a result, previously unrelated features and functions are brought together and need to be aligned. The coupling of two (or more) of these require a highly contingent, techno-economical process, a process that is difficult to design and cater for. Cable TV and the telephone have a long-standing history of distinctly different networks. They were conceived of, designed, and appropriated in quite distinct ways. Only as a result of technological development and legislative deregulation has it become reasonable to link them. This has given rise to an *ecology of networks* that may be linked together later by gateways.

5

Actor-Network Theory and Information Infrastructure

The study of the economics of infrastructure has already begun to show how the development, introduction, and use of an information infrastructure are an involved socio-technical process of *negotiation*. The open-ended character of this process—the stumbling, the compromises, the way non-technical interests get dressed up in technical disguise—calls for an analytic vehicle that helps tease out interesting and relevant issues related to the 'management' of such processes.

This chapter introduces, outlines, and illustrates one such vehicle—namely, actor-network theory (ANT). We introduce ANT by briefly positioning it within the broader landscape of conceptualizations of technology and society. This exercise is intended to be neither comprehensive nor systematic. It is aimed at spelling out those underlying aspects of an information infrastructure towards which ANT makes us sensitive.

First and foremost, ANT, especially in the minimalistic version outlined here, offers an illuminating vocabulary to describe information infrastructure. It provides a language to describe how, where, and to what extent technology influences human behaviour. This is valuable when identifying the influence of seemingly grey and anonymous technical components such as standards or systems modules that are already installed. In particular, it allows ANT to zoom in and out of a situation as required.

This implies that the granularity (that is, the scope, depth, and level of detail) of the analysis is flexible. Sometimes a comprehensive set of interconnected modules and systems is collapsed into one node; sometimes the focus is on the relative contribution of each of the modules; sometimes a detailed analysis is needed of the design of one specific module. This kind of flexibility is indispensable in any analysis of information infrastructure.

The reason for outlining ANT in relation to the development and establishment of information infrastructure is the need critically to assess the descriptions of this issue provided by traditional management literature. This literature—as discussed in Chapter 2—is dominated by top-down, rational, decision making.

There are, of course, alternative perspectives on strategic information systems in general and information infrastructures in particular. For example, there exists an

interesting body of literature on critical management thinking related to information systems. This literature is sensitive to issues of power distribution (Knights *et
al.* 1997), the lack of top-down control (Walsham 1993; Ciborra 1994), and rhetorical devices (Alvesson 1993). An ANT-influenced perspective on information
infrastructure provides a fruitful supplement to such a body of literature. In particular, it provides a different insight into how information systems and business
strategies are 'aligned' (see Chapter 2). Rather than portray 'alignment' as traditional
management thinking, ANT offers a different account. Alignment in the sense of
ANT, to be spelled out in greater detail below, differs along several, crucial dimensions, which turn the notion of alignment into something else. It is heterogeneous,
meaning that there is an open-ended array of 'things' that need to be aligned,
including work routines, incentive structures, training, information-systems modules, and organizational roles. It follows immediately that there can be no strict top-
down control over such a collection of 'things'. Hence, ANT leans heavily towards
a bottom-up concept of alignment and strategy formation. Furthermore, ANT
emphasizes strongly the performative or process aspect of alignment. Alignment,
according to ANT, is not the result of any top-down plan or decision. It is the
achievement of a process of bottom-up mobilization of heterogeneous 'things', as
Latour (1996: 86) underlines in his phrase 'every day is a working day'.

   ANT belongs to the strand of thinking that questions given categories. It is
accordingly more geared towards *performing* order through the establishment of
facts, effects, beliefs, or technological solutions. Order is the effect of an achievement—it is not given a priori. The challenge is to develop an understanding of
what this achievement is made up of, to unpack the dynamic, socio-technical
process unfolding over time that as a net result constructs reality and order. This is
an operationalization of the essence of social constructivism: it is waging war against
essentialism and is devoted to 'understand[ing] how it is that durability is achieved'
(Law 1999: 4).

   The remainder of this chapter is structured into two parts. First, ANT is located
within a broad strand of critical thinking around information systems and technology. We then turn to the core of this chapter, and outline a selection of key concepts and issues in ANT relevant to a grasp of the challenges of establishing a
working information infrastructure. In so doing, we will draw upon illustrations
from the cases described in greater detail in the case studies in Part Two of this
volume.

ANT in Context

The non-technical in information systems research

The relationship between technology and society may be conceptualized in many
ways. We embrace the fairly widespread belief that IT is a—perhaps the—crucial
factor, as it simultaneously enables and amplifies the currently dominating trends
for the restructuring of organizations (Orlikowski 1991; Applegate 1994). The
problem, however, is that this belief does not carry us very far; indeed, it is close

to becoming a cliché. To be instructive in an enquiry concerning current organizational transformations, one has to supplement it with a grasp of the interplay between IT and organizations in more detail. We need to know more about how IT shapes, enables, and constrains organizational changes. A continuum of alternatives can be illustrated by two extreme end points. On the one hand, there is technological determinism, which holds that the development of technology follows its own logic and that the technology determines its use (Winner 1977); on the other hand, there is social reductionism or constructivism (which comes close to technological somnambulism (Winner 1977; Pfaffenberger 1988)), which holds that society and its actors develop the technology they 'want' and use it as they want, implying that technology in itself plays no role. A series of Braverman-inspired studies appeared in the late 1970s and early 1980s biased towards a technological-determinist position, arguing that the use of IT was but the latest way of promoting management's interests regarding deskilling and control of labour. Later, a number of studies nearer to the social-constructivist end of the continuum were produced, which focused on diversity of use among a group of users and displayed use far beyond what had been anticipated by the designers (Henderson and Kyng 1991).

A more satisfactory account of the interwoven relationship between IT and organizational transformations is lacking. More specifically, we need to learn, not just that this interplay exists, but how it works. This implies that it is vital to be more concrete with respect to the specifics of the technology. As an information system (IS) consists of a large number of modules and interconnections, it may be approached with a varying degree of granularity. We cannot refer to it indiscriminately as IS, IT, or computer systems. Kling (1991: 356) characterizes this lack of precision as a 'convenient fiction', which 'deletes nuances of technical differences'. It is accordingly less than prudent to discuss IS at the granularity of an artefact (Pfaffenberger 1988), the programming language (Orlikowski 1992), the overall architecture (Applegate 1994), or a medium for communication (Feldman 1987). To advance our understanding of the interplay it would be quite instructive to be as concrete about which aspects, modules, or functions of an IS enable or constrain which organizational changes—without collapsing this into a deterministic account (Hanseth *et al.* 1996).

The majority of scholars in the field adhere to an intermediate position somewhere between the two extreme positions outlined above. Their accounts end up with the very important, but all too crude, insight that 'information technology has both restricting and enabling implications' (Orlikowski and Robey 1991: 154). This insight—that IT enables and constrains—is reached using a rich variety of theoretical frameworks.

ANT represents one framework within this restricting/enabling regime outlined above. Given the interdisciplinary character of information systems research, there has never been a lack of candidates for theoretical frameworks. There has always been a steady import as indicated in the discussion above. ANT has been employed neither for a long time nor extensively within information systems research. It has been used in a few interpretative case studies (such as Timmermans *et al.* 1995; Hanseth and Monteiro 1996; Walsham 1997; Jones 1998), but must still be said to remain on the margins.

In what follows, we argue that ANT is particularly relevant to developing information infrastructures, because of the way it lends itself to empirically underpinned studies (Monteiro and Hanseth 1995; Jones 1998).

Science and technology studies

ANT has not, of course, developed out of nowhere. To trace its roots in any detail would quickly take us beyond the scope of this chapter. Still, a brief look at the background will be useful.

ANT was born out of the interdisciplinary field of science and technology studies (STS). This field, which emerged in the 1970s, is grounded in a fairly simple observation. The way science is actually done—not how it is normatively supposed to be carried out—and the way technological artefacts are actually designed—not how textbooks in engineering instruct us—have largely been ignored by the social sciences and the humanities. The essence of STS, then, is to ask the following question: if we sideline all espoused theories about this realm and instead bring along the critical and empirically underpinned apparatus from sociology, history, and anthropology, what does the process of producing science and technology look like?

Looking back, a handful of approaches can be identified under the general label of STS (Bijker *et al.* 1987; Law 1991; Bijker and Law 1992; Williams and Edge 1996):

- the systems thinking developed by Hughes (1983, 1987, 1994), which describes the historical development of technological infrastructure by emphasizing the issues of inertia and heterogeneity;
- the social construction of technology (SCOT), which emphasizes the interpretative flexibility that the relevant actors have in ascribing meaning to a technological artefact (key contributors are Bijker, Pinch, and Woolgar);
- actor-network theory (ANT), as developed by Latour, Law, Callon, and Akrich, and as presented further below;
- the sociology of scientific knowledge (SSK), which is devoted to unravelling the infights and manoeuvring that go into the establishment of a scientific fact (key contributors include Collins, MacKenzie, and Traweek).

Related to STS, but largely decoupled from it, there is a strand of thinking that has been influential, not least within IS research—namely, socio-technical systems thinking. This approach has, however, seemed to fade away. Socio-technical systems thinking has lost its ground—and, ironically enough, its old abbreviation, STS. In fact, by the end of the 1990s the label STS was to an increasing degree associated with science and technology studies. From the point of view of ANT, Law (1991: 8) underscores the main problem with socio-technical systems thinking—

namely, that, 'despite the pioneering work on sociotechnical systems by the Tavistock group in the 1960s, *technology does not appear to be productively integrated into large parts of the sociological imagination*' (emphasis added).

Key Concepts (the Minimalistic Version)

What is an actor network, anyway?

The term 'actor network', the A and N in ANT, is not very illuminating. It is hardly obvious what the term implies. The idea, however, is fairly simple. When going about your business—driving your car or writing a document using a word processor—there are a lot of things that influence how you do it. For instance, when driving a car, you are influenced by traffic regulations, previous driving experience, and the car's manoeuvrability; the use of a word processor is influenced by earlier experience, the capabilities of the word processor, and so forth. All of these factors are related or connected to how you act. You go about your business not in a total vacuum but rather under the influence of a wide range of surrounding factors. The act you are carrying out and all of these influencing factors should be considered together. This is exactly what the term 'actor network' accomplishes. An actor network, then, is the act linked together with all of its influencing factors (which again are linked), producing a network.

An actor network consists of and links together both technical and non-technical elements. Not only the car's engine capacity, but also your driving training, influence your driving. Hence, ANT talks about the heterogeneous nature of actor networks. In line with its semiotic origin, actor-network theory is granting all entities of such a heterogeneous network the same explanatory status, as 'semiotics is the study of order building . . . and may be applied to settings, machines, bodies, and programming languages as well as text . . . [because] semiotics is not limited to signs' (Akrich and Latour 1992: 259). It is 'a ruthless application of semiotics' (Law 1999: 3).

It might perhaps seem a radical move to grant artefacts the same explanatory status as human actors: does not this reduce human actors to mere objects and social science to natural science? We do not intend to pursue this rather dogmatic issue and fully embrace Law (1992: 383) that this 'is an analytical stance, not an ethical position'. Interested readers should consult Callon and Latour (1992) and Collins and Yearley (1992).

For the present purposes, what is important is that this move has the potential to increase the level of detail and precision. More specifically, if we allow ourselves not to distinguish a priori between the social and technical elements of a sociotechnical web, we are encouraged to undertake a detailed description of the concrete mechanisms that combine to glue the network together—without being distracted by the means, technical or non-technical, of actually achieving this. If we are really interested in discovering influential factors regarding the way we drive, we should focus on what turns out to be actually influential, be it technical (the engine's capacity) or non-technical (the driver's training).

In relation to the development of a working information infrastructure, how should we think about actor networks, where are they, and how should they be identified? A fruitful way of approaching this, which links up with the more general arguments that IS design and use have to be contextual and situated (Suchman 1987), is to view the actor network as the context. An actor network is literally the network of heterogeneous materials that make up the context. This can be illustrated from the IBM case study (see Chapter 7). The actor network related to the customer-relationship-management (CRM) effort includes: the contracts where middle managers pledge their commitment, the jungle of existing modules and systems, the hierarchical power structure, incentives, the habit embodied in employees of seeing organizational efforts come and go. Hence, the actor network is those elements in a context that shape action; 'the argument is that these various networks *participate* in the social. They *shape* it' (Law 1992: 382).

Equating an actor network with the specific characteristics—some technical, others not—of a context says something about what an actor network is. But it does not say what it is not or, more precisely, how to delineate one actor network from the next. The notion of an actor network, quite literally, instructs us to map out the set of elements (the network) that influence, shape, or determine an action. But each of these elements is in turn part of another actor network, and so forth. Hence, if you take this in too literal a sense, unpacking *any* actor network will cause an explosion in terms of complexity. You end up with the whole world in your lap every time. To illustrate this, tracing the actor network related to CRM would lead to the disciplinary regimes of structured methods, the political-economical manoeuvring to preserve IBM as a potent, US-based company, the processes by which IBM's portfolio of data communication protocols connect to external protocols such as the Internet, the military-industrial heritage of the Internet, and so on. In terms of methodology, this apparently makes the analytic tool of an actor network utterly unmanageable. This, however, is a distortion of ANT. It is rather the case, we argue, that it is overly ambitious (or naive) to expect ANT (or any other theoretical framework for that matter) to instruct you how to separate foreground from background (Bijker 1993). Employing ANT still requires a researcher to make critical judgements about how to delineate the context of study from the backdrop.

Inscription and translation

Two concepts from ANT are of particular relevance: inscription (Akrich 1992; Akrich and Latour 1992) and translation (Latour 1987; Callon 1991, 1994). The notion of inscription refers to the way technical artefacts embody patterns of use: 'Technical objects thus simultaneously embody and measure a set of relations between heterogeneous elements' (Akrich 1992: 205). The term 'inscription' might sound somewhat deterministic by suggesting that action is inscribed, grafted, or hard-wired into an artefact. This, however, is a misinterpretation. By balancing the tightrope between an objectivistic stance where artefacts determine their use and a subjectivistic stance holding that an artefact is always interpreted and appropriated flexibly, the notion of an inscription may be used to describe how concrete anticipations and restrictions of future patterns of use are involved in the development and use of a technology. Akrich (1992: 208) explains the notion of inscription in the following way:

Designers thus define actors with specific tastes, competencies, motives, aspirations, political prejudices, and the rest, and they assume that morality, technology, science, and economy will evolve in particular ways. *A large part of the work of innovators is that of 'inscribing' this vision of (or prediction about) the world in the technical content of the new object* . . . The technical realization of the innovator's beliefs about the relationship between an object and its surrounding actors is thus an attempt to predetermine the settings that users are asked to imagine . . . (emphasis added)

   Stability and social order, according to ANT, are continually negotiated as a social process of aligning interests. This takes place in 'the process that is called translation, which generates ordering effects such as devices, agents, institutions, or organizations' (Law 1992: 366). As actors from the outset have a diverse set of interests, stability rests crucially on the ability to translate—that is, re-interpret, represent, or appropriate—others' interests to one's own. In other words, with a translation one and the same interest or anticipation may be presented in different ways, thereby mobilizing broader support. A translation presupposes a medium or a 'material into which it is inscribed'—that is, translations are 'embodied in texts, machines, bodily skills [which] become their support, their more or less faithful executive' (Callon 1991: 143).

   In ANT terms, design is translation: users' and others' interests may, according to typical ideal models, be translated into specific 'needs'; the specific needs are further translated into more general and unified needs, so that these needs can be translated into one and the same solution. When the solution (system) is running, it will be adopted by the users, who translated the system into the context of their specific work tasks and situations.

   In such a translation, or design, process, the designer works out a scenario for how the system will be used. This scenario is inscribed into the system. The inscription includes programmes of action for the users, and it defines roles to be played by users and the system. In doing this, the designer is also making implicit or explicit assumptions about the competencies required by the users as well as by the system. In ANT terminology, he or she delegates roles and competencies to the components of the socio-technical network, which includes the users as well as the components of the system (Latour 1991, 1999). When a program of action is inscribed into a piece of technology, the technology becomes an actor imposing its inscribed program of action on its users.

   The inscribed patterns of use may not succeed because the actual use may deviate from it. Rather than following the assigned programme of action, a user may use the system in an unanticipated way; he or she may follow an anti-programme (Latour 1991). When studying the use of technical artefacts, it is necessary to shift back and forth 'between the designer's projected user and the real user' in order to describe this dynamic negotiation of the process of design (Akrich 1992: 209).

Some technologies inscribe weak/flexible programmes of action; tools are typical of this, with the hammer a classic example. Other technologies inscribe strong/inflexible programmes, with the assembly line of Chaplin's *Modern Times* a standard illustration. Inscriptions are given a concrete content because they represent interests inscribed into a material. As Law (1992: 387) points out: 'Thus a good ordering strategy is to embody a set of relations in durable materials. Consequently, a relatively stable network is one embodied in and performed by a range of durable materials.'

The flexibility of inscriptions varies: some structure the pattern of use strongly, others weakly. The strength of inscriptions, whether they must be followed or whether they can be avoided, depends on the irreversibility of the actor network into which they are inscribed. It is never possible to know beforehand exactly what is needed, but by studying the sequence of attempted inscriptions we can learn more about exactly what inscriptions were needed, and how they had to be inscribed, to achieve a given aim. To exemplify, consider what is needed to establish a specific work routine. First, for example, the skills needed for the routine can be inscribed through training. If this proves to be too weak, the routine can be inscribed in a textual description in the form of a manual. If this is still too weak, the work routine can be inscribed by supporting it with an information system. Hence, through a process of translation, one and the same work routine can be inscribed into components of different materials, with the components linked together into a socio-technical network. As these inscriptions are added and superimposed, they accumulate strength (Latour 1999: 158).

Latour (1991) provides an illuminating illustration of this aspect of ANT. It is an example intended for pedagogic purposes. Hotel managers want to ensure that guests deposit their keys at the front desk when they leave. The way to accomplish this objective, according to ANT, is to inscribe the desired pattern of behaviour into an actor network. The question is, however, how to inscribe it and into what. This is impossible to know for certain beforehand, so the management has to make a sequence of trials to test the strength of different inscriptions. In Latour's story, the management first tried to inscribe the pattern of behaviour into an artefact, in the form of a sign behind the counter requesting all guests to return the key when leaving. This inscription, however, was not strong enough. The management then inscribed it into a key with a metal knob of some weight. By gradually increasing the weight of the knob, the desired behaviour was finally achieved. Hence, through a succession of translations, the hotel's interest was finally inscribed into a network strong enough to impose the desired behaviour on the guests.

Inscriptions invite us to talk about how various kinds of materials—artefacts, work routines, legal documents, prevailing norms and habits, written manuals, institutional and organizational arrangements and procedures—attempt to inscribe patterns of use (which may or may not succeed). Inscribing patterns of use is a way to confine the flexibility of use of an information infrastructure.

Inscriptions have many forms, quite a few of which are not easily spotted. We are accordingly particularly concerned with uncovering the different materials for inscriptions—that is, how and where patterns of use are inscribed. But first it is necessary to study how interests get translated—that is, how they are inscribed into one material before getting re-presented by inscription in a different material.

There are four aspects of the notions of inscription and translation to note:

- the identification of explicit anticipations (or scenarios) of use held by the various actors during design—that is, standardization;
- how these anticipations are translated and inscribed into the standards—that is, the materials of the inscriptions;
- who inscribes them;
- the strength of these inscriptions—that is, the effort it takes to oppose or work around them.

Consider an example drawn from the Statoil case (see Chapter 9), which deals with how the infrastructure based on Lotus Notes actually got 'diffused'. The IT department (SData), in an effort to gain greater organizational visibility, lobbied for the introduction and use of Notes. In terms of inscriptions, SData attempted to inscribe a scenario of extensive Notes use in Statoil. To achieve this, SData needed materials for the inscriptions. The pressure for quality improvement in the sense of ISO certification was exploited to this end. To spell it out in terms of inscriptions, the thrust behind ISO certification—initially spawned by the scandalous sinking of an oil platform belonging to Statoil—was translated and inscribed into a specific Notes application (called Elark) for electronic archiving. This was a viable strategy, as enhanced quality through the ISO certification had already been translated into stricter documentation procedures.

Irreversibility

A key feature of information infrastructure, as discussed in Chapter 3, is the difficulty of making changes. With the use and extension of the core ANT vocabulary developed above, this vital aspect may be lifted forward to occupy centre stage. An information infrastructure is an aligned actor network. The constitutive elements of an information infrastructure—the collection of standards and protocols, user expectations and experience, bureaucratic procedures for passing standards—inscribe patterns of use. But is it not possible to express this more precisely, somehow to 'measure' the net effects (a dangerous expression, but let it pass) to which these superimposed inscriptions actually succeed in shaping the pattern of use—in other words, to measure the strength of an inscription?

Callon's (1991, 1994) concept of the (possible) irreversibility of an aligned network captures the accumulated resistance against change quite nicely. It describes how translations between actor networks are made durable, how they can resist assaults from competing translations. Callon (1991: 159) states that the degree of irreversibility depends, first, on the extent to which it is subsequently impossible to go back to a point where that translation was only one amongst others and, secondly, on the extent to which the network shapes and determines subsequent translations.

Hughes' (1983, 1987, 1994) historical studies of infrastructure technologies underscore the irreversibility of actor networks through his notion of 'momentum'. The crucial difference between Hughes and Callon is the way in which the dynamics of momentum unfolds. Hughes (1994: 108) describes momentum as very much a self-reinforcing process, which gains force as the technical system grows 'larger and more complex'. It is reasonable to take the rate of diffusion of the Internet during recent years as an indication of its considerable momentum. Major changes that seriously interfere with the momentum are, according to Hughes, conceivable only in extraordinary instances: 'Only a historic event of large proportions could deflect or break the momentum . . . the Great Depression being a case in point' (ibid. 108) or, in a different example, the 'oil crisis' (ibid.112). This, however, is not the case with information infrastructure. Momentum and irreversibility are accordingly contradictory aspects of an information infrastructure in the sense that, if momentum results in actual—not only potential—irreversibility, then changes are impossible and it will collapse.

The issues of irreversibility and the alignment of actor networks provide an entry into the debate in the management literature on the (misleadingly similar sounding) notion of 'alignment' (see Chapter 2). An ANT perspective makes it strikingly clear that this 'alignment' is neither straightforward nor controllable in any strict sense. As ANT instructs us, it is not so much an exercise in juxtapositioning two neatly packaged entities as an attempted orchestration of all the elements of a truly extensive, heterogeneous actor network.

The degree of irreversibility of a network may be regarded as a process of institutionalization (Latour 1999: 155–6). This operates both ways: an increased degree of irreversibility is signalled by a firmer institutionalization, and, from the other point of view, the construction of institutions functions as a way to align the network and make it increasingly irreversible. The establishment of a new arena between Norsk Hydro and Statoil (see Chapters 8 and 9) to exchange experience, ideas, and worries related to Notes provides an example of this. The construction of an institutional cooperation aligns the initially independent efforts in the two companies and accordingly increases their irreversibility.

Black-boxing

The flexibility in the granularity of the analysis is essential in the description of information infrastructure. This is because information infrastructure, in a quite straightforward sense, is simultaneously a micro-phenomenon (detailed design, formats, protocols, patterns of local use) and a macro-phenomenon (the actual infrastructure, the collection in total, cutting across local contexts). There is a pressing need to curb the inclination that macro-oriented analyses are biased towards cause and effect of factors, whereas micro-oriented studies notoriously speak of contingency, interpretative flexibility, and social construction (Callon and Latour 1981; Misa 1994; Smith and Marx 1994).

In much the same way as ANT refuses to distinguish a priori between humans and non-humans, so it refuses to distinguish a priori between small and big networks. There is, in other words, no a priori distinction between the micro, meso, and macro level. ANT offers a uniform framework regardless of the unit of analysis.

The problem of information infrastructures, possibly global ones, seemingly inevitably leads to a macro-level analysis with relevant actors such as whole companies, even business sectors, governmental regulating bodies, and broad trends in consumption and production (see Chapter 4). This is important because, as Misa (1994: 119) points out:

Besides taking a smaller unit of analysis, such micro studies tend to focus solely on case studies, to refute rationality or confute functionality, and to be disorder-respecting. Generally, macro studies make it easy for historical actors to appear rational, purposeful, and as key agents of change, whereas micro studies make it difficult or impossible for historical actors to have these same attributes.

The challenge, then, for any critical analysis of evolving, 'global' information infrastructure is to unpack the seemingly macro-elements down to their empirical constituents (see the argument for qualitative research methods in Chapter 2)—that is, their underlying actor network. In this way, ANT provides a uniform framework, in connecting the local and the global, to identify the local in the global, and vice versa.

To illustrate how this works when moving up and down in the analysis, consider the early phase of the introduction of Lotus Notes in Statoil (Chapter 9). A crucial element in the analysis is the way a macro-factor—falling oil prices—got translated into a need for uniformity and subsequently inscribed into a Lotus-based platform. In this way, there are empirical links between the macro and the micro. This link tends to be blurred when resorting to different framework for the micro and the macro: 'Too often sociologists . . . *change their framework of analysis* depending on whether they are tackling a macro-actor or a micro-actor' (Callon and Latour 1981: 280).

Law (1992: 380) also underlines the need to be critical of the unit of analysis. In ANT 'it is a good idea not to take it for granted that there is macro-social system on the one hand, and bits and pieces of derivative micro-social detail on the other', because, if we do so, 'we close off most of the interesting questions about the *origins* of power and organizations'. It is, accordingly, the result of an effort to construct oneself as a highly profiled organizational actor on behalf of others; it is not given beforehand.

The alternative to distinct frameworks that ANT represents is to make the notion of an actor network scalable. This implies that one actant of an actor network may be expanded into a new, complete actor network. Or, conversely, a whole actor network may be collapsed into a single actant. 'To summarize, macro-actors are micro-actors seated on top of many (leaky) black boxes' (Callon and

Latour 1981: 286).

What, then, does this imply in an analysis of information infrastructures, what does this zooming in and out of actor networks look like? It entails that the 'actor' of an analysis is of the 'size' that the researcher chooses as most convenient relative to the direction of the analysis. Hence, an actor may be a given person, a whole group or community of practice including its working technology, a whole organization, even a profession. Similarly, a researcher would vary between a focus on a technological platform as a whole, including the aligned, administrative routines, a focus on some of its applications and patterns of use, down to a focus on the details of integration mechanisms, functionality, and protocols.

Conclusion and Links to the Previous Theories

The way economical, strategic, social, and technical issues profoundly mesh in information infrastructure calls for a framework from which to launch a critical, empirically founded analysis. The ability of ANT to cut across these issues, zoom in and out and make sense of the unfolding process including how irreversibility is constructed, makes it a promising candidate. ANT provides an effective platform from which critically to assess and unravel a set of problematic explicit and implicit assumptions made from the management perspective on information infrastructures as outlined in Chapter 2.

The basic message of ANT related to management and strategy is a cautionary one. ANT is a strategy for unpacking the complexity of our everyday life. Abbreviations, short-circuits, and simplifications are always *produced*. They are the (up till now, successful) result of a mobilization process with black-boxing effects. The ordering these simplifications produce is neither neutral nor 'obvious'. They are *made* obvious or natural in order to achieve an effect—namely, to curb opposition or alternatives. For example, the utterly 'obvious' requirement for global information infrastructures to tidy up the existing mess, fragmentation, and local variety is not obvious at all; it is constructed as obvious.

Relationships with the Other Theories

We conclude by looking briefly at how the theories presented so far can be linked together. They have different origins and are developed to describe or explain different phenomena. However, they all point out important aspects of information infrastructures, and the difficulties and challenges related to the design and management—or control—of such infrastructures. And we also believe that the theories may be interpreted and used in ways so that they all fit together into a richer framework for understanding infrastructures.

One way to make them fit is to see actor-network theory (ANT) as a theory upon which reflexive modernization as well as information economics can be based. ANT can be used to describe in detail and in a coherent way how large heterogeneous networks are built through the ongoing modernization and globalization processes, and also how these networks can be interpreted as actors when side effects are propagated through the networks and new events—also having side effects—are triggered.

Network externalities can be looked at as side effects, and self-reinforcing mechanisms are specific patterns of side effects where one action creates them, and they further trigger new actions similar to the original ones, which again create the same side effects as the first, and so on. When a standard is adopted by one more user, a side effect is that the standard's value for its users increases, which leads to new adoptions, and so on.

Large systems, like the Internet, are built by many independent actors over time. Such systems appear as independent living actors for several reasons.

- The number of actors shaping the system/network is so high that it is impossible for any of them to overlook the actions of all others. This makes the network change in unpredictable ways.
- Side effects of known as well as unknown actions make the network change in unpredictable ways.
- One change—including its side effects—to the network triggers new changes.

Hughes (1983, 1987, 1994) has developed the concept of momentum to describe the development of large technical systems. This is a concept integrating the theories presented so far. He describes momentum as close to a self-reinforcing mechanism as outlined by the economists; at the same time he defines large technical systems as heterogeneous networks in line with ANT (this similarity is pointed out by Hughes 1994 and Callon 1991, as well as by Latour 1999).

Finally, Giddens' image of contemporary phenomena (technology, organizations, institutions, personal careers, identities, and so on) as a juggernaut that is an independent actor partly shaping us and partly shaped by us seems to match perfectly the basic perspectives underlying ANT.

PART TWO

Cases

6

Conservative Success: Organization and Infrastructure Evolution at SKF

BO DAHLBOM, OLE HANSETH, AND JAN LJUNGBERG

SKF is world leader in the production of ball and roller bearings, having 15–20 per cent of the world market. Ever since it was established in 1907 it has been a global, production- and distribution-focused company, selling the very same type of products all over the world. Of course SKF has changed throughout this period. However, what is most striking with the company—in particular compared with the picture of modern global organizations painted by current management literature—is its stability. SKF is changing, but in small steps.

As with the overall company, the information technology (IT) infrastructure has evolved slowly and in relative harmony with the organizational changes. This chapter will outline the successful co-evolution of SKF and its infrastructure. We shall see how, in recent decades, SKF has relied on a strategy for building infrastructures focusing on standardization and hence stability, in effect having an institutional perspective on its organization, focusing on inertia and the cultivation of entrenched infrastructures (Hanseth 1996). This is in obvious conflict with the focus of modern management literature on dynamics and flexibility and on radical and rapid organizational change, designing infrastructures from scratch.

Even when SKF seems to be following modern infrastructure strategies, aligning infrastructure and business strategy, following a top-down, centrally controlled, approach, it does so by developing slowly, without radical breaks with its past. But how long will such a conservative approach be possible? Can SKF meet an increasingly global competition by simply making its production and distribution organization more efficient? Or is there a need for more radical changes at last?

The field study at SKF was carried out in Sweden, Belgium, and Italy. It included seven site visits with observations and about twenty-five interviews with local IT managers, people from the IT headquarter, project leaders, the European sales manager, and managers of production planning, product lines, and warehouses. Visits were made to the IT headquarters, two ball-bearing factories, and a local distribution centre in Göteborg, Sweden, to the European Distribution Centre in Tongeren, Belgium, to the factory in Torino/Airasca, Italy, and to the sales office in Torino, Italy. We are extremely grateful to Olof Berg of SKF for being such a great guide to his company and to the Swedish Transport and Communications Research Board for funding the Internet project (http://internet.informatik.gu.se), of which the research reported in this book is a part.

SKF: History and Evolution

SKF was founded in 1907 by a young engineer, Sven Winquist, at Göteborg, Sweden, but immediately became a multinational company. Its main product is ball and roller bearings. In addition, SKF produces steel and seals. The steel is raw material for the bearings and the seals are to a large extent produced to match the bearings. The bearings' part of the company (which is the subject of this chapter) is organized into six divisions: Automotive, Electrical, Industrial, Asia and Pacific, Speciality Products, and Emerging Businesses. The current strategy focus is on expansion in the growing markets in Asia and Central and Eastern Europe.

SKF's sales reached SEK38 billion in 1998 (in 1996 SEK34 billion), and the number of employees 45,000. At the time of writing, the company is operating in more than 130 countries. Production is taking place at more than eighty-two plants, in fifty-four locations in twenty countries. Customers are reached through 10,000 distributors and approximately 100 SKF sales offices. There was a negative balance of SEK2 billion in 1998 because of investments of SEK3 billion in a global restructuring programme, but in 1996 the profit margin was SEK2.4 billion.

SKF produces (and sells) about 22,000 different bearings. The smallest one is about 2 mm in diameter (used in aeroplane gyroscopes). The largest one is about 7.2 m in diameter and its weight is about 45 tons (used in tunnel drilling machines). In its first year SKF produced 2,200 bearings. At the end of the 1990s it produced 227,000—per hour!

SKF considers its strengths to be technical superiority, quality, and a worldwide distribution system. A well-qualified workforce of application engineers is ready to solve customer problems, give advice, and provide solutions. The high quality is possible only because of excellent engineering competence. Thus, much of the production equipment is manufactured by the company.

SKF began in 1907 with fifteen employees and a yearly production of 2,200 bearings. In its first three years, it was established in France, Germany, England, Finland, Australia, and the USA. Then SKF moved into Norway, Belgium, Holland, Russia, South Africa, China, and Austria. In 1918 SKF had twelve factories around the world, 12,000 employees, and sales in 100 countries. Accordingly we might say that SKF has always been a global company. However, what it means to be global has changed—and keeps changing rapidly.

One way of being a 'global' company—in fact, the most accepted way—is global presence, which is achieved primarily by selling the products globally. Strategies for organizing and operating SKF as a global organization have changed as transport and communication technology has evolved. They have also changed as SKF's customers have become more global.

SKF has continuously globalized through expansion. Although the company has always been global, its activities have remained based in Göteborg. The closer to Göteborg, the larger the market share. For instance, in 1996, 72 per cent of production and 55 per cent of sales were in Western Europe. On the other hand, SKF activities in this area are not growing. The growth is located in the new markets in Central and Eastern Europe and Asia.

In Central and Eastern Europe, SKF is to a large extent expanding by buying factories that used to be run by the governments. In 1998, for instance, SKF took over a factory in Ukraine. SKF has had production units in operation in India since the 1960s, in Singapore since the 1970s, in Japan since the 1980s, in Taiwan and Malaysia since the early 1990s. In China, a new plant began production in Shanghai in early 1997, and another one in Nankou (together with the Ministry for Railroads in China).

At the time of the study, expansion into new markets is taking place primarily through joint ventures. For instance, SKF has bought a 20 per cent share in the leading bearings manufacturer in China, Wafangdian Bearings Company. SKF and this company are together setting up new joint-venture production companies. SKF will be the majority owner and responsible for leadership in these companies. Similarly, SKF is establishing a joint-venture company with ANZAG for the production of seals. A new factory started up in early 1997 in Korea. This is also a joint venture, where SKF is the majority owner and responsible for the leadership.

In the USA, SKF is strengthening its position by alliances. Thus, a new distribution concept has been introduced together with Rockwell Automation. Since the companies are serving their markets through the same distributors all over the USA, SKF and Rockwell have formed a transport alliance, which means that their products are distributed together from one warehouse in Crossville, Tennessee. There are possibilities for including new companies in the logistics system.

When establishing joint ventures with local companies, investments in factories, machines, equipment, and so on are not the most important aspects. What counts rather are investments in quality education, competence, information, and training. Competence development is becoming increasingly more important.

In its early period, the 'global' SKF was organized in independent, local (national or regional) organizations. These organizations were self-contained in the sense that each one included all functions: production, distribution, marketing, and sales, each with its own plants, warehouses, and sales offices. Only product development was centralized at corporate level.

With time, improved transport and communication technology enabled coordination as well as better distribution services across longer distances. Eventually this led to a major shift in strategy. In the early 1970s it was decided to introduce an organizational model in which all production and distribution were integrated. The mother–daughter organization was to be replaced by a divisional organization. The idea was to continue being a full-range producer of bearings, but to cut production costs by specializing production. In principle, each bearing should be produced at only one place, in one plant. That plant should supply all customers, globally.

Of course, the change from independent self-contained national or regional companies into one such globally integrated company could not be made instantly. And, in keeping with the SKF ideology of introducing changes slowly and carefully, this change keeps going on. The new organizational model was not implemented immediately, but rather served as a long-term vision for change. Once the change was begun, it proceeded step by step, with activities being integrated gradually and the area within which activities were operated being extended by one unit at a time.

Growth in the new markets requires a global production, distribution, and sales organization. The customers to be served by SKF are becoming more global. Accordingly, it is important for SKF to be able to respond to customer needs, wherever the customers happen to be.

In addition to globalization (through expansion and integration), SKF has, of course, always worked on making the organization more efficient through increased productivity, less products in stock, and improved customer service through increased reliability (delivery at the time promised) and shorter lead times.

One Information Infrastructure

The decision to adopt a new organizational model in the 1970s also had implications for IT strategy. As long as the national (or regional) companies had been independent and included all functions, they had developed their own IT strategies and solutions. The new integrated model required an integrated IT infrastructure.

Global forecasting and supply system

The first IT-related decision to be made was to start the development of the Global Forecasting and Supply System (GFSS). Such a system was necessary to increase coordination of production and distribution. This system was to be shared by all units in SKF, so it required a shared underlying infrastructure linking the units together. The decision also said that, as far as possible, SKF should build its own infrastructure rather than use commercially available infrastructural services. The infrastructure was considered so important for the business that the company could not depend on external providers for the necessary services—except for the most basic telecommunication services.

The infrastructure was implemented based on a global SNA network. In fact, SKF was a pioneer in establishing a proprietary international data communications network. The first set of leased lines was established in 1976, providing rudimentary mainframe-to-mainframe connections (Hagström 1991). In 1977 the decision was taken to build a proprietary data communications network.

A number of communication services were established, such as file transfer, remote job entry, and message transmission. In 1979 the SKF Group Telenet (Teleprocessing Network) was created to provide basic telecommunications services. Five computer centres in five countries were included: Sweden, West Germany, Italy, France, and the UK. A set of corporate applications and systems was supplied as a part of Telenet. One example was the message transfer system MEST (SKF Electronic Message Transmission). The first backbone network linked the five main European bearing manufacturing units by a set of leased lines from Göteborg to Schweinfurt, Turin, Clamart, and Luton. In 1985 the large computer office at the head office of bearings in King of Prussia, Pennsylvania, was tied to the network through a leased satellite link.

Common Systems

By tradition, computerized information systems had been handled locally. With the establishment of Group Telenet, those days were gone (Hagström 1991). Coordinated production and distribution required shared information services. In principle, coordination would be best supported by just one global system. However, centralizing all computing to one unit was impossible. A more distributed model, including some local computing resources, was necessary. But even if computing power was to be distributed, there would be only one system in use. Such a strategy was defined in terms of 'Common Systems' for all units. All the different systems that were in operation were replaced by a portfolio of systems that was common all over the corporation. The purpose was to link customer orders to production scheduling by intercommunicating systems along the value chain. The new systems portfolio was named the New Material Flow Concept (NMFC). This Common Systems strategy was definitely fundamental to SKF's IT strategy at the time of the study.

The set of integrated Common Systems has been a very important infrastructure for SKF since the 1980s. In the vocabulary of strategic alignment (Weill et al. 1996), these systems primarily constitute a dependent infrastructure. However, the infrastructure has also been enabling, since organizational integration has increased considerably since the first version of Common Systems was launched. Furthermore, the systems have served as a utility, reducing cost through integration, shortening lead times, and decreasing stock. We will now briefly describe the most important systems in the Common Systems portfolio, from the customer side to the supplier side (see Fig. 6.1).

The Sales Company Service System (SCSS) was first installed in Brussels in 1987. It encompasses all administrative functions in a sales company except salaries—that is, it covers marketing support, sales budget and support, customer order handling and invoicing, warehousing and accounts, and even transport scheduling. The main function is to allocate products to customers. By early 1990 it had been implemented in all countries with main node national networks.

SCSS is installed at sales subsidiaries local computers (AS400), which also function as peripheral nodes in the data communications network. Distributors, agents, and local sales offices can place orders, check delivery status, and make enquiries. SCSS will first try to fill an order from local bearing services stock. If this is not possible, then SCSS automatically continues to search for stocks belonging to the bearing industry's warehouses. The SCSS system cannot give the answer 'no'; it can answer only when bearings will be available. If bearings are not available in warehouses, the specialized manufacturing unit replies when the required bearings will be produced.

The International Customer Service System (ICSS) was installed in 1982. It is the key interface between the sales and manufacturing organizations—that is, it

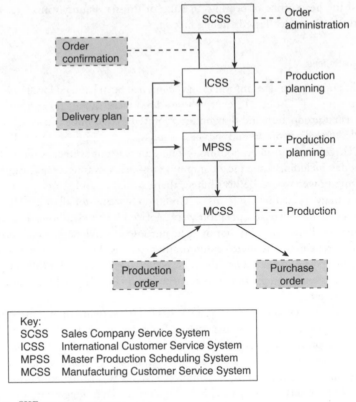

Fig. 6.1. SKF common systems

books orders against internal supply not available from the domestic ware-houses. Its main functions are order entry, delivery time fixing, pricing, order acknowledgement, and export documents creation (including allocation, packing, invoicing, and so on). By 1983 all manufacturing companies in Europe had their own installations (mainframes with MVS). All organizational units connected to Telenet could use ICSS, by having batch as well as on-line connections for trans-mission of orders, packing specifications, and invoices. For the time being the on-line facilities were pretty advanced.

The Master Production Scheduling System (MPSS) is a system for overall plan-ning and production. MPSS was installed between 1987 and 1989 in the main European manufacturing companies. The intention with MPSS was to improve production flexibility without losing any of the efficiency improvements gained by production specialization. MPSS identifies resource requirements and checks them against available manpower and machine capacity, and then generates a master pro-duction plan, attempting to keep the scope for possible intervention as wide as pos-sible. ICSS can intervene in the process about one month before assembly. The

MPSS system is guided by information from both ICSS and PFS—the Product Forecasting System, the latter calculating product forecasts and safety stocks.

The Manufacturing Customer Service System (MCSS) supports shop-floor activities—that is, the day-to-day running and costing of manufacturing. Implementation of MCSS started in 1986 and it was installed in the main European bearing production companies by the beginning of the 1990s. MCSS schedules operations, checks on capacity and workload, monitors work and resource consumption, records changes in inventories, and so on. MCSS regularly generates reports, which are sent to the divisional head office. MCSS is running on mainframe (MVS), and the company-wide responsibility for maintenance and support is assigned to the Turin node.

A Global Organization

When the Common Systems were installed, significant organizational change took place in the form of global harmonization and integration of activities. However, change in organization and infrastructure continues. We will here look at the two most recent major change efforts at the time of the study, both of which took place in the 1990s: first, the introduction of the production channel concept and, secondly, the New European Distribution Structure project (NEDS).

Production channels

The concept of 'production channels' was developed and implemented over a period of years around 1990. Up to then, SKF produced bearings according to (as they describe it themselves) a Taylorist model. This meant specialization to get economies of scale. Each plant (or production unit) produced only one piece—for instance, balls of one specific size, inner rings of specific size and material quality, etc. Then the specific parts were delivered to the locations where the specific bearings were assembled. This model was considered inappropriate and replaced by the channels model—which meant that complete bearings were produced out of the raw material at each channel.

The production-channel concept was introduced in the large-size bearings factory in Göteborg in 1990-1. This factory produces bearings with a diameter of more than 50 cm. Producing such bearings is something of a craft, since each bearing might be unique or produced in very small series. In general, the smaller the bearings are, the more automated the production process will be.

The manufacturing of a large-size roller bearing includes the following steps: cutting on the lathe; ultrasound examination, looking for possible defects in the material (this is sometimes a two-step process; if it is not possible to draw a clear conclusion after the first 'automatic' check, a closer manual examination is made); hardening; grinding; polishing; assembling the pieces together into a complete bearing; and packaging. Between each operation, the bearing components are stored in buffer areas in the factory. According to the general model, there is one area for components on which the operation is finished and one for incoming components. However, the areas are usually 'merged', so that one area containing outgoing components from one operation is also the buffer area for incoming components for the next.

The channel system was introduced in two main phases. In the first, the channels were established, using only existing production equipment. This implied that several channels shared equipment, making optimization and control of the production process quite difficult. The next phase was to introduce new machines so that every channel had its own machines, and to tune the processes. This increased the production capacity. It also made coordination between channels, and accordingly production planning, significantly easier. After the introduction of the channel model, production time in some factories was reduced by 50 per cent.

The introduction of the channel system of course implied that the production-related information systems had to be changed as well. In the large-size bearings factory, new production planning systems were installed in the late 1980s. These systems were designed to contain information about every piece in the production, registering everything done with it at every station. This would enable managers and machine operators to get an overview of the jobs to be done at every station— how many pieces were in line and what to do with them. More aggregated information could also be produced concerning the overall production load and estimated output in the next hours, days, weeks, and so on.

However, the information systems were not put into operation in this extensive way. To do so would have required substantial amounts of information to be entered by the machine operators and a PC (terminal) would have been required at every station. Production managers were convinced that this would cost more than it would pay. Instead, a more simple production control system has gradually grown out of a combination of old ways of working and the new systems.

Orders are collected from a computer system and the production managers use the orders as a basis for putting together a six-week production plan, based on the capacity of the production channels, filling in with demand estimates to round off production. The six-week plan is a simple sheet of paper, sometimes made on a word processor, sometimes produced by the computer system (in which case, the relevant production manager will have made his own personal program to produce it). The production plan sheet is distributed to all the operators in the channel and it is the basis for discussion at the weekly general channel meeting. The operators will mark their sheets as production takes place, and they will share this information at the meetings.

The actual activities on the shop floor are controlled using a simple idea that revolves around 'material as information carrier'. Based on this idea, what the production managers call a 'material information system' has gradually evolved, with the following elements:

- Just looking at the amount of material stored in the various buffer areas gives the information needed about possible bottlenecks in order to utilize the machines optimally.

- Information about what should be done with the individual pieces is written directly on the material:
    - any area that contains a defect is marked (using a piece of chalk); the area is then checked later to see if the defect disappears as the material is cut down;
    - after the cutting process, inner and outer rings are paired together and given identifiers (post-it notes are stuck to the surface);
    - after the grinding process the rings are marked (with ink pen) to indicate how much extra material there is left before the polishing.

This production control system seems to be very straightforward and works well. The interface between the material and the computerized information system is simple (just a sheet of paper). It supports all operations by introducing as few additional activities as possible. It is simple and easy to use by the production workers at the shop floor. And it is very cheap.

The system is heterogeneous, involving humans, computers, paper, and the metal material of the production process itself. In this way, the steel rings are not only the objects to be worked on and 'manufactured'; they take an active part in the production process, informing the operators what to do (see Chapter 5).

The engineer in charge was extremely happy with his system and was adamant in pointing out how much better this 'material information system' was than the computer-based production control system (MCSS) people wanted him to use instead. But looking a little closer at the situation may well make one wonder. The six-week production plan sheet is, of course, the interface to a system that might very well have been run on a computer. And if the operators had to make their marks on such a computer interface rather than on the sheet of paper, then the information about the production process could have been read off the computer rather than being shared at weekly meetings at which people had to read from their sheets. It is all very well using the buffer areas as a means for calling bottlenecks to everybody's attention, but without the sheets it is impossible to know how production is really going.

This example also illustrates the fact that a shared infrastructure based on integrated Common Systems is not constituted by one universal system installed in an identical way at every location. The various factories are indeed different. To make a shared system work, every unit has to implement its part of it. In doing that, each unit might choose to do that in a way that optimized local needs, or in a way that optimized 'external' needs. The large-size bearings factory chose the first alternative. By using paper sheets rather than the common production control system, the large-size bearings factory has really taken control of its operation away from the main office. As long as it is only on paper, there is no way the production can be closely monitored from the main office. The material information system really has the same sort of *raison d'être*. By marking only the material itself, all information about the actual production process is kept on the shop floor, away from the eyes of the main office. This material information system was optimized according to the needs of the local production manager. However, it did not contribute in the best way to a shared infrastructure for the whole of SKF.

There are two sorts of systems compared to each other in this case:

- a material information system with manual routines advocated by engineers and operators on the shop floor;
- a computer-based, powerful, somewhat old-fashioned, production control system advocated by the main office.

In our discussions at SKF only one sort of argument was heard for or against these systems: the argument of practicality. It may seem obvious that the powerful computer-based production system is impractical in a craftlike production, but this is exactly the issue.

To the extent that the manufacturing of bearings retains elements of craft, then computer-based systems will seem impractical. If we side with the engineer on the shop floor, then we seem to have a good argument in favour of the material, manual system. But if we take the perspective of the main office, with the ambition to automate production further, then we might very well say that the disadvantage of the material, manual system is large enough to warrant a more forceful intro-duction of the computer-based system. And, if that system could be made more like the manual paper sheet system they use in the factory, then perhaps it would be even more practical. And, they might even save time by not having all those meet-ings!

The manufacturing of bearings at SKF is undergoing continuous automation. The level of central control is such that there is room for decentralized autonomy in the factories, where the central information systems are not used to their full capacity: 'We have common systems, but lack common policies, common pro-cedures.' In some cases, like in the production of large-size bearings, the craft-like elements of production are still strong. And in most factories there are several gen-erations of production technology working side by side. Thus there is room for fur-ther automation and more intense use of information technology.

The new distribution structure

In the 1970s a major effort was made to coordinate production and distribution in Europe. This activity was a part of the implementation of the new organizational model described above. International warehouses were built and production was specialized for the different factories in Europe. All of Europe became one inte-grated production and distribution system. In the early 1990s this production and distribution system was further refined, in the so-called New European Distribution Structure (NEDS) project, in 1992–6.

When the NEDS project started in 1992, the seven factories in Europe each had their own international distribution warehouse, and all the eighteen local sales offices in Europe had their own warehouses. When the project was finished, four of the fac-tories had international distribution warehouses and all the local warehouses had been shut down while one European Distribution Centre (EDC) had been built in Tongeren in Belgium. At the time of study, big volumes (few order lines) were delivered directly from factories and the four international warehouses, while small volumes (many order lines) for the after-market were delivered from EDC.

The new distribution system requires a new information system architecture. Before NEDS, every sales unit had its own complete version of the Common Systems for handling customer orders with EDI connections to the many factory warehouses. With NEDS a more centralized system has been introduced, described as a client–server architecture, with clients for order and purchase handling at the sales units and central server systems for delivery at the distribution centres. Order handling and delivery involve several systems that have to be able to communicate.

- An order is registered in the sales order system at a sales unit. In this system there is a database with information about customers, products, and pricing.
- A message is sent from the sales order system to one of the distribution centres (selected by the system depending on customer and product) and the order is booked.
- The server system returns a message to the sales unit, confirming the order and giving time of delivery.

There are about twenty installations of the sales order system at sales units around Europe, and there are five installations of the distribution system (at Tongeren and at the four international warehouses). New installations are easy to implement; new sales units and distribution channels can easily be introduced independently of each other. The new system provides improved information about products, delivery times, and order status directly to customers, plants, and distribution and sales units all over Europe. Statistical reports show the number of messages sent, the types of messages, the sender, the receiver, and process times.

This project has been very successful. It was well planned and preceded by benchmarking. Other international companies, including SKF's bearing competitors, had already performed similar changes with good results.

SKF and the IT Revolution

Being one of a handful of quickly growing industrial companies when Sweden was industrialized, and producing a vital component in virtually all machinery, SKF was a major force in the industrial revolution. In many ways it has been an exemplary industrial company. Focusing on production and distribution of its products, with large factories and small offices, SKF was built by engineers and has been run by engineers. It remains a production-focused company. The educational level is relatively low, and the company has a typical blue-collar feeling. What will happen to a company like this in the information-technology revolution?

With the introduction of information systems in the 1970s and 1980s, offices and office work began to grow. Many engineers left the factories to begin to collaborate more closely with economists in the offices. In many industrial companies there was even a power shift from engineers to economists. This trend grew stronger with the document management systems of the early 1990s, increasing the

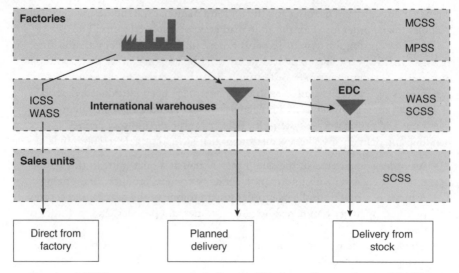

FIG. 6.2. NEDS system structure, including the Warehouse Support System (WASS)

amount of document processing in many companies, making them focus even more on office work.

SKF has been slow in following these trends. Its information-technology use remains focused on production and distribution—production planning, ordering, logistics, and so on. Its offices remain relatively small. Even if it has introduced document management technology like Lotus Notes, it is not really used. In many ways, SKF is an industrial company that has used information technology to support and strengthen its production orientation. Information systems have been introduced as part of more general organizational trends towards centralization and globalization of production and distribution.

So far this strategy has been both necessary and successful. With large industries (automotive companies, electrical appliance companies, paper mills, and so on) as its major customers, the SKF product line can develop relatively slowly and the profit margin is small, so there is neither need nor money for a large office organization. What is important is to be able to continue to produce high-quality bearings more and more efficiently with less and less production disturbances. This means that all infrastructure changes have to be introduced slowly and with the active collaboration of the engineers involved, taking into consideration the old infrastructure and giving room for individual bricolage and preferences.

In this way, SKF has been steadily developing its organization and infrastructure in the direction of a more and more closely knit global production unit for bearings. Nothing that information technology has brought has really changed this traditional approach. SKF remains an industrial company with the same old ambition: to produce high-quality bearings and deliver them reliably and quickly, meeting competition by automating and cutting costs.

This traditional approach has worked well and kept SKF at the top among its competitors. But one may well wonder how long this approach will continue to be successful. At a time when information technology is rapidly turning into a global marketplace, with electronic commerce, one-to-one marketing, and an increasing focus on sales and services rather than production and products, industrial companies like SKF are beginning to lose their power. No matter how efficient they become at manufacturing and distributing their products, their profit will remain slim. So what should a company like SKF do?

From Production to Service

The standard introduction to consultancy books and articles in the early 1990s told about how things were changing. In the past, they would say, it was possible for companies to rely on a stable market with faithful customers. But all that is different now, they went on to say, with global competition on a global, deregulated, and open market, empowered customers demanding tailor-made products and services of high quality, a rapidly developing information technology, more knowledge intensive work, and therefore a more educated workforce.

The global challenge

If, in the past, the most successful organization was the huge factory, mass producing one and the same product to the same customers year after year, it appears that in the 1990s the only surviving companies were those that were able to adjust quickly to an increasingly changing market, with changing demands for new products and services. The recommended recipe for survival was then to move away from the industrial factory organization towards a more loosely organized, fragmented enterprise with alliances, external networking, and outsourcing as major ingredients (Peters and Waterman 1982; Drucker 1988).

The machine bureaucracies typical of large industrial companies were well suited to the demands of the industrial age. Companies producing large quantities of bearings for other industrial companies rather than for consumers ought not to be particularly worried by the warnings of 1990s consultants. Thus, it may perhaps be a bit silly to take seriously the warnings of consultants who are suggesting a development that will turn bearing-producing companies into mobile, networking, knowledge organizations.

SKF focuses on production, and this means that managers close to the production in the factories are empowered to influence the actual nature of the company infrastructure. The culture of the company is such that the experience and competence of the engineers directly involved in production shape the whole company. The way Common Systems have been implemented is a good example of how SKF remains a company where the head office is careful not to enforce its ideas on the engineers and operators on the factory floor. As an indication of the culture of SKF, everybody speaks about production and distribution when they describe their company.

With industrial companies as its major customers, the market is relatively easy to manage. Even if SKF has 25,000 customers, this is really a small number compared to the global market of a pharmaceutical company or a PC company. And among these 25,000 customers there are very few consumers, if any. Thus, when we look at the global challenge to turn into a customer- and service-oriented, distributed, mobile, sales organization, this does not really affect SKF.

And yet, this may not be the whole truth. Globalization means increasing competition and, when several companies are selling similar products, prices will drop and only one will survive. Surviving means focusing on 'adding value' to the customer—that is, offering the customer a product satisfying its needs in a way that competitors cannot match, and for it is willing to pay a good price. In the view of Reich (1991), those surviving in the global competition are turned into service companies. Service delivery is the opposite of mass production. Key characteristics are customer or client interaction, as the service is consumed when it is produced.

Becoming a customer-oriented company

At the end of the 1990s SKF was far from being a service provider. However, there were some indications that it was moving towards the images presented of modern, global organizations. 'Customer in focus' had been a slogan for quite some time. Eventually it started to mean something. There were all sorts of signs of a growing customer awareness in the actual factories. (Hanging from the ceiling above the production channels, one could see signboards with the names of the current customers of each channel. When one of the foremen was asked to name the companies on the board, he got two out of four right without looking.) These signs may seem innocent, but if they are taken seriously they point in a direction that will break up the integrated production and distribution system of SKF, strengthening direct lines of communication between customers and individual factories, and thus threaten the traditional production-oriented philosophy of the company.

Such close cooperation is something big customers were beginning to expect and demand. Thus, for instance, Ford plants in Germany expect the bearings factory in Airasca, Italy, to check the inventory control system at Ford twice a day to determine Ford's needs for bearings, and make deliveries accordingly. Sales management at the factory assumes that most of their customers (mainly car manufacturers) will have similar requirements.

This trend towards more customer orientation is explicit in official SKF documents. Here is the 1996 annual report: 'Sales people are organized into market segments around customers rather than products in order to offer best possible service, solving their problems rather than offering a product.' One example of such customer orientation is the interaction between SKF and Volvo's motor plant in Skövde, Sweden. In this factory, 1,500 motors are manufactured every day. The machines are using SKF bearings. SKF has developed a computerized monitoring system to enable Volvo to have exact on-line information about the status of the bearings. The machines are equipped with sensors communicating directly with the plant's computer system and this system is connected to an SKF computer system, transferring the information to SKF. When a machine begins to malfunction, SKF can advise Volvo on what actions to take, providing a service rather than just selling a product.

This is only one example of a new and rapidly growing market for SKF in products and services for preventive maintenance. These services include everything from small portable equipment for collection of information to on-line systems continuously collecting information and automatically stopping processes when necessary. In 1996, SKF installed one of the most advanced monitoring systems in the world at the Star Petroleum Refinery in Thailand. The system monitors, and prevents breakdown of, all rotating equipment at the refinery such as generators, turbines, gear cases, and pumps. The market for such systems is also growing rapidly in the paper industry. Many of the products for this market involve a large amount of services, setting up continuing cooperation and interaction between SKF personnel and the customer company.

Increasing customer orientation places new and different demands on SKF and on its personnel. From being experts on the production of bearings, SKF has to learn more and more about its customers and their business. At the European sales office in Turin, for example, more and more people are becoming engaged in direct customer interaction. A help desk has been set up for customer advice on design, helping customers identify the bearings that best fit the requirements of the product under design and giving advice about how bearings' requirements affect the design. And for the Italian customers, an organization has been set up making sure that all customers are contacted by telephone or visited on a regular basis, and a detailed database about these customers has been compiled.

Some of these changes may seem innocent and marginal, but together they add up to a radical change in the SKF company culture, changing its focus from production and distribution to customers and service. As of the time of study, this change was only hinted at, with occasional examples and experiments like the ones reported above, but already this new focus had put a strain on the traditional production orientation and the infrastructure that had served it so well.

Developing a service infrastructure

Through its Common Systems strategy SKF has developed a corporate infrastructure that includes all major applications—not only basic communication services, but sales order systems, production planning systems, and the like. This strategy has been very successful. Over the years, the systems have been adapted to changing needs without dramatic crises. The information-systems infrastructure has been aligned with business strategy and under management control. This approach has been possible, however, only because SKF has remained a traditional production company with a relatively narrow range of relatively simple products. While staying within the old production paradigm, SKF has avoided the requirements for a flexible organization and radical changes. SKF has changed its organization at slow speed, a speed the infrastructure could follow.

During the late 1990s SKF seemed to be flirting with a more radical change, however, in the direction of a service- and customer-focused organization. Such a change is difficult to take slowly, involving as it does a more radical change of organizational paradigm, from a production organization to a more diversified and flexible structure. And the infrastructure has to follow. The computing set-up (mainframes, text-based terminals) also has to be replaced. The new infrastructure has to support the new organization. It is more heterogeneous and it must be far more flexible. Like the organization itself, it has to be more customer oriented to support a closer customer interaction. The monitoring system installed at Volvo in Skövde and integrated with SKF's own systems in Göteborg is one example. Such an infrastructure cannot be owned by SKF alone. It must be based, as far as possible, on public infrastructures like the Internet. Such a heterogeneous, rapidly changing infrastructure based on publicly available services can only be controlled by SKF to a limited degree.

SKF is also approaching the end of its computing paradigm, because that is built on a dying technology. Graphical interfaces, client server architectures, and multimedia technology will be required. Such a change in technology will be a major challenge independently of new organizational requirements. But it will contribute to a speeding-up of the changes already begun in the organizational culture.

At the time of writing the challenge is this: a production-oriented company with industrial customers can operate on a global market with its own internal infrastructure, and it will do well to turn its company into one integrated production and distribution organization. The drawback of this approach lies in the normal dangers of centralization: it creates a slow-moving colossus with few local initiatives and little sensitivity to local variations. SKF seems to have handled these dangers well enough in the past, giving its factory engineers a substantial amount of autonomy. But that was when production was the focus.

A service-oriented company, on the other hand, will have to be very different. Its operation on the global market is made possible by public infrastructures, and its focus is sales and services rather than production and distribution, which it presupposes are already well managed. Were SKF to move in this direction, it would have to create a networked sales organization, which would use public systems rather than Common Systems. That sales organization could either be closely tied to production and distribution or it could operate at a distance from the factories, treating them as outsourced partners.

To create such a sales organization is no easy task. When companies try to get closer to their customers, providing services, anticipating needs, being more aggressive in their marketing and sales efforts, company boundaries begin to dissolve. But those boundaries dissolve for other reasons as well, as when companies want to change by increasing personnel turnover, by encouraging collaboration across company borders, by relying more on consultants and independent operators, and so on. In all of this, there is a trend away from the self-sufficient, formally organized, closed factory, to a more nervous, fragmented company, opening up to the world surrounding it. It is very difficult to see how such a fragmented organization could be tolerated within the SKF family.

Conclusion

The engineer is still king at SKF, and it will not be easy to change that. But the profit margins for old industrial companies like SKF are slim. And more forceful automation of the production to cut costs, necessary to meet global competition, will not change this fact. In this, companies like SKF resemble their poor cousins the textile factories. Those factories are now functioning as low-profit outsourcing operations in the hands of high-profit design, sales, and marketing companies. Will the mechanical industry go the same way as the textile industry? If so, then SKF may very well be wise to begin setting up its own more customer-oriented marketing, sales, and service organization close to the market. The experiments with more active sales initiatives and customer services seem extravagant, but maybe they are a first step in the right direction. Some of the ideas of the IT people at SKF (as summarized in a study they made in 1995, called 'The Future IS Study') seem much too trendy for a company like SKF—mobile computing, multimedia, and virtual-reality technology—but maybe they are actually right. And maybe pressures from customers to cooperate more closely, if only by simple means such as e-mail and telephone, and by sharing information systems, will eventually bring forth a new, more service-oriented SKF?

But then, on the other hand, there are of course good reasons for SKF to stick to its successful tradition and remain what it always has been: a powerful industrial company focusing on production and the quality of its products. As long as SKF's major customers—such as the automotive industry, electrical companies, construction companies, paper mills, and so on—do not change, it does not make sense for SKF to change.

Eventually it may very well be the case that the business focus in the world will shift from powerful industrial production companies like SKF to powerful sales, marketing, and financial operators. Certainly there is such a shift going on within the automotive industry from the production end of the companies towards the design and sales end. But this does not mean that the production part of an automotive company will have to, or even should, change. And SKF may very well remain a machine bureaucracy, producing high-quality bearings. But in order to remain in power, it would have to ensure it maintained control of the sales of its bearings. And to do so it would have to turn its sales organization into a much more powerful and customer-oriented operation and increase its power over production.

How easy would it be for SKF to change its sales and marketing organization into a network of networking organizations? Well, first it would have to accept the power shift from production to sales and services, without at the same time giving up its high standards of product quality. Perhaps the only way it could do this would be by making the sales and services offices more independent, distinguishing them more clearly from the production divisions. Perhaps, they ought to be able to sell products from other companies. Perhaps, SKF should divide into two company structures, one for production and one for sales and services. If it is true that the IT revolution will make the old and powerful industrial production companies lose their power to networking sales and service companies, then SKF might do well to ensure it has a powerful company of the latter sort when the time comes for the power shift.

7

Infrastructure as a Process: The Case of CRM in IBM

CLAUDIO U. CIBORRA AND ANGELO FAILLA

> The capability procures for itself organs;
> it is not the organs that possess capabilities.
>
> M. Heidegger

The early 1990s were years of tremendous change and turnaround for IBM. The growth of this high-tech industry giant was shaken dramatically. In the year after IBM had had the highest profits of its long history, Big Blue went into the red. A radical change at the leadership level was swiftly implemented, and Lou Gerstner arrived—a manager who came, not from inside the company, or even from the IT industry, but from the consumer product industry. The organization structure, which had been on the brink of being totally decentralized through the creation of several separate and independent companies, was suddenly recentralized. Various workforce reduction plans were enacted to change the culture of the corporation and the expectations of its employees. New priorities were defined, but their translation into concrete measures took time. This led to a shifting internal organization. For the first time in its history, IBM was perceived, even internally, not as a smoothly running hierarchy, but as a confusing, if not downright messy, organization. The swift reforms delivered: a dramatic turnaround brought the company back to profitability, and its share price rose to surprising levels that left stunned those observers who had been too quick to suggest that Big Blue was on an irreversible decline.

This study was conducted during 1997 and 1998 in the following countries: the USA, Italy, France, Sweden, and the UK. More than fifty people were interviewed: regional and area managers (Europe); senior heads of vertical businesses (USA); those responsible for organization and IT (USA and Europe); CRM top consultants (USA and Europe); local sales-force managers (USA); CRM training managers (Europe). Interviews lasted on average two hours. Three major feedback sessions were held based on an earlier manuscript with CRM and regional managers in Europe. The authors wish to thank IBM and specifically all the personnel interviewed. Special thanks to Giulio Koch for his continuous support of the project, and to Gianni Camisa, Dario Colosimo, and Pierangelo Sartori for their constant help in the fieldwork.

This case reports on the implementation of one of the main strategic priority programmes that were introduced in the early 1990s by the new leadership. This particular programme set out to develop the 'new plumbing' of IBM—that is, to redefine and build anew the business process that links customers with the company. This newly designed process is called customer relationship management (CRM). It was defined and launched in 1994 and features a complex web of activities, roles, and IT tools, affecting thousands of employees. Like the other main programmes, its deployment has been followed closely by top management: an IBM Executive Board has been responsible for the overall implementation activities of CRM.

The case looks at CRM as a major new infrastructure, consisting of processes, people, and technology, and analyses its inner dynamics of conception, launch, deployment, use, and ongoing modification. It shows that the term 'infrastructure', or the more colourful ones of 'plumbing' and 'pipeline', may not be the right metaphors to describe CRM 'in action'. Though ideally CRM looks like an orderly, streamlined sequence of processes, it actually functions more like an 'unfolding event' or 'a process in itself'. The continuous revisions and adjustments reveal an immense effort of learning by making ad hoc adjustments, fine-tuning, and even tinkering. The implementation of CRM is striking because of the amount of 'care' (Ciborra 1996c) required by all the stakeholders involved, the effort expended to 'align' the various parts of the organization, and the technology needed to make the initial concept an organizational reality (Latour 1987).

The case raises, but does not resolve, various questions. CRM is aimed at streamlining and shortening the key business processes that define IBM's relationship to the markets of its various products and customers in a way that will be truly global. But the process of implementing CRM itself is far from being streamlined and fast. Many informants at all levels of the organization have repeatedly said that 'there is no alternative to CRM. Thus, no matter the time it will take, it is the only way to go.' Learning, adjustments, and changes along the route are inevitable, and in any case after four years the newly designed process was beginning to deliver the expected results. So, is it fast enough? Does it pay off? Can it be fully implemented? Do these questions express the voice of those 'angry orphans' touched negatively by the new standard (David 1986)? Or, do they point to inner difficulties of the original CRM design? Could there be alternatives? The case cannot draw any conclusion, but hopes to clear the way for further discussion and questioning.

Globalization and its Consequences

In order to appreciate why there would be no alternative to CRM, and to the other major re-engineering initiatives en route at IBM, it is vital to understand the competitive trends in the industry and the ensuing need for a strategic response called 'globalization'. But the attempt to transform internal operations and identity has also played a crucial role in the positioning of Big Blue versus the outside competitive forces.

Despite the total quality management (TQM) programmes started in the 1980s, systematic benchmarking and auditing of customer opinions in the early 1990s convinced the new leadership that IBM needed further to streamline and speed up its internal operations in order to provide faster and better-quality customer service. Secondly, the service idea itself had to become a common IBM approach. Customers seemed to appreciate having a consistent interface with the company, and valued its brand-name reputation, rather than having to deal with multiple, separate organizations. Soon, the challenge appeared to lead to the reinvention of a highly efficient global company, able to service customers worldwide in a uniform manner, with overheads and speed of response as good as the next, newer competitors. Certainly, the challenge seemed to imply a better redeployment and use of IBM internal competencies, resources, and skills.

Global products offered by a global company, able to service customers worldwide, became the new business idea for IBM. That idea had to be translated into a set of internal changes. Among them, a dozen consisted of BPR initiatives affecting the main processes through which IBM was doing business. If the thrust of the changes was a better alignment with the market, their overarching philosophy was to redefine the new, global way of operating through cross-functional processes. Vertical businesses were identified (instead of the previous product or business units, or separate companies), together with new geographical areas. The resulting organization is characterized by a three-dimensional matrix structure, made of processes, vertical businesses, and geographies. To implement the new arrangements, the previous ones had to be gradually dismantled. In particular, the existence of unitary, global, and transversal processes required abolishing the hierarchy of national and area sales organizations, which previously handled customers' requests. Thus, country organizations such as IBM Italy, or area organizations such as IBM Europe, were to lose most of their content, and their managers were to perform mainly political or symbolic roles, compared to the previously much more hands-on assignments.

In particular, the goal of CRM was to outline the sequence of activities needed to complete a negotiation cycle that starts from identifying a business opportunity, and continues through making an offer, writing the contract, and delivering the solution procured internally and/or through the business partners, up to the monitoring of customer satisfaction. The roles of units and people who perform the activities were specified together with a broad set of IT applications to support the various activities and processes. The full layout of CRM is very complex and some of its diagram incarnations can cover a whole wall. In Fig. 7.1 a summary version is reproduced. In CRM representations the other dimensions of the matrix are seldom shown—that is, no reference is made to geographies or vertical markets. This is done intentionally, since CRM has been conceived and is being implemented as a common, corporate way of doing business, valid for any type of deal, business, and country. It is through processes like CRM that IBM wants to become a truly global company.

CRM: An Overview

In an earlier document (1994) CRM was described as a project aimed at redesigning IBM sales processes. The final goal was to standardize all the activities related to sales and customer support across all geographic areas where IBM used to operate. As an extra, a new IT infrastructure (or IT tools) was to be introduced to support the key activities of identifying new customers, defining new market opportunities and skills required successfully to execute a transaction, and, more generally, to allow thorough information sharing across the organization concerning commercial transactions.

The ambitious redesign was motivated by the urge to offer an adequate answer to what the market demanded. What the customers wanted from IBM in the early 1990s was pretty clear. They asked for a vendor able to keep its own promises; to offer customized solutions; to provide in the earlier stages of a transaction a full range of opportunities in terms of prices for different products/services; and to be capable of communicating effectively and of understanding the specific needs of businesses and individual customers, so as to be ready to assemble and deliver all the competencies and resources needed to solve the client's problems.

At the very basis of CRM there is the original effort of having had to rethink the whole set of relationships with the customer. At the time of writing this process is still underway and it is transforming the entire IBM organization.

As shown in Fig. 7.1, CRM is composed of eleven main processes. The activities grouped in these processes concern the front office, with relationship manage-

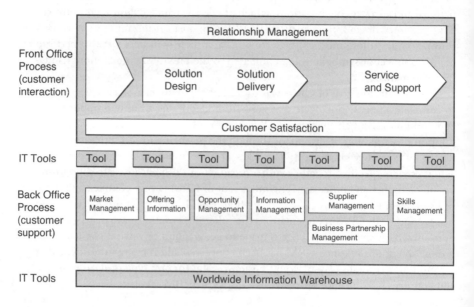

FIG. 7.1. A general view of CRM

ment, the design and supply of a solution, and various support activities up to the customer satisfaction evaluation. These front-office processes are complemented by six back-office processes that range from market management to skills management. Knowledge about the available internal resources is a key aspect of CRM, and the archive of existing competencies includes thousands of skills profiles.

The processes as outlined in Fig. 7.1 were pretty much defined in 1996, including the support of a variety of IT tools and an 'Information Warehouse'. The latter would work as an 'organization memory' (Prusak 1997), able to keep track of the relationship histories with customers, including initial deals, signed contracts, satisfaction levels, and so on.

Starting from the original, overall architecture, each process has been micro-designed so to make it fit the business requirements. Consider, for example, the process concerning skills and resources management (see Fig. 7.2). The latter are seen not just as final conduits to distribute products/services, but as professional resources able to devise solutions and create services that can add value to the customers. The process goal is, then, to take the right skills, required by the market at the right time and location, and make them available worldwide. In order to reach this objective, the process is decomposed into four different sub-processes. The first, linked to the market-management process, consists in a careful analysis of the skills and resources as requested by the market. This allows management to identify the gap between the skills that are available and the market demand. On the basis of such an analysis, it is possible to specify interventions and corresponding investments. The second sub-process evaluates the existing individual skills profiles and sets up training and development programmes. The third sub-process supplies the specific training and development interventions by using the available resources and coordinating the effort of the internal units concerned. The final sub-process deals with the optimization of the use and development of the human resources globally.

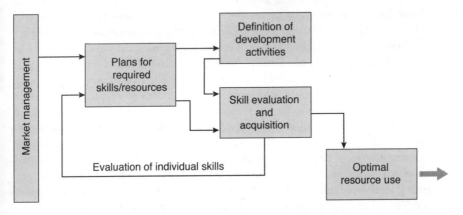

FIG. 7.2. The skills and resources management process

The microdesign is constantly aligned with the overall CRM goals, and each process or sub-process has to meet the overarching requirements of three different kinds of customer relationships—namely, off-the-shelf sale, mass customization, and 'one of a kind'.

In general, a typical CRM transaction would start with the opening of a new opportunity (that is, a customer interest is identified regarding a product/service) by a role (a function to be performed by a manager or employee) called the 'Opportunity Identifier'. Subsequently, the follow-up of the initial contact is attended to by another role, the 'Opportunity Owner', appointed by the local employee responsible, or the 'Opportunity Manager'. Typically, at any point in time, there are thousands of opportunities in the 'opportunity database' (another key IT tool).

Given the complexity of the process and the multiplicity of roles, a short example will help to illustrate the main stages of CRM. The IBM sales representative (in this case the 'Opportunity Identifier') who deals with a major client detects an interest in that company for an IT application for its sales-force support. She has no special knowledge about such an application. Before CRM, the sales representative would have assembled a solution on her own to be submitted to the client. Following the CRM guide, instead, the representative registers the request as a new opportunity in the opportunity database. This database is 'owned' by the Opportunity Management process and the employee responsible. The Opportunity Manager evaluates the lead in the context of the marketing plan concerning that market segment, IBM's current offerings, the skill availability, and other relevant variables contained in the Information Warehouse. If the business lead is commercially interesting, the Opportunity Manager allocates it to an Opportunity Owner who is competent to deal with that kind of application. The Opportunity Owner informs the sales representative and the customer, and takes responsibility for carrying out the whole project. During the execution of the project he uses the organizational memory to retrieve similar solutions that have already been implemented with other customers, and also to find details about the relationship history between the customer and IBM, its most meaningful events and trends. To facilitate the latter process, so-called Customer Rooms are being set up where those within IBM responsible for dealing with the same customer can meet and share information. Finally, the sales representative can proceed to identify the next business opportunity with the same or other customers.

The example shows how CRM pursues the objectives of a typical BPR design: the decrease of low value-added activities; optimization of other activities; and the refocusing of the main business drivers. Moreover, doing business is not just reacting to a customer's request, but being constantly engaged in a proactive search for opportunities according to market segments and targets. Necessary preconditions for such a design are the worldwide standardization of the market segments; the sharp separation of roles (for example, on the one hand, market analysis and opportunities evaluation; on the other, contract execution); and the allocation of the right competencies to the pending jobs by optimizing the use of available resources, again worldwide. Whenever an opportunity becomes a successful transaction, the experience is memorized, and the relevant knowledge, competencies, and intellectual capital are shared across all the geographic areas. The Information Warehouse is a key tool in this respect (actually a foundation tool, since it lies at the bottom of all back-office processes (see Fig. 7.1)). It is not surprising, then, that a regional manager concludes that 'IT and CRM walk hand in hand'.

CRM and IT

Surprisingly, although CRM has been conceived from the very beginning within a coherent strategic vision, the construction of the IT infrastructure has not been a seamless process, despite the ubiquitous and foundational role attributed to IT in the original design (recall the scope for the Information Warehouse). Specifically, while CRM was presented and perceived as an orderly sequence of activities, or at least as a grid where it was always possible to find the right place, role, and process, the various IT tools emerged gradually, mostly out of contingent choices, opportunistic moves, and short cuts. Certainly, the *installed base* made things more complicated: for example, seven different computer architectures would coexist in a typical national IBM organization. The process of building the technical infrastructure, which was still ongoing at the time of study, can be described as an enormous 'learning-by-doing' process, which was inevitably taking quite a long time to be completed. In an earlier phase, almost as a reaction to the failure of a grand new design project (see below), management tried to use existing tools, which came from disparate functions and areas. This is because, in each country, there is an abundance of local business applications, which are one of the outcomes of IBM's excellence in systems and applications development savvy. Why, then, not pick and choose the best among the local applications and make it the worldwide standard for each CRM (sub-)process? The price for this diffusion strategy has been the scarce level of integration of the systems and applications selected. On the one hand, the implementation of CRM as a business process could not 'wait' for the completion of the IT tools set. On the other, in order to provide some IT support, ad hoc solutions had to be adopted to fill the overall applications portfolio of the Information Warehouse (see Fig. 7.3). The general design indicates that the Information Warehouse supports the transactions with the customers according to the three main types of market contracts (see above). Data in the Warehouse concern market segments; customer profiles; solutions already tested, available skills, and so on. The construction of such an organizational memory in a context that is not a 'greenfield site' appears to be quite vast and complicated: for example, existing regional and functional databases need to be accessed and merged intelligently. The level of difficulty of such a task can be better appreciated if one considers the case of the skills-management database (one key component of the Warehouse). Originally, the application was developed by IBM Australia, and then adopted globally after some local adaptations. However, that application was not fully integrated with other tools present in the same Warehouse, such as Omsys, for

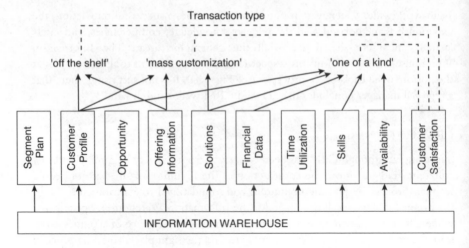

FIG. 7.3. Main functions of the Information Warehouse

keeping track of the business opportunities; RTM for customer information; or Dashboard for internal progress reporting.

In a subsequent phase, streamlining the emerging infrastructure was the main focus of activity. Three goals were set forward by management: architectural coherence, the maximization of user satisfaction, and the integration of CRM tools with the surrounding business systems. At the time of study, budget expenditure in this area had begun to decrease, signalling that the integration effort was approaching completion, but not without pain and cost.

It goes without saying that moving from the initial phase of the separate tools to one of integration has radically redrawn the boundaries between local and central powers concerning IT. The enormous effort required to streamline and integrate systems into a coherent infrastructure has gradually reduced the margins for local autonomy. For example, ad hoc applications cannot be developed locally any longer. Everyone (in IT services) is instead called to contribute to the definitions of new global standards and systems: only through this consultation process can the local voice be exerted. The success factor for a new application shifts dramatically: to be viable it must first be consistent with the global architecture. To get a new application approved, or better accepted, depends upon it working its way effectively through the extant global management system.

Intellectual Origins

Ironically, CRM started small, and before it was included in the portfolio of the BPR projects to enact the 'new, global IBM'.

In fact, the CRM team was an outgrowth of an existing local, almost self-appointed small group of managers in the USA who wanted to rethink the marketing processes and activities. With Gerstner's arrival and the launch of the major BPR initiatives, the initial small team was extended to include both US and Europe managers, and assigned the mission to design CRM. Thinking in terms of processes was, of course, not something new for IBM managers. At that time the inheritance—at the least the intellectual one—of the quality movement was still much in evidence. In order to improve the quality of operations, managers and engineers were urged by the TQM philosophy to focus on whole processes rather than particular tasks. Thus, at that time part of the corporate approach was the fact that 'process management will be the principal IBM quality focus in the coming years' (internal IBM memo reported by Davenport and Short 1990: 11–27).

Besides TQM, other intellectual origins and interventions can be tracked down. Above all, CRM is the intellectual product of the vast wave of the corporate restructuring movement called BPR. It shares most of its basic tenets with BPR, such as a process orientation, a radical and global approach to redesign, and the key role assigned to IT. Indeed, BPR was supposed to be using 'the power of modern information technology to radically redesign our business processes in order to achieve dramatic improvements in their performance' (Hammer 1990). CRM was first conceived in the name of a global and radical change of processes. Technology—or, as defined in the CRM jargon, 'tools'—has from the start been regarded as a way to freeze the new processes in silicon and software. On the other hand, CRM was not really designed to achieve 'quantum leaps' in performance, since from benchmarking studies IBM could match competitors' performances in most, though not all, areas. Rather, the vision driving CRM envisaged goals such as: establishing a global, uniform way to deal with customers; being able to complete and monitor a commercial transaction from end to end; being able to measure overall process performances centrally; and, of course, being able to do all this equally well or better than the next competitor. Only in some specific activities, like invoicing, could one observe the kind of goals, consisting of dramatic cuts in time and costs, usually instigated by a BPR programme.

CRM was also launched conforming to the tenets of how to start a good BPR exercise. A top-level management team representing the experiences of the key functional areas was set up with the mandate of breaking loose from outmoded ways of doing business and searching for new ways to achieve results. The team was urged to 'think big' and had the support of top management, the factor 'that is necessary for reengineering to succeed: executive leadership with real vision' (Hammer 1990). There were explicit actions taken in this respect, with a highly symbolic value. The CEO designated a senior manager as the 'owner' of the process and invested him with full authority and responsibility over the process implementation.

In defining the actual content of CRM, specific BPR design tenets were also adhered to: to organize around outcomes, not tasks; to subsume information processing into real work; to treat geographically dispersed resources as though they were centralized; to link parallel activities; to capture information once and at the source, and so on.

However, we submit, if one looks at the original conception of CRM, some of the BPR principles are seen to have been emphasized, while others were, if not downplayed, at least adapted to an in-house interpretation of how to organize the relationship with the customer. To wit, while the principles listed above were strictly followed in designing the new processes, others were not considered so closely, such as: 'Have those who use the output of the process perform the process'; or, 'Put the decision point where the work is performed and build control into the process'. Instead, instances where certain roles have to send information upwards, to allow superiors to exercise control over larger portions of the process, can still be found in CRM.

In other respects, CRM shares with the BPR philosophy the fact of being an instance of 'discontinuous thinking', breaking away from the fundamental assumptions that underlie operations (Hammer 1990). For example, the original CRM team availed itself of the consulting advice of Fernando Flores, to tap his radical ideas about management as a 'network of commitments' (Winograd and Flores 1987), and IT as a means of coping with the breakdowns that interfere with the smooth completion of a commitment. Indeed, despite the maze of sub-processes and roles in CRM, its basic idea is relatively straightforward: to identify and organize consistently all those activities that are needed to complete a transaction with the customer from the initial lead to measuring final satisfaction. The collaboration with Flores and his consulting firm lasted until the definition (but not the execution) of the vast CRM training programme for IBM personnel.

The Implementation Process

Apparently, its designers were conscious that CRM would imply vast, radical changes that could take place only with time. And the detailed design effort did not hide the fact that CRM was 'a journey, rather than a destination', in the spirit of a true learning organization.

At the end of 1997 and the beginning of 1998, estimates of how much of CRM had been implemented varied, depending on the level, role, and country of the informant. If 'implementation' is divided into two phases—deployment and execution—most informants agreed that CRM was between 80 and 90 per cent deployed, and between 40 and 50 per cent in execution. Where does this difference come from? In the 1997 corporate reports, CRM is presented as a new way of working that is here to stay. At the same time, these reports are adamant about the fact that there were still many ways in which the use of CRM could be improved, in areas such as tools, a reduction of internal red tape in 'passing the baton in the relay race', an uneven workload in the sales force, and so on. Hints about the discrepancy between deployment and execution can also be found in the training cases used in the CRM courses. These are real cases in which all the main characters assume CRM roles and fulfil them but more as a ritual than as an actual way of working. Indeed, execution as portrayed in the cases features the traditional bureaucratic way of running the business: the customer comes last; there is a lot of scapegoating and discharging of corporate responsibilities from one role or office to the other, and so on. The cases remind the trainees that people within IBM may be able to fill the roles according to the CRM language, but may then act in the old bureaucratic way. The result is that the customer remains baffled and the 'old IBM' re-emerges behind the newly deployed CRM.

At this point, only the study of the implementation process can provide a qualitative clue about the discrepancies just mentioned. The deployment of CRM is evidently a long and complex learning process. Schematically, it is possible to distinguish two stages of the journey, which for the sake of clarity can be labelled 'mechanistic' and 'adaptive'.

The main thrust of the mechanistic stage was the straightforward application of the CRM model, once the key management factors had been ensured in terms of strategic alignment, top-management support, and allocation of the resources, skills, and competencies needed to develop the new infrastructure. This stage, which lasted for about three years, was characterized by some aspects that were overlooked and a few snags that delayed implementation and ultimately brought about major changes not so much in the original model, but in the way it was implemented. By spring 1998 deployment was still ongoing, after the major changes introduced at the end of 1997.

The mechanistic stage was spent in 'spreading the message' throughout the corporation. More than 100,000 employees had to be exposed to the new model as a first, essential step to making it truly globally understood. Training was organized top down: first, all senior managers worldwide were offered a short introductory course; then the message was gradually diffused down the hierarchy, relying on the fact that, once senior managers had been exposed to the new concept, they would start autonomous training courses in their businesses. After this first phase had been accomplished, the next task consisted of spreading the message in the country organizations. Dedicated training materials (cases, videos, and exercises) were conscientiously prepared and utilized. The complexity of the process and even the sheer mental effort required to learn by rote all the facets of CRM, meant that training had to be relatively intense, structured, and backed up by manuals, press releases, and systems that prompted decision-makers to act according to the CRM philosophy and operational requirements. As seen above, though the idea underlying CRM is pretty straightforward in business terms, the details of the process involve a special language, and not everybody is able to memorize by heart such a new language when executing a customer transaction. On the one hand, the vast training effort signals once again the determination and commitment from management to diffuse CRM as the new lifeblood of the corporation. On the other, CRM may be somewhat difficult to 'understand'. To wit, CRM can be clearly described and communicated thanks to plenty of explanatory material of good quality available on multimedia supports (including a web site). But this is just the first level of modes through which people can take care of complex systems and processes (see Ciborra 1996c). For CRM to be used in action, roles need to deal with breakdowns of systems and processes in a skilled way (and not just by being able to recall by heart all the sequences and terms). At the limit, and this is the level of true understanding, people should execute CRM without thinking about it. In all the instances explored during this study, it seemed that employees were far from having reached such a high level of understanding. CRM, though valued in certain contexts, still seemed to be 'incongruous', standing out from the normal way of working; it still had to be referred to explicitly, since it was not yet part of the implicit or tacit way of working. The subtle threshold that separates CRM from being not just a mechanical sequence of procedures but a routine embedded in the workflow and daily practices, had not been crossed, except in certain levels of the organization and in selected countries (essentially the USA (see below)).

It is hard to say whether the higher level of understanding will happen with time and more practice backed by further training or whether this is intrinsic to the process. What is certain is that CRM seems to have no built-in acceptance mechanism by which it acquires its own momentum and its diffusion becomes a self-feeding process.

A series of new mechanisms and interventions were devised by top management for stepping up the level of care for CRM. Such higher care, supported by large-scale interventions, is what characterized the second stage of implementation.

This later stage featured a complex set of moves aimed at overcoming some of the obstacles that had emerged during the previous one and at pursuing the further implementation of CRM. In general, what had been perceived as missing were 'dynamic mechanisms' or 'engines'. The use of metaphors hinted at the fact that CRM had not unfolded automatically or autonomously. It had lacked momentum for various reasons, the key ones being people, tools, and cultures.

The people factor refers to the lack of compliance at all levels. Here, the reform envisaged comprised new sets of incentives tied to the CRM organization, so that, by working according to the new standards, people would get rewarded. But incentives do not suffice at the higher levels of the hierarchy. Here, other 'engines' are being used. For example, top business unit managers are requested to make a formal commitment (by signing a CRM charter) to implement the new process. Commitment is thus 'signed in blood', to become (hopefully) irreversible.

The IT tools were another major terrain of intervention for the adaptive stage. With the new applications not yet in place, and after the failure to build a totally new platform to support CRM, there was little way to enforce or at least 'prompt behaviour through the technology'. The arrival of Lotus Notes has provided the basic content for the second reform: the new applications are built on Notes, addressing the main steps of CRM one after the other. But there is a more general dimension of interest: the role played by corporate IT. This has been redefined quite dramatically: since the end of 1997 corporate IT has been formally associated to the BPR projects, and it actually has to report to the BPR management team. This formal realignment has been deemed necessary, since CRM, like other projects, met unexpected difficulty in having corporate IT coping with the new exigencies triggered by the business process transformation.

Finally, the cultural reasons refer to the multiple 'national' reactions to CRM and the varying degrees of implementation in different countries, so that CRM may mean something very different in the distinct national contexts. Some see globalization proceeding 'no matter what the sceptics say': it is the only way to do 'e-business'. Any slowdown or local resistance is seen as an aberration, especially from the US point of view. Others hint at the fact that one has to live with an uneven level of implementation (grades are informally given to the various geographies and even to individual countries). For some areas it is again suggested that it will be a matter of time, although for others it should be assumed that they would never use CRM. If the latter opinions have any validity, the feasibility of the new managerial vision supposed to steer the company towards globalization would be in doubt.

The adaptive stage shows that management is learning some important lessons, and recognizes that the initial, rather mechanistic implementation of the BPR principles was blinded by excessive enthusiasm. Note how the second stage is characterized by a more realistic approach: it is putting order in the ways to deal with the incentives for human resources and the technical platform, and in general adjusting expectations. At the time of writing progress seems to be good. Still no precise 'completion date' is in view; nor is any explanation provided about why some key aspects of design and implementation were overlooked in the early days of CRM implementation.

First Results

Four years after its initial conception, CRM was delivering its first substantial results, especially in those geographic areas where its deployment was further ahead—namely, the USA. Positive outcomes could be noticed both at local and headquarters level.

At a local level, the regional sales offices could get from CRM an updated status of advancement of key measures regarding the number of opportunities in store, their allocation, and their progress. CRM was being used as an Executive Information System, which helped the local decision-maker to allocate resources and efforts to reach his or her targets. The management and follow-up of the opportunities was then carried out according to the axes of the overall matrix organization.

At the headquarters level, each vertical market could have the overall figures of its business worldwide, in terms of the CRM macro indicators (how many opportunities were in store; how many were being realized; and so on). On the basis of these indicators, it is now possible to measure on a factual basis the performance of all the key decision-makers, up to the head of each vertical business. CRM managers and internal consultants submit that this is the biggest pay-off of CRM: the opportunity of centralized factual performance measurement, which leads to the possibility of providing a rigorous discipline and steering of the business on an unprecedented global scale.

The gradual implementation of Notes applications to support CRM was beginning to offer another opportunity: that of freezing the CRM discipline in silicon, thus 'enforcing' globally behaviours on how to run the business. A virtuous circle was thus finally emerging. The growing base of Notes applications would make the measurement possibilities deeper and enlarge their scope over more and more CRM processes. This would further increase the scope and depth for control, both at local and central level.

There are, however, many difficulties along the way. As mentioned above, national/cultural factors make the deployment of CRM somehow uneven. Some geographies (like Japan) have been considered as 'opaque' areas that fall outside the CRM reach. Also, the European front is pretty fragmented in the extent and style of CRM actual use. This varying degree of implementation makes CRM, as a 'global' process, still quite fragile, at least at the time of writing.

Given the fragmentation of the sources (in terms of their CRM 'maturity'), what is the level of confidence of the data that make it to the headquarters? How well can they portray the real dynamics of the business worldwide? How reliably can they be used to evaluate the performance of the top managers responsible for the vertical markets? Some informants suggest that, despite the commitment to make evaluations based on facts, the data at the headquarters level provided by CRM should be taken with a grain of salt; or it should be remembered that they might be subject to interested, or controversial, interpretations.

Moreover, the new Notes infrastructure may not work as a panacea to the CRM tools blues. There are still a few hurdles along the way, to which we now turn.

The Ambiguous Role of IT

As already mentioned, IT and BPR are seen by the management literature to have a 'recursive relationship': each is a key to thinking about the other (Davenport and Short 1990). And it should be our imaginations guiding our decisions about technology—not the other way around (Hammer 1990). Furthermore, IT promises to be a powerful tool for reducing the costs of coordination, provided that information technology is seen in terms of how it supports new or redesigned processes, rather than existing business functions (Davenport and Short 1990). That is the theory, as perfectly acknowledged by the CRM team thinking and management. The BPR literature also offers advice on how to deal with, and specifically organize, IT internally to make it a powerful force in redesigning processes. Thus, IT services are seen as a behind-the-scenes adviser and advocate of BPR, able to promote, build, and deliver platforms, architectures, and standards on which process-specific applications can be quickly constructed. Note, however, that these recommendations do not seem to address some political issues, such as: who is in charge of BPR? Where are the IT services placed in relation to that authority? Where should the BPR design and consulting competencies lie? Who will solve the conflict between the constraints and opportunities set by the technology and those set by the process? Will 'brainstorming' of solutions (again as advocated by the literature) be enough? In major, global redesign processes, these issues may be large and crucial, so the potential conflicts.

Consider, then, the role of IT in relation to CRM. It would be unfair to state that the CRM design team underestimated IT to support the new process. Indeed, one can find from the very beginning on the CRM chart that the bottom, infrastructural line is made up of a variety of interlinked IT tools (see Fig. 7.1). Moreover, a separate project team was immediately set up to develop an overall IT–CRM platform: a fully dedicated CRM application. The project was discontinued because the sheer complexity of the application did not allow the building of a comprehensive and robust data processing (dp) environment.

Hence, the deployment of CRM was carried out on shaky, or fragmented, IT foundations, until the emergence of Lotus Notes as a suitable platform pointed to a new way to approach the whole tools issue systematically. But the context has never been one of a virgin ground lacking skills and resources. In other words, CRM and the new IT tools have not been developed in a dp void. On the contrary, the diffuse IT capability of IBM has over the years populated the internal dp landscape with a very high density and variety of systems and applications. For example, at the time of writing, there are up to 5,000 different accounting applications within the company worldwide. A large, ramified, and deeply rooted 'installed base' is what any new CRM application has to fight its way through, and against. The installed base has been a vast, silent, but effective force slowing down the deployment of CRM during the whole 'first stage' of implementation. Only later was the drastic move to realign the top responsibilities of corporate IT carried out in order for the new organization to master the installed base and harness it towards the new strategic intent of true globalization (see Chapters 4 and 5).

The plan is obviously to unify the sparse databases systematically: for example, multiple customer records are to be unified worldwide, and thousands of systems reduced to one. This job, however, takes considerable time (on the scale of one year). The new vision of a ubiquitous Notes platform does provide the global environment ready to support CRM-like applications. At the time of study, work was well under way in this direction; new, major CRM applications are rolled out regularly each half year or so. But all these efforts and unquestionable achievements reduce the influence of the installed base more slowly than might be expected. For many new CRM-like Notes applications, the raw data must come from somewhere. The somewhere is once again the installed base. Hence, Notes is no quick fix. In itself, it is fairly easy software to install and use. The problem is the data content: here the installed base of data and applications comes back into the picture, slowing down the deployment of the new platform as a useful tool. Consider a brand new Notes application for contract negotiation: it is global and can be used by any IBM business and geography according to the CRM logic. However, it also has to be compatible with the existing local applications that are geared to local legal and business contexts. Certainly, the local context is frozen into a variety of country-specific installed bases. Building the global Notes contract application (one year of development) turns out to be the easy part, the tip of the iceberg. On the other hand, nobody seems to be able to predict how long it will take it to make it interoperable with the local applications. The risk is that the new application will remain 'floating' above the local installed bases, and applied only on a piecemeal basis.

Finally, many of the other BPR initiatives are going to be supported by standard applications, especially ERP packages like SAP. The implementation of these complex applications encounters all those difficulties and slowdowns that are typical of ERP systems. Again, technology seems to represent an unexpected bottleneck for the BPR initiatives.

Notes and SAP are being implemented in order to provide IBM with a new infrastructural IT capability. What the management literature on the development of IT infrastructure seems to underestimate is the pre-existing IT capability required to generate the new one: where does it come from? How does the existing pool of competencies and tools nurture it? And, conversely, to what extent is it hampered by the huge installed base?

Opposing Views

Recall all those practices against which BPR engaged its sweeping crusade at the beginning of the 1990s (Hammer 1990):

- the blurring of accountability in executing work;
- the fragmentation of business processes and the ensuing, desperate attempt of management to piece together the fragmented bits;
- the inefficient effort to adapt processes to changing circumstances, creating more and more layers of new practices over the existing ones;
- the fact that most procedures are not even designed, they just happen—that is, they are the result of local improvisations;
- that fact that there is a tendency to institutionalize the ad hoc and enshrine the temporary, both leading to the sedimentation of inconsistent practices.

Certainly, the BPR literature discusses the difficulties in managing IT-driven redesign processes. Most frequent 'key success factors' listed are: 'keeping management commitment'; being competent in governing a cross-functional implementation process; being able to cope with the sheer complexity of the new global process; aligning the multiple stakeholders; explaining the need for redesign to the workforce; addressing and solving conflicts by constantly referring to the needs of 'the customer' as the final reference point; recognizing the importance of the constant attention of the CEO ('If managers have the vision, re-engineering will provide a way', and 'Only if top-level managers back the effort and outlast the company cynics will people take re-engineering seriously') (Hammer 1990). But, despite the full management backing, there are still diverging opinions about CRM. What do they say?

The principle of parallel coordination of functions during the process (and not after it is completed), as suggested by BPR, seems to be in conflict with the mainly 'sequential' nature of CRM. The delicate point is how, when, and to whom to pass the relay 'baton' during the multiple-stage race to complete the transaction: no special ways of how to work and communicate in parallel are emphasized by CRM. The implicit assumption is that passing the baton will be a pure 'technicality' in process execution, which evidently is not the case in practice. Here, the issue is one of coordination and IT support: the correct application of this BPR principle presupposes that communication networks, shared databases, and teleconferencing can bring the independent groups together so that coordination is ongoing (Hammer 1990). While the ways of communicating within IBM are diffused, this is one of the many instances where the existing IT infrastructure (especially the databases) does not allow a smooth and full sharing of the data that lie at the basis of parallel work.

The economic literature on infrastructure (see Chapter 4) points out that any standard enforced through an infrastructure (network, type of records, processes, and so on) creates as a side product 'angry orphans'—that is, groups of agents who have somehow been damaged or at least do not see any pay-off out of the effort of adapting to and adopting the new infrastructure. As mentioned above, one big angry orphan is the IT installed base itself, which requires 'to be taken care of' specially. The diverging and sceptical voices may be the expression of some of these angry orphans.

The very same CRM features can be seen and described from opposing points of view. For example, what CRM consultants call 'engines' (to make CRM work) get called 'patches' by other informants (possibly the 'cynics' to whom Hammer 1990 refers). Patches recall a traditional way of coping with complex and controversial issues within IBM: conflict cannot be allowed to reach levels where it becomes disruptive, and everybody is asked to cooperate towards a unified goal. However, this takes place through various forms of compromises, called 'patches'. While 'patching up' maintains internal cohesion, it can stifle innovation, by gradually diluting it. Deprived of its most controversial aspects, the innovation may drift into a 'philosophy', and become marginalized (as happened to the TQM initiative). On the other hand, top management and CRM consultants repeat that the CRM choice is irreversible, and in fact there is so much at stake in terms of investments, both real and symbolic, that it cannot be abandoned. On the other hand, this does not rule out the possibility of its transformation into a philosophy accompanied by the opportunistic performance of rituals.

The two main achievements of CRM—streamlining processes on a global scale and generating business performance measures—can also be seen in a different light. CRM should help IBM to operate in an industry where years are becoming 'web years'—that is, three months. Unfortunately, the pace of its deployment seems to be slow even in 'normal' years. Will the embedding of CRM into the fabric of the extant IBM practices and operations be a never-ending journey (thus increasing the risk of the sublimation of CRM into a philosophy)?

As mentioned earlier, the measures delivered by CRM are regarded by some with suspicion, and their validity is questioned internally, since they are based on a gathering process that is far from being truly global and robust. Again timing is essential. If the convergence of approximate measures is fast enough, doubts and scepticism will vanish quickly. But what if measures stay approximate?

Despite the emphasis on decentralization of decision-making and teamwork, CRM is a powerful weapon for centralization. On the one hand, regional feuds and hierarchies are de facto abolished in favour of transversal processes. The weight and control scope of headquarters are greatly reinforced. But, such a centralization needs complete local cooperation to be effective—for example, when inputting data for every single phase of the process. Here, CRM seems to share the stigma of the old centralized MIS procedures: they would allow terrific opportunities for management governance at the centre, provided people did their homework in inputting data at the periphery. Unfortunately, such new tasks can become a bureaucratic burden (some local decision-makers are complaining about too much 'electronic paperwork' in feeding the new processes). Thus, cooperation is not enthusiastic, which means that data are not updated promptly, or to a sufficiently high standard. This fact, or just the doubt about its occurrence, could endanger the whole process. Many of the reforms introduced in the adaptive stage of deployment are aimed at ensuring that this negative outcome will not occur, or will at least be contained.

The voices of the angry orphans seem to testify that some of the drawbacks of the pre-BPR world that CRM wanted to address and eliminate may still lurk behind what is considered in the industry and by most IBM management as a successful application of BPR principles.

Concluding Questions

Throughout the 1990s the management literature advising companies on how to set up large infrastructures and link them to BPR projects (Davenport and Short 1990; Broadbent and Weill 1997) was based on a set of shared assumptions. Turning a traditional hierarchy into a process firm enables the achievement of dramatic efficiency gains. IT is the essential tool to enact and support such transformation, and, more generally, to endow the process firm with an infrastructural capability to pursue further changes and organizational innovations. What is required from management is the sound application of BPR principles, guided by a clear strategic intent and the development of an appropriate set of IT tools (platforms, architecture, and infrastructure). The implementation process should be based on spreading the message, designing appropriate roles, and securing strong senior management support. The new processes and tools are the foundations on which IT and business capabilities will be grounded to enact effective competitive strategies.

At the end of our case study we would question this dominant approach, and take the trajectory of CRM as a partial illustration in this respect.

The major conceptual flaw of the literature, management models, and relevant consulting practices is an inversion of factors alluded to in our initial quote. The crux of the matter is not only whether the new infrastructure will deliver the hoped-for capabilities. Rather, it is the quality of the pre-existing capability of the organization to procure itself the tools, or 'organs', it needs. This pre-existing capability is deeply rooted in the extant formative context (Ciborra and Lanzara 1994) of the corporation. By formative context we mean the set of institutional arrangements and cognitive frames (culture) that govern not only the execution of current routines, but also more importantly the enactment of any socio-technical innovation. The challenge facing IBM is, then, both to design the infrastructure that will make a new way of operating possible, and to go beyond, especially during the implementation stages, the capabilities moulded by the extant formative context. It may be hard to change the very (bureaucratic) context that breeds the (anti-bureaucratic) innovation. Complex exercises of (radical) organizational learning may be required in order to exit the extant formative context, when the latter is deemed dysfunctional. Moreover, as the experts of organizational learning know, new visions, routines, and systems are more likely to deliver the status quo than radical reforms (Argyris and Schön 1996).

The case does not question the power of the new capabilities that are being obtained through the new 'organ' of CRM and its associated tools. The end point is clear and the ultimate vision seductive: an agile, highly centralized but lean corporation, able to operate globally, and open to change. However, the implementation of the vision is the outcome of the pre-existing capabilities and context. These may exercise subtle influences and reverse, from the inside out, any revolutionary design. The study unveils some practices of this kind, though it cannot indicate whether they are a marginal phenomenon, or whether they might have a major impact in the long run.

The organizational-learning and formative-context literatures can be of help in better assessing such inertial practices. They do not lie in the errors that are made during implementation (like those now admitted publicly by IBM management characterizing the mechanistic stage of CRM deployment); nor in what the sceptics say (though their presence signals resistance and friction). Rather, they can be detected in the way past errors are being corrected. Indeed, if one scrutinizes the way the errors committed during the mechanistic stage were fixed during the adaptive stage, one can find moves dictated by a drive towards centralization, standardization, and a better harnessing of the technology to enforce behaviour. We submit that what these moves bring to the surface is an old, not a new, capability of IBM: to be a well-managed, centralized bureaucracy. Certainly, such a capability evolved over the years in a multinational context thanks to a certain degree of decentralization. During the 1990s all this changed, in a way in which pre-existing capabilities get mixed with new ones, such as 'teamwork', 'process orientation', and 'decentralization'. The message being spread may get blurred. For example, processes are perceived as somewhat bureaucratic and procedural, while the new talk is about teamwork. Is such confusion the price that has to be paid for the transition? And how long will the transition last? Should IBM governance mechanisms be adjusted to this permanent transition, instead of being aligned towards an end state that will never obtain?

Will the new infrastructure be composed of processes and tools, never fully implemented, or will it be constituted by employees and managers busy working to patch it up (Ciborra 1996c; see also Chapter 12 below)? As mentioned above, while the managerial literature assumes that everything—processes, technology, roles—are tools to be harnessed in order to enable a capability or achieve a strategic intent, the economic literature on infrastructures is much more cautious (see Chapter 4). According to the latter, infrastructures belong to multiple stakeholders; they are never built from scratch; they belong to an installed base; they may have 'a logic of their own'; they possess inertia and momentum; they are embedded in an institutional context (DiMaggio and Powell 1983). All these features suggest that large infrastructures can be only indirectly 'cultivated' (Dahlbom and Janlert 1996), and not built from scratch. The case shows how the force of the installed base is relevant in influencing the implementation of CRM: it can dramatically slow things down and dampen the efforts towards a swift deployment.

Note that economics also indicates that, once an infrastructure has taken off, its diffusion is self-feeding: standards get widely accepted and the increased business generated induces other agents to use the new infrastructure. Inertia turns into a favourable momentum. Acceptance becomes automatic.

CRM shows that complex, corporate infrastructures tend *not* to be managed this way: they are implemented top down and continuous management support is required. Unfortunately, this resembles too much the 'old' way of trying to build large, centralized Management Information Systems (MIS): resistance, lack of cooperation at the grass roots, uneasiness with the extra bureaucratic burden, and so on have been typical factors building up against the implementation of such large systems, despite the significant shifts in the substance (process instead of function) and the technology (Notes instead of centralized databases).

CRM is here to stay. The new process is acquiring irreversibility. But so far it is not a self-feeding process. It does not enjoy increasing returns (Arthur 1996). On the contrary, it absorbs a vast amount of resources (and the sceptics are ready to ask: what is the ratio of results versus the resources spent for CRM; or, more naughtily: where are the measures about the performance of CRM itself?). Its advocates state that there is no turning back in sight, since the industry privileges this type of lean-process organization. Still, the question persists: is this emerging industry model aligned with the IBM existing capabilities?

8

Who's in Control: Designers, Managers—or Technology? Infrastructures at Norsk Hydro

OLE HANSETH AND KRISTIN BRAA

This chapter presents and discusses globalization and the definition and implementation of corporate information infrastructures within Norsk Hydro. Standards are widely considered as the most basic features of information infrastructures—public as well as corporate. This view is expressed by a high-level IT manager: 'The infrastructure shall be 100 per cent standardized.' Such standards are considered universal in the sense that there is just one standard for each area or function, and that separate standards should fit together—there should be no redundancy and no inconsistency. All actors within a use domain are assumed to share all the standards, and the standards are equal for all of them. Our study illustrates that the reality is different. The idea of the universal standard is an illusion, just like the treasure at the end of the rainbow.

As suggested in Chapter 4, information infrastructures are not a closed world defined by a closed standard. They should be seen rather as open networks—that is, as networks that are linked to other networks, which are again linked to other networks, and so on, indefinitely. As networks become larger and more linked to and embedded into other networks, they become harder to control. A network can be changed by those who are explicitly trying to change it (for instance, software engineers designing infrastructure standards). But what may be more important, a network can also be changed indirectly, as networks it is connected to are changed. As networks become larger and more interconnected, so effects of events—effects of an earthquake, or the rapid diffusion of the Internet, and so on—are spread more quickly and across longer distances, leading to less predictability of effects of actions

The data on which this chapter is based were collected primarily through interviews. We interviewed a total of thirty people (working in Norway, Italy, Belgium, and the USA); the length of the interviews varied from one and a half to four hours. We had follow-up telephone conversations with some of the people interviewed. In addition, we had shorter meetings and telephone conversations with about fifteen people. The information from the interviews is supplemented by internal documents from the Bridge project and the newsletters distributed to Hydro employees. The presentation also draws upon the work of six students who have written their Master's thesis on the implementation and use of SAP and Lotus Notes applications in Norsk Hydro. The authors wish to thank Norsk Hydro and, in particular, Jan Christiansen for generously giving us access to all the information we needed, Claudio Ciborra for establishing the InfraGlobe project (http://internet.informatics.gu.se) and giving us constructive criticism, and finally the KTK programme at the University of Oslo for financial support.

and accordingly more unintended side effects. Indeed, side effects can be the most important driving force in our globalized society (Beck 1992; Beck *et al.* 1994).

This chapter will illustrate the 'embeddedness' of infrastructures and how this makes infrastructure *design* difficult if not impossible. An infrastructure is designed just as much through the side effects of changes to other infrastructures to which it is connected as through any efforts aimed deliberately at designing the infrastructure. The dynamics created by unintended side effects turns infrastructures into independent actors (or actor networks) which again are 'designing' other actors (humans as well as non-humans) (see Chapter 5).

Building large, powerful global infrastructures is important for global corporations. And doing so is in line with traditional modernization as rationalization—extending and improving the control structures and technologies. But this case will also show that doing so is a reflexive activity—infrastructures are *reflexive*. Making larger infrastructures—to obtain enhanced control—means making larger and more interconnected networks. Larger networks are harder to change and the role of side effects increases—which leads, paradoxically, to less control.

The embeddedness of infrastructures will be illustrated first by one case—the definition and implementation of the Hydro Bridge standard. This case shows that any new infrastructure has to be linked to and change existing infrastructures (or other networks), which may be very resistant to change because of their size and embeddedness. Furthermore, as an infrastructure is used, the need to link it to other networks is revealed, so that the infrastructure has to increase its own embeddedness. The last point in particular will be illustrated through the implementation of a SAP system in one of the divisions within Hydro. First, this SAP installation crumbles into several interdependent ones; then it gets linked to SAP installations in other divisions and corporate ones. The SAP installations also get tightly interlinked with Bridge. This shows that systems and infrastructures that are considered completely separate and independent in fact become closely linked and interdependent. Together these systems constitute a huge heterogeneous infrastructure. Controlling the development of this infrastructure seems much closer to Giddens' description of 'riding the juggernaut' (see Chapter 3, and Giddens 1991) than the way we usually think of IS design.

(A) Norsk Hydro

Norsk Hydro was established in 1905. Until the 1950s the only business area was fertilizer, but then Hydro started to expand, moving into light metals, and later oil and gas. These are the core business areas.

Hydro grew rapidly during the period 1972–86; its income increased from NOK 1 billion to NOK 60 billion. The growth was brought about by acquisitions in agriculture (fertilizer) and light metals, and also by building up brand-new activities within oil and gas. Hydro's tradition was to run its factories with a 'hands-off' style of management. This changed in 1985, when it was decided to stop expanding and to concentrate on consolidating the existing business.

Although there was a corporate IT department, called Hydro Data, running the factories 'hands off' meant that there were independent IT strategies and solutions. This also changed in 1985. Top corporate management acknowledged that IT was an important issue, so divisions had to work out IT/IS strategies, and evaluate the value of their own IT solutions for the company.

A central institution was established, called IS-Forum, responsible for working out common strategies and policies concerning IT, and a 'Corporate Steering Group for IT' was set up as the legitimate unit for making decisions at the corporate level. Members of IS-Forum were primarily top IT managers in the divisions, while the Steering Group was composed of high-level business managers in the divisions. The head of the Steering Group was one of the corporate vice-presidents.

In 1990 a consensus process around common IT architecture started. Consensus was reached in 1991–2 about the importance of standards in general, the establishment of a shared TCP/IP based network, and the need for corporate standards concerning office automation/desktop applications. The corporate standard, defined a bit later, was named Hydro Bridge. Hydro Bridge is the standard on which we focus in the following discussion. During the 1990s the globalization process gained momentum, and so did the focus on collaboration across all divisions and the development and use of a shared infrastructure.

Throughout the 1990s collaboration and knowledge sharing between divisions as well as outside organizations (like engineering companies in the oil sector) were increasingly focused. Lotus Notes and the rest of Bridge were seen as important tools supporting this. In the late 1990s Hydro was also involved in building a considerable SAP infrastructure. The approach was bottom up, as decisions were distributed to the divisions. Thus, the infrastructure was emergent rather than deliberately planned and designed. The first SAP applications were installed in France in 1990. SAP was settled as the corporate standard in 1994. The decision was based on cost considerations. It was cheaper to have one licence for all divisions than for the divisions to buy different systems or even to buy SAP individually. At that time—and later on too—SAP applications were seen as separate, individual information systems, and *not* as infrastructures. The divisions decided completely on their own how to implement and use SAP.

The Hydro Bridge Standard

We will now turn to the Hydro Bridge standard—its conception, definition, implementation, and use. Bridge is seen within Hydro as the standard defining the infrastructure that is shared by the whole corporation.

The first PCs arrived at Hydro in 1983. PCs were introduced based on local initiatives. The oil community, being 'allergic to mainframes' because it had to 'turn around fast', was the first adopter. New PC technology was acquired as it appeared on the market: file servers and PC LANs, network operating systems, and so on. The first Novel Server was bought in 1987. The variety of products, applications, and configurations exploded, and the need for standardization was acknowledged. Standards for document templates, partition of disks, back-up facilities, and routines were defined and enforced. The pendulum moved back and forth between standardization and diversification for each new major generation of PC technology. The definition of the Bridge standard can be seen as a step in this process; at that time it seemed appropriate to standardize PC desktop applications.

By 1992 the IT managers in IS-Forum widely acknowledged that poor integration was a major obstacle for the smooth operation of the company. There was a lack of integration and communication across divisions and between the divisions and the corporate headquarters, costs were too high, use of resources was suboptimal, and so on. The most obvious answer to this problem was—for those concerned—standardization.

The IS-Forum agreed about the need to develop one corporate standard for desktop applications, but, as it was well aware, others had a different view. The Hydro Bridge project was set up in November 1992 to look a little more deeply into the issue, analysing costs and benefits, important obstacles, possible solutions, and so on. The project was staffed by IT personnel. The leader was the IT manager in the oil refining and distribution division. The project soon proposed to the Corporate Steering Group that a corporate standard should be defined and implemented.

Once it was decided that a standard should be settled, the next step was to define its content. It seemed obvious for all involved that this was a choice between Microsoft and Lotus products. Most saw Microsoft products as the clear winner. The Bridge project, however, decided, mainly because of costs, to go for the Lotus SmartSuite applications. The project members knew that this decision would be difficult to sell. To make that easier, they turned the issue about which producers' software to buy into a strategic one. To succeed in that effort, they allied with Lotus Notes: Lotus was chosen because Notes was perceived as a strategic tool!

Even with the content of the standard decided, there were still many issues to take care of. Among these were the scope, the reach, and the range, in Keen's (1991) terms, of the standard. Who should use it and in which functions or use areas? Initially, those advocating the Bridge standard intended that there should be no other systems used by anybody inside Hydro for functions that Lotus SmartSuite products could cover. However, to obtain the required acceptance for the decision, the Bridge project group had to agree to the use of Microsoft products in some areas. These included areas where large software applications were developed—for instance, Excel applications for the interpretation of data from lab equipment and for currency transformations in some budgeting support systems. Word was also accepted as the preferred word processor in several joint projects with other oil companies, where the others required Word (or other Microsoft products) to be used as a shared platform.

The Steering Group for Information Systems formally approved Bridge as a corporate standard on 29 April 1994. But, even in the very first version of the Bridge standard, the ideal of having just one corporate standard had in fact already been given up.

Product development: opening Pandora's box

The first step after the formal approval of the (first version of the) standard was to implement it into a 'product'. As the standard specified only a set of commercial products (applications) to be used, this might seem to have been unnecessary. But that was far from being the case. Applications such as those involved here can be installed and configured in many different ways. For the benefits in terms of less costly installation, maintenance, and support of these products to be experienced, the applications had to be installed consistently on all computers. Such a coherent installation was also crucial to establish a transparent infrastructure where information could be exchanged smoothly between all users. A considerable development task had to be carried out to reach these objectives. The task included primarily bundling work in the form of developing scripts so that the applications would automatically be installed in the same way. Developing these scripts was quite a challenge. Lots of unforeseen problems cropped up, but the implementation of the first Bridge version of the desktop applications package was declared finished by January 1995. When the product was launched, it was, however, far from being free of errors.

Until the product implementation project started, Bridge had been seen (or at least treated) as a self-contained package. During the product development it was 'discovered' that that was definitely not the case. To work as a shared infrastructure, this infrastructure itself required an extensive underlying and supporting infrastructure. However, the infrastructure underlying Bridge was far from standardized within the company. The major problems during the product development project were in fact seen as caused by the lack of standardization of their underlying infrastructure. The implementation project tried to solve the problems by standardizing each layer as it was uncovered.

The first, and immediately underlying, layer to be discovered was the operating system. Virtually all PCs were running DOS or Windows, so agreeing on Windows as the operating system standard was not controversial.

A large number of PCs were running in local area networks running LAN software and possibly a networking operating system. This 'layer' also had to be standardized for several reasons: most Bridge applications would be installed on a file server and not on each individual PC; the applications (users) were storing their files on such servers and using other shared resources such as printers, and so on. On this level, a standard based on Novel's LAN products was specified. This included a design of a specific LAN topology to be implemented everywhere.

Dealing with the PC hardware layer was certainly the most demanding implementation challenge. PCs were discovered to differ significantly with respect to external device adapters (LAN, screen, keyboard, mouse, and so on) and their drivers, BIOS, memory, etc. This was so, in spite of the fact that they were all 'IBM standard' PCs. Later on, when laptops were included in the platform to be supported, PCMCIA cards created severe problems. To standardize this layer would necessitate changing most of Hydro's PCs. This was obviously an impossible short-term solution because of its costs. But it was considered a necessary long-term solution—that is, one to be phased in over time.

The intention to impose strict standardization of PCs was given up. It was simply beyond reach. At the time of the study, the specification of the latest version of Bridge said that it should support any 'standard' PC from any 'major' manufacturers selling PC's 'globally'.

In parallel with the implementation of the Bridge infrastructure, communication generally became more important. This implied that the global IP-based network being built, Hydro InterLAN, was also included in Bridge. The underlying layers are indeed heterogeneous: two MBits leased lines, telephone services, broadband networks (ATM), radio and satellite communication (to oil platforms, for instance), and so on. However, this heterogeneity has not caused any trouble, since TCP/IP runs smoothly on top of all of them.

All the major difficulties that occurred during product development were related to the desktop applications—and not to Notes. The desktop applications were brought into focus basically because of the fact that there was already an infrastructure—although a fragmented one—in place. The implementation of the Bridge standard implied that the existing infrastructure should be turned into a new one. In this process many users in several divisions had to stop using their existing applications and switch to others. Concerning Notes, however, the infrastructure was designed from scratch. There was no infrastructure to be replaced—no *installed base* to fight (see Chapter 4). Replacing one infrastructure by another is the most challenging issue, technologically as well as politically—technologically because the transition takes some time, and during this period both the old and the new have to work and maybe even have to interoperate; politically, simply because most users prefer the products and applications they are experienced in using.

The lack of standardization of an infrastructure's underlying layers will often be visible to those using and maintaining the infrastructure. So the infrastructure may not appear as unified and coherent, but rather as several separate and different structures. The Hydro Bridge standard was initially defined to save expenditure on maintenance and support work. This expenditure was certainly lowered, but not by as much as planned, because several different Bridge implementations had to be maintained and supported on different platforms.

Diffusion, adoption, and use: the 'global' meeting the 'local'

The common view that looks at standards as universals assumes that a standard is just one thing, equal for all. That is not how Bridge appeared as the adoption process unfolded. It was seen very differently by the different units, because of differences in the existing computing environments, the resources available in terms of money and competence, the cultures concerning management styles as well as use of technology, the feeling that an improved infrastructure was needed, and so on. The speed and style of adoption also depended on the distance from the main office of Hydro Data. For those already using Lotus products, adopting Bridge meant doing almost nothing. Others had to change considerably. Bridge soon came to encompass several different systems. This implies that some implemented the whole package, others just a few components. In the latter group you would find smaller offices in Africa, for instance, typically having just a few stand-alone PCs.

Strategies adopted for implementing Notes, on the one hand, and the rest of Bridge, on the other, were very different. The desktop applications were pushed intensively from the top. Notes, however, was initially not pushed at all. Later on it was pushed as an e-mail system. Differences in strategies among the different units have implied that Bridge has been implemented not as one coherent universal package, but rather as many different ones that need to be integrated and linked together to make the overall infrastructure work.

The desktop part of Bridge diffused pretty fast. In April 1998 there were about 18,000 users, which meant that it had diffused throughout most of the Hydro corporation. However, the diffusion speed and patterns varied a lot among the divisions.

The Oil & Gas division has always been the first to adopt any new technology—and so it was with Bridge. However, Oil & Gas was a heavy user of Microsoft products, so the adoption of Lotus SmartSuite products was somewhat mixed. The Lotus package was installed and used to some extent, but Microsoft products were still used extensively. This was partly due to local resistance among experienced Microsoft users, but also, more importantly, to the close collaboration with other oil companies using Microsoft products. The general rule established within this collaboration is that the company that is to operate an oilfield to be developed determines what tools to use. This means that Lotus products are used in the projects where Hydro is the operator, but in cases where a company using Microsoft products is the operator, Hydro has to use these products as well.

Within the oil sector it has always been important to be advanced in using new technology to stay competitive. The actors in this sector have lots of money, and most employees are highly educated engineers, who are always focused on finding better tools.

The large fertilizer divisions also adopted Bridge very quickly. The adoption was pretty smooth and easy, as they already used Lotus applications, except for the word processor. For them, adoption of Bridge basically meant switching from WordPerfect to AmiPro. They also already used Novel's LAN technology. Their existing network topology, however, was different from what Bridge specified. So, they had to restructure their network. This meant hard work for the technical personnel.

Other divisions were more reluctant, because they had an installed base of solutions that was significantly different from what Bridge specified. In particular, adoption of Novell was challenging and expensive for those having large Banyan Vines installations. The transition to the Novell-based Bridge standard took time, and happened stepwise. Throughout this process, lots of different network structures were in operation. This required local customizations of other parts of the Bridge standard to make them run on top of the local networks.

The light metal (aluminium and magnesium) divisions were slow in adopting Bridge. The aluminium divisions were the last to join the company, and had systems that were very different from those found in most other divisions. In addition, they have a culture that stresses local independence. For this reason, they were always negative towards Bridge and resisted adoption. The magnesium division was also slow in adopting Bridge. For this division, the basic problem was the costs. It has a constant struggle with low incomes and had problems in finding space for Bridge investments in its budgets. This was in strong contrast to the Oil & Gas division.

There was also variation in the speed of diffusion within divisions. All new products and versions were first installed in Hydro Data, being the permanent pilot site. The next units were those physically located at Vækerø in Oslo, which is the largest Hydro Data site and the largest office in Norway, housing major parts of the Oil & Gas and Technology & Projects divisions.

To make this heterogeneous infrastructure work, filters and converters for word-processing formats still had to be used. In addition, different viewers were included in Bridge so that users could easily get access to documents produced by tools they were not using themselves.

One of the desktop applications was more difficult to implement coherently in the organization than any other: e-mail. Companies always communicate with externals. With the diffusion of the Internet, supporting such communication by computers gained much attention. Hydro also adopted the Internet and integrated it with Bridge (see further below). However, it was already using several other computer networks for various purposes. It developed a considerable network together with other oil producers and engineering companies working within the oil sector in Norway. It was using an X.400-based network as carrier for EDIFACT messages.[1]

In finance and trading activities it had been using Telex for a long period, and it was using a proprietary system delivered by Digital for communication with the aluminium exchange in London. It had even bought a new computer-based Telex system, running on a PC under the CP/M operating system! Some of these various e-mail and messaging systems were being used separately, with quite a few users using several of these systems. Other systems were integrated and interconnected through gateways. The new Telex system, for instance, was integrated into the overall message-handling infrastructure. Telex messages could be sent and received as Notes e-mails through an X.400 system.

Hydro's policy, saying that only Notes (and cc:mail at that time) should be used for message-based communication, implies that these systems should be replaced. At the time of the study, there was no indication that it was going to happen. The use of most of these systems has deeply penetrated the work practices within which they are used, as most infrastructures do (Joerges 1988). And because Hydro is only one of many organizations involved in these practices and networks, it is far beyond Hydro's power to replace Telex technology by other systems.

---

[1] X.400 is the ISO and ITU standard for e-mail.

Non-technical services

The Bridge infrastructure requires more supporting layers than operating systems, network services, and so on. It also requires non-technical services: user training, maintenance, and support (see Fig. 8.1). Such services are just as important as the technical layers such as operating systems and networks. The non-technical supporting infrastructure required by Bridge has been hard to establish. In fact, these are the required underlying infrastructures that Hydro has been least successful in implementing. We will here mention three reasons for this.

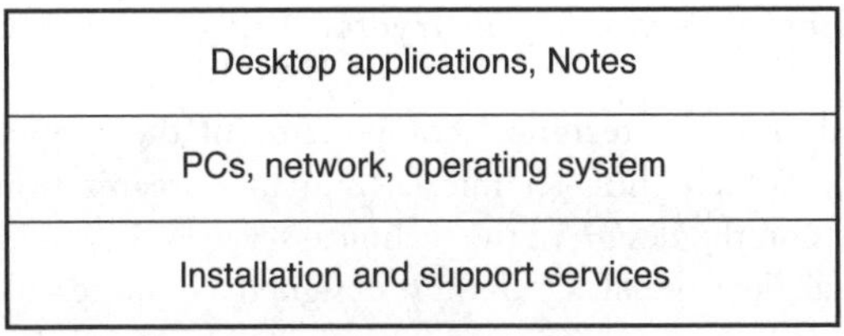

Desktop applications, Notes
PCs, network, operating system
Installation and support services

FIG. 8.1. Applications and required underlying services

First, these infrastructures are beyond the control of the Bridge team. This is illustrated by the SAP project that will be presented below. For most divisions, the support services required by Bridge are seen just as part of the overall IT support services within a division. How these services are set up—for instance, whether they are provided by an internal IT department, bought from Hydro Data, or outsourced to another organization—is (as in the SAP case presented in the next sections) mainly based on what is believed to serve the 'mission-critical' applications best.

Secondly, most of those involved in the design of the Bridge standard were technicians and were blind to the non-technical elements in the infrastructure. The problems related to lack of user support and training have been addressed only as far as technological components can be presented as proper solutions. Advanced tools for IT infrastructure management, systems for the 'automatic' downloading of applications, and a CD-ROM-based training programme are some of the solutions that have been developed and included in the Bridge package. However, very little seems to have been done to identify the needs for support and training, and how services satisfying these needs could be established.

This blindness to non-technological elements is related to the third issue we will mention. There is the huge local variation in the kind of services that are required, as well as the bases on which they can rely. Requirements depend upon factors such as what kind of work is done, what kind of applications are used, which parts of Bridge are accessed, the general competence of the users, and—last but not least—the users' knowledge about IT. How to establish support and training services

depends, among other things, on what kind of resources—human and technical—
are available. The kind of support services Hydro can offer its users in, say, Africa
is rather different from what is easily available to those with an office in the same
building as most Hydro Data people.

Hydro Data serves as the permanent site for pilot testing. As it is an IT department, the staff are very knowledgeable about how to use the Bridge tools.
Furthermore, the computing equipment and competence of the support staff are
the best in Hydro. And it is certainly far beyond what is found at smaller offices in
remote locations. The competence level and services provided are taken for
granted. The technicians do not see the role the support personnel are playing and
how Vækerø differs from other sites in this respect. This fact is reflected in a statement expressed by users working in Hydro: 'Bridge is the world as seen from
Vækerø.'

The technical and non-technical components of the supporting services are
interdependent. Which non-technical (human, organizational) services are
required depends on the design of the technical services. For instance, the need for
user training will decrease if a carefully designed computer-based user training
package is provided. Further, the need for support also depends on how the technology is designed. Hydro Data has experienced, for instance, that equipment running at remote locations with limited support needs to be set up in a way that makes
it more robust than otherwise. Disk drives are duplicated, more processing and
storage capacity is provided, and so on.

Infrastructures Meet

SAP in HAE

The Bridge infrastructure was built in parallel with a large SAP infrastructure.
These infrastructures were initially considered completely separate, but they have
become increasingly intertwined as they have grown. The first SAP applications
were installed in the agriculture division in France in 1990, and SAP was settled as
the corporate standard in 1994. At that time SAP implementation projects were
going on in parallel projects in several divisions.

Hydro Agri Europe (HAE) is the largest division in the company and is the
owner of the most ambitious SAP project. HAE includes nineteen production sites
and a total of seventy-two sites throughout Europe. Since the 1980s Hydro has
bought several fertilizer companies all over Europe. In line with traditional Hydro
management policy, the companies bought were run in a 'hands-off' style. In 1992
prices were very low, bringing the whole division into a crisis. In this situation the
division management launched a very ambitious re-engineering project, aimed at
integrating the independent national companies into one operational unit.

But the implications of the envisioned changes were grossly underestimated.
Local managers and virtually all the employees did not see the need for integration.
They focused on caring for their territories. Thus, no change took place.

In parallel with the integration activities in Europe, Hydro set up or bought new factories and sales offices outside Europe. So the importance of closer cooperation between the European division and other units was constantly increasing.

When the re-engineering started, IT management soon reached the conclusion that the division could not be integrated, on the basis of the heterogeneous collection of systems used throughout the division. Each company had its own portfolio of applications. For each company, the basic infrastructure in terms of computers, operating systems, database management systems, and communication networks was delivered from different vendors. Virtually any available technology was in use somewhere. In January 1994 HAE launched a new IT strategy project, announcing that the whole division should go for an ERP package, and that this package should be SAP. Based on this package, one set of applications should be common for all units. In August 1994 top division management decided to adopt this advice. The SAP project started in early 1995, and the plan was that it would be completed by mid-1999. The project was split into three phases: developing and implementing a pilot, validating the pilot and developing the 'final' version, and finally implementing that version in the whole division.

When the validation started, five regional project teams were set up to take care of this. The project for the Scandinavian region, for instance, had more than 100 members. The validation identified more than 1,000 'issues', each of which required changes in the system. In total this meant that the design and implementation of the 'final' version required much more work than expected.

When the SAP project started, the original re-engineering project was subsumed into it. The original objectives from the re-engineering project were, however, still alive—now expressed as 'One single integrated European learning organization'.

The focus of the re-engineering work has been the establishment of 'common processes' across the whole organization. Once in place, it is assumed that they will serve as a platform for closer integration.

The original re-engineering project was intended to bring about radical change fast. In reality, the organization remained the same. The SAP project, on the other hand, was initially intended to support the new re-engineered organization. Although the SAP project has been ambitious and permanently close to collapse, it has worked as a vehicle for organizational change. The organization is indeed changing—much more slowly than the top management believed would happen when the re-engineering started, but much more quickly than before the SAP project was launched.

The change model in the SAP project was a two-stage rocket. First, common work processes were established, supported by a common SAP solution throughout the division. In the second stage the common processes were to serve as a platform for further integration. The common work processes were meant to facilitate coordination between the different units, while some processes might be extracted out of the individual units and located to just one site, taking care of the process for the whole division.

A technology like SAP is more than a pure software package to be tailored to specific needs. Embedded in the technology are established ways of using it as well as of organizing the implementation project. This 'formative context' (Ciborra and Lanzara 1994) is inscribed into the larger actor network of which SAP software is a part (see Chapter 5). This network comprises SAP documentation, existing SAP implementation, experience, competence, and practices established in the SAP 'development community'. The SAP implementation has been a guiding tool for selecting activities to address, and in which sequence to address them. It has also been a tool and a medium for representing, 'designing', and implementing new work processes. As the process unfolded, SAP made issues appear. Should these processes be common across all Europe? Should a shared European function be established taking care of these jobs? Several tasks have been found that could be centralized into one European unit. As the SAP implementation has a complexity almost beyond what can be managed even when the organizational changes are at a minimum, most issues are postponed until the SAP implementation is considered finished. However, for a couple of the issues identified, it was decided to implement new integrated services. One such service is the Single Distribution Centre (SDC).

SDC is a new unit through which all transactions between marketing and production units are channelled. It was established as a legal company, located in Paris, although it was without any staffing. This operation was established because a better-structured way of dealing with internal transactions was needed, but most of all because this unit was 'logically' required by SAP to avoid a tremendous amount of transactions, which would slow down the system and confuse those involved or responsible. SAP is weak on supporting distribution and logistics. SDC compensates for that weakness. In this way that change is very much designed by SAP. SDC has been in operation since November 1997.

When the re-engineering project started, the different units inside the division were all unknowns to each other. Tight integration means close collaboration. Close and efficient collaboration requires that those involved are parts of the same community, knowing each other well and having a shared background, culture, and identity. Establishing such a shared 'platform' takes time and can happen only through collaboration.

SAP has been the most important shared activity involving people from most parts of the division. Through the project people all around Europe have become acquainted with each other, learning about each other's ways of working and doing business; 'best practices' are identified, tried, and transferred to other locations. Through this process the different units get ideas about how to improve their own work far beyond what is addressed by the SAP project and they discover new areas where cooperation and integration would be beneficial. Collaboration on other issues has been initiated—and also supported—by Notes applications.

Applications integration: including the environment

The Bridge case illustrates how a smooth implementation of a standardized infrastructure on one level recursively requires a standardized infrastructure on the level below. A similar problem is found along the border between an infrastructure and its context. When using the term 'context' we are here referring only to *applications* that are not part of the Bridge standard but are related, in one form or another, to the applications included in Bridge. An application becomes a part of Bridge's environment when it is used within the same or related tasks.

There is an important difference concerning the relations between the Bridge standard infrastructure and its underlying infrastructure, on the one hand, and Bridge and the other applications in its environment, on the other. Bridge *requires* an underlying infrastructure—otherwise it will not work. Which applications populate its environment, however, is accidental. These are applications that the Bridge users decide to use, so making them related or linked to each other. How these links are addressed and managed is accordingly different.

The applications that are included in another's environment can to some extent be specified at the same time as the decision is taken to adopt an application. But the collection of applications used varies over time and so does how each application is used. Further, the way a user really uses his or her tools is to a large extent tacit. This means that an application's environment will be disclosed as the users actually use it.

Dealing with borders is also closely related to learning. As an infrastructure is used, new ways of using it are discovered; it drifts and 'meets' other infrastructures. And this happened with the Bridge applications. One strategy for dealing with evolving use and drift is to include an application in the environment in the standard. For instance, as the Internet was growing in popularity, its relationships to the Bridge applications became closer, leading to the situation where it was included in Bridge. Among others, a package of administrative applications (for smaller offices), called SUN, was also included. When several applications are linked together in a way that makes them interdependent, it becomes necessary to standardize the interfaces between them and their use.

Other applications are included because of relationships on a more abstract level. For instance, applications that are already included and some that are outside may be seen as 'really of the same kind'. So, if one is included, then the others should be included as well.

In some cases, this strategy—that, when a relationship between one application inside the standard and one outside is discovered, the latter is included—might be the best one. But it does not work as a general strategy. Each component in a standard has its own environment, and different components have different environments. This means that environments are indefinite. Trying to solve this problem by extending the standard to cover what is linked to it will lead to indefinite regress. This means that this 'border' problem cannot be solved. Further, borders cannot be drawn once and for all. They have to be renegotiated continuously and maintained through more or less ad hoc links and various forms of gateways.

There is often an overlap in functionality between components of an infrastructure and components in the environment. This raises the issue about which components should be used, when, and for which purpose. The relations between the

Internet/Web and Notes are very much of this kind. Where to draw the border between the areas where each of them should be used is hard to specify. In almost any case when the development of a Notes application is considered, one could just as well use Internet/Web technology. This means that where the border should be drawn has to be defined in every single case. Over time, an organization changes and technology evolves, implying that the border can drift (Ciborra 1996a) significantly.

To avoid making the definition of the border a time-consuming effort full of conflicts, a smooth interface is required. Inside Hydro, Internet technology has been used to develop an 'Intranet'. Web technology overlaps a lot with Notes, so the Web-based Intranet and the Notes infrastructure were integrated. In many cases it was considered a fairly open question whether to use Notes or Web technology. A Web interface to all Notes databases (through Domino) was provided. The divisions developing Notes interfaces to their applications did the same for the Web.

As the integration between Notes applications and the Internet (technology) was growing rapidly, Internet technology was also put into the Bridge standard. The close links between solutions based on Internet technology and Notes applications also included positive interference by causing a spill-over (Steinmueller 1996), in the sense that solutions available in the Internet world were also developed for Notes. For example, Hydro developed a search engine similar to those found on the Internet for searching across all Notes databases.

We will illustrate in more detail the relationships between the inside and the outside and how changes on one side interfere with and affect what is on the other by looking at the integration and links between the Bridge infrastructure and SAP implementations in Hydro.

SAP and Bridge meet

As Bridge and SAP were implemented in Hydro, they were also tied closely together, as illustrated by Fig. 8.2. However, Hydro never considered including SAP in Bridge. SAP is outside the scope of Bridge and it is too big and complex an issue to be seen as just a part of Bridge. Thus the relationships between SAP and Bridge have to be managed without being part of the same standard.

During the SAP implementation process a wide range of links between SAP and Bridge was uncovered. Some of these links were in fact 'known' in advance and taken care of in the design process. These cover the part of Bridge that implemented infrastructural services required by SAP such as PCs, operating system, data communication network, and so on. Other links emerged during the process. These include services such as maintenance and support. Some important links may also stay invisible to those involved. And the links do not always cause trouble. In some instances, SAP and Bridge are even mutually dependent and are mutually enhancing each other's development and use.

Some divisions, for instance, discovered that the SAP applications have rather complex user interfaces. For infrequent users this constitutes a big problem. Some divisions tried to solve this problem by developing Notes interfaces to their SAP applications as well as to others. This turned out to be quite a challenge, not least because of SAP's policy regarding permission for their customers to integrate SAP and other applications.

For some needs, data from SAP applications are extracted and made available through the Web-based Intranet. Data are exchanged between SAP applications and others, in particular spreadsheet (1-2-3) and other Bridge applications. In some cases, data are transferred manually by means of cut-and-paste operations. In others, scripts and programs are developed to transfer data more or less automatically.

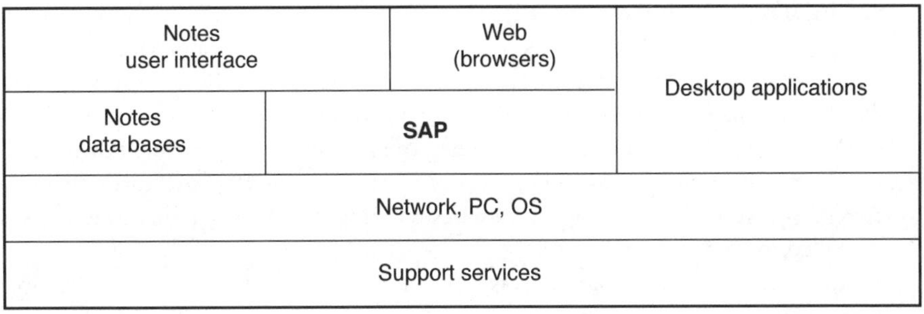

Notes user interface	Web (browsers)	Desktop applications
Notes data bases	SAP	
Network, PC, OS		
Support services		

FIG. 8.2. SAP's embeddedness in the Bridge infrastructure

When the Bridge standard was extended to include PCs, operating systems, and network protocols, that part of the standard was defined with a focus on the requirements of the Bridge applications. However, it was obvious that this part of Bridge also had to support other applications used by Bridge users, and accordingly it defined the infrastructure underlying SAP as well. Further, in some cases, SAP and Bridge had to rely on shared underlying services, as, for instance, user support. We will now look in more detail at the interference between the SAP implementation in HAE and Bridge.

The SAP transaction processing was to run on computers physically located at a large processing centre in the UK. When the decision about outsourcing SAP processing was taken, the IT management in the division thought that it would be an advantage if the same service provider also delivered the required network services connecting the client software on local PCs to the servers. So it decided to outsource that as well. Moreover, it also believed it would be beneficial to have just one provider responsible for the whole chain from the servers running the SAP databases through the network to the hardware equipment and software applications used locally. Accordingly, a contract was signed covering three areas—called processing, network, and (local) site management respectively. At the time of the study, Bridge had been extended to include Hydro's global network. This contract meant that the design and operation of the Bridge network was handed over to the service provider outside Hydro. The same thing happened for the responsibility for installation and support of all elements of Bridge locally (PC operating systems, desktop applications, the Notes infrastructure and applications, Internet software and access, and so on). In practice this meant that local sites had great difficulties even getting the Bridge up and running.

The outsourcing experience has been a mixed blessing. The network and processing services were fine, but site management (that is, local support) was problematic. The major issues seem to be related to the fact that the actual global service provider organized its business in independent national subsidiaries, and was not able to carry out the required coordination across national borders. In addition, some problems were related to the fact that the site management contract specifies that users should call the help desk in the UK when they needed support, even if they were situated in Norway close to Hydro Data. The threshold for doing this was quite high for large user groups not speaking English, although the help desk should have had people speaking all major European languages. Problem solving was found to be much more difficult when the help desk was contacted than when assistance was sought from local support personnel. In this way SAP made the support of Bridge far more complex than desired. The site management contract was cancelled towards the end of 1998.

We often think about side effects as negative—as was the case in the example above. However, there are also examples showing that side effects from interdependencies of infrastructures can be positive. To make the SAP project succeed, people from all sites had to be involved to provide the project with the required knowledge about how tasks were performed and business was conducted at different sites. For a project of this size and geographical distribution, smooth communication is mandatory. Notes applications have been used as e-mail system, project document archives, and discussion databases. As such, Notes has been a crucial infrastructure making possible the required cooperation between those involved all over Europe.

Notes has been widely used by virtually all SAP projects in Hydro, and in many divisions SAP projects were the first users of Notes. In this way SAP has been an important agent in making Notes diffuse. The initiatives for using Notes have been taken by IT personnel familiar with the technology and optimistic about its potential contributions to Hydro's overall productivity and efficiency. As all SAP projects are large and involve numbers of different user groups, knowledge about and practical experience with the technology becomes widely spread. SAP projects seem to be the most intensive users of Notes, and accordingly SAP one of the most important actors in making Notes diffuse in Hydro.

Infrastructures as actors

Having illustrated how infrastructures such as SAP and Bridge are playing different roles as actors, it remains to be understood how their agency is played out together with other actors, as one unit in a larger network—as a member of a larger community (see Chapter 5). In this community, each member acts individually. The effects are not caused only by SAP or Bridge. They are the result of actions involving others—a network of aligned actors, or a number of actors having joined forces in alliances. As in political theory, actor-network theory considers power as being related to the ability to align other actors to your own interests—that is, making them your allies. For any actor, non-human (i.e. technological) allies are just as important as humans (Latour 1988; Introna 1997).

Actors in the 'SAP community' are designers, users, and managers. In the early phase of the re-engineering project, the managers were key actors. IT managers were important in making the SAP decision. As the SAP project evolved, lots of actors entered the stage. First project managers, then consultants, were hired as designers and programmers. Later on users and local managers were involved in the four regional projects, taking care of specifying local requirements and then the local implementation of the SAP system. These regional projects involved a significant number of people.

When the SAP system was installed, even more actors appeared on the arena. An important one was the provider to whom the computing services were outsourced. Central servers, local PCs, and the networks entered the scene as SAP's underlying platform. And, as the users started adopting SAP into their working practices, these practices also started to play an active role in the project. These practices included other tools and systems. To make SAP work smoothly, all these had somehow to be aligned. As SAP approached its use environment, it became increasingly embedded into the socio-technical web constituting Hydro Agri Europe.

During the evolving SAP implementation, alliances were built and changed as new actors were enrolled. In the early part of the project, SAP was a close and important ally of top management to get the change process moving. And SAP was a powerful actor to make this happen.

Two alliances are worth mentioning here. First, there was an alliance between the user groups and SAP. The user groups were to specify local requirements. These included identifying the needs of each office. Such specific needs were due to established local practices—which could be changed into common ones. Others, however, were outside Hydro's control. These include differences in national legislation concerning accounting, taxes, environmental issues, and different transport systems in different nations/regions (railway, ships, trucks, riverboats, and so on). In addition there were differences in business cultures and market structures in different nations or regions. These local aspects had to be accounted for in the design. And in this process locals played a key role. They took control over the design process, and also turned SAP into an ally to help them get control over the overall change process. The early alliance between SAP and division management was broken. This made the change process slower, just as the locals had initially wanted. Through this process the SAP solution was customized for each individual site. It changed from one shared, universal solution into one variant for each site. These variants had much in common and they were linked together. The SAP solution had changed from one coherent common system to a complex, heterogeneous infrastructure.

SAP applications installed in different divisions were considered isolated and independent of each other. Later, SAP applications were linked together, hence emerging as a corporate infrastructure. The Technology & Project division (HTP) builds most of Hydro's installations (mostly plants and oil platforms). In doing so, it buys the equipment and materials needed. At the time of the study this was done by means of the procurement systems of each division. To make these tasks easier, HTP was developing its own SAP-based procurement system. This system was going to be integrated with the procurement systems in all other divisions, many of which are SAP applications. Further, a corporate Human Resource system was under development, as was a shared module supporting plant maintenance.

To enable smooth integration of SAP and better utilization of resources, shared processing centres are needed, as well as a shared infrastructure of development and maintenance resources. The lack of such an infrastructure has been acknowledged as a problem, since most SAP applications development has been provided by consultants, who are hired for a project and leave when it is finished.

Some divisions are developing Notes interfaces to all their applications—including SAP—for infrequent users. Data from SAP applications are extracted and made available through the Web-based Intranet; data are also exchanged between SAP applications and applications such as spreadsheet (1-2-3) and other Bridge applications. Some SAP applications are then integrated with extensions tailored for specific sectors. One of these is an accounting module, called IS-OIL, supporting joint-venture production of oilfields. When different SAP installations are linked together with each other and with SAP extensions like IS-OIL, the process of moving from one version of SAP to the next becomes difficult. Those responsible for the different parts will continuously wait for each other in order to align versions. Moving from one version to another is in addition very expensive and comprehensive. These problems are also acknowledged in the SAP literature (Bancroft *et al.* 1998).

With the emergence of this complex infrastructure, SAP appears to be increasingly difficult to control—becoming a more independent actor. Which role this actor will play is hard to predict. One role, however, can be discerned: it is difficult to change; it might well turn into a powerful actor resisting all organizational change. And to integrate HAE into one unit as envisioned requires radical change beyond what is supported by the SAP solution. Further challenges were already appearing at the horizon: 'We have made things difficult for ourselves. We have customized SAP too much.' The customization, however, seems to have been the price to pay to enrol local users and managers into the project, and to counter the objections that SAP was a significant step back in functionality compared to existing local systems.

The difficulties in changing SAP installations have been experienced by all divisions that have reached this stage. At Hydro Agri North America, after two years of deployment, the users finally understood the technology and were able to see how it might be used to improve their work. However, when changes are proposed, the response is that the SAP application is so complex that it all costs too much to change it. Experiences are similar in the oil division: 'SAP is like concrete—it's very flexible until it sets. Then there is nothing you can do to change it.'

It is worth noting here that seeing SAP implementation as a form of 'electronic concrete' might accurately describe how SAP appears to designers when they are trying to change it. SAP implementations do change, but these changes usually take the form of a sequence of small steps, where each step is to a large extent a side effect of changes in its environment.

These experiences are all related to isolated SAP installations. As more SAP installations are put into place and integrated into a corporate infrastructure, the individual modules become important actors influencing the future development of the others in unpredictable ways.

Who's in control?

A SAP installation in a global organization can easily become a large infrastructure. It is an infrastructure designed and controlled by managers and IT personnel, but also an actor shaping its environment as well as its own future. Like any actor, the technology builds alliances with others. However, the alliances might shift over time. In the case reported here, SAP was first allied with top management, playing the role of a powerful change agent. Later on SAP was allied with local managers and users, helping them to bring the change process under their influence and at a speed they preferred. But SAP keeps changing its role as it is installed and integrated into a larger corporate infrastructure. Briefly, it becomes everybody's enemy by resisting all organizational transformation.

The shifting roles of the SAP installations are basically due to its emergent infrastructural character. The SAP installations have been seen as ordinary information systems and were designed as such. In the beginning of the project, the SAP implementation had the form of a systems design activity. However, this form vanished. The shift from system to an emergent infrastructure can be outlined as a four-step transformation. First, the set of SAP applications got a flavour of infrastructure, because of its big size, the number of units and functions to be supported, and the number of users, managers, and developers involved. The second step was the crumbling of the SAP application as one common universal and system for all units. During the validation and the following implementation process, major customization of the application to different local needs took place. During this customization, the application changed from one universal and common application towards one for every single organizational unit. The overall result is a large number of overlapping and interconnected applications—a complex heterogeneous infrastructure. The third step was the integration of SAP and the Bridge infrastructure, and through this integrations even with the Internet. Finally, the SAP installation in HAE became integrated with others.

Standards Evolution: The Reflexivity (Double Hermeneutics) of Infrastructures

The Hydro Bridge standard has changed considerably from its initial conception. Several new versions have been defined, partly as a result of learning and of Bridge's own success, and partly as a result of the need to adapt to a continuously changing world (as also illustrated by the Internet example above).

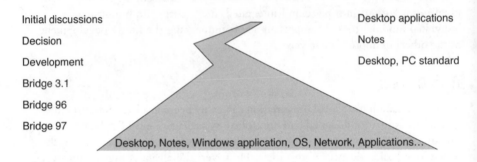

Initial discussions   Desktop applications

Decision   Notes

Development   Desktop, PC standard

Bridge 3.1

Bridge 96

Bridge 97

Desktop, Notes, Windows application, OS, Network, Applications...

FIG. 8.3. The evolution of Bridge in terms of growth in number of modules

Previous sections have reported several components that have been included in Bridge since its initial definition. Here we will mention some more. A second version of the Notes infrastructure was operational in May 1997. It introduced a new service providing high-speed replication of databases following the established structure of hubs and spokes and a service providing replication directly between servers (bypassing the hierarchical structure of hubs and spokes). Hydro templates for standard documents such as letter, memo, fax front page, summons to meeting, minutes of meeting, and so on were defined, and a central directory service for resources across Hydro's different technologies is under development at the time of writing. The components included in Bridge are split into two categories: Basic Bridge and Bridge Extensions.

Changing from one Bridge version to the next is a challenging task. Migrating to Bridge 97 means moving from Windows 3.1 to Windows 95 or NT. This implies that all applications have to be ported. This did not cause much trouble for most commercial products. But Hydro is using a wide range of PC software developed in-house. Porting this software has been a major task.

The Bridge standard has grown considerably since its initial conception, as illustrated in Fig. 8.3 and Table 8.1. The character of the Bridge standard and infrastructure has also changed similarly. While it was clean and well structured at the time of conception, as a result of its changes the increasing number of parts have become overlapping and are linked together in an evermore complex lattice, as illustrated in Fig. 8.4. Bridge has been growing along several dimensions: users and

Table 8.1. *Bridge 97*

Area	Products			
Information sharing	Notes	Web		
Desktop applications	Lotus	Windows		
E-mail	Notes	cc:mail	X.400	Telex
OS	Novell	Win95	WinNT	
PC	All major vendors			
Network	TCP/IP	Novell		
Telecom	Telephone	ATM	Radio	2 MB
Support	Local	Hydro Data	Outsourced	
Versions	Bridge 3.1	Bridge 96	Bridge 97	

use areas, the number of applications, the degree of duplication, and the inclusion of the required underlying services.

In addition to the evolution of Bridge from one version to another, the different speed of adoption of version updates among the divisions adds to the 'chaos' of the Bridge infrastructure. Some divisions move quickly to new versions, others are

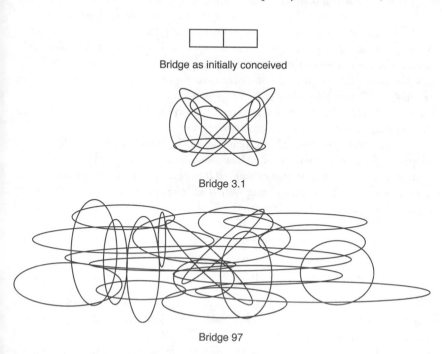

Bridge as initially conceived

Bridge 3.1

Bridge 97

FIG. 8.4. The evolution of Bridge in terms of internal structure

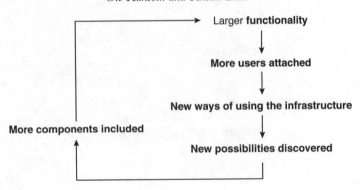

Fɪɢ. 8.5. Learning reinforcements mechanism

very slow. The file formats of desktop products change from one version to the next. The products are usually backward compatible, so that later versions may read files produced by older ones. The opposite is not the case; accordingly new product versions mean incompatibilities between tools used in different divisions. Bridge is evolving from one version to the next. But a new version only partially replaces the old. The old ones are still in use—which means that the new versions are introduced *in addition* to the old ones. All this means that the complexity, heterogeneity, and incompatibility of the infrastructure have been growing very fast.

This increase in complexity is largely driven by the infrastructure itself, as its users learn to use it. This illustrates the reflexivity of infrastructures (see Chapter 3). As illustrated in Fig. 8.5, when an infrastructure grows in terms of users/nodes connected and applications/components included, new user groups adopt the infrastructure and start to use the infrastructure in new areas. This leads to the generation of more new ideas and new possibilities about how the infrastructure can be used, which in turn lead to improvements of the infrastructure to fit the new use areas better and increase the functionality, and so on.

Infrastructures and standards are reflexive in the sense that their diffusion and adoption drive their own change. Fast and successful adoption implies radical change. In this way *an infrastructure standard is becoming obsolete by its own success.* And this reflexivity implies the following: When an infrastructure is enhanced—that is, extended and linked to more infrastructures, to get better control of organizational processes—it leads to more and faster propagation of side effects as the networks become larger. This further implies that the infrastructure becomes harder to control, as do the organizational processes it is supposed to support.

Conclusion

Standards and infrastructures interfere with other standards and infrastructures. Sometimes a simple interface can easily be specified, while the infrastructures remain independent. In other cases, they interfere in such a way that they actively support each other, so that each makes the other more useful. However, in some cases they cause trouble for each other in a way that requires careful attention. The site-management problems prove that what seemed to be wise decisions from a SAP point of view were at the same time bad decisions from the Bridge perspective.

Standards are settled in order to create order. A smooth interaction between standards requires a global order. But such a global order is beyond reach in our complex world. We define local standards to create local order. But each local order interacts with others and, as long as there is no global order, one local order—however well it is designed—will create disorder in its environment. SAP's order was Bridge's disorder (Timmermans and Berg 1997; Berg and Timmermans forthcoming). The more connections, the more unintended side effects—and the more disorder is created when pursuing local order.

So what? Going deeply into discussions about what kind of design strategies should be derived from the theories of reflexive modernization and actor networks is beyond the scope of this chapter. However, it is possible to make a few comments on how to deal with infrastructures and their irreversible installed base. A twofold strategy could be envisaged. On the one hand, it is important to fight against the power of the *installed base* by building an infrastructure in a way that makes it possible to avoid being trapped into it. This means making it as *flexible* as possible. Flexibility can be obtained through general strategies such as *modularization* and *simplicity*. In the context of infrastructures, this means that it is advisable to develop independent systems for smaller units and define simple interfaces between them, rather than develop one common universal system that includes all functions needed by anybody. When modularizing infrastructures to make them flexible, *gateways* are key tools (David and Bunn 1988; Hanseth and Monteiro 1998).

The other part of the proposal is somewhat the opposite. Make the installed base your ally by designing the new infrastructure in a way that builds upon the installed base as it is, rather than establishing a new one. The development and diffusion of the Web demonstrates the success of this strategy in the way the Web protocol (HTTP) and its data format (HTML) are designed to build upon the Internet's basic protocol (TCP/IP) and its format for multimedia information (MIME).

9

Infrastructure Strategy Formation: Seize the Day at Statoil

Eric Monteiro and Vidar Hepsø

Oil and gas operations are a key industry in Norway, representing 15.5 per cent of GDP. At the time of writing, Statoil is the largest producer in Norway and the second largest exporter of oil worldwide. Statoil—the State of Norway's Oil Company Ltd. (Den norske stats oljeselskap A/S)—is in the middle of a metamorphosis. After years sheltered from unbiased competition guaranteed through a broad, political coalition, Statoil is transforming itself into an internationally oriented, competitive enterprise. Statoil is learning to operate in a competitive market at the same time as it diversifies. It is no longer only an oil producer, but supports a whole chain of businesses from exploration of oil and gas fields, to the development of field installations and transportation systems, and the operation and maintenance of a number of offshore production platforms and pipeline systems. Statoil is changing into an integrated energy supplier. As well as diversifying its business areas, Statoil is also rapidly globalizing its operations through concentrated upstream activities in the Caspia, Angola, Nigeria, Venezuela, the UK, Vietnam, and the Gulf of Mexico. The globalization of Statoil is vital in increasing the robustness of its operations.

The development of comprehensive, versatile, well-aligned, and communicative information systems—in short, establishing an information infrastructure—is identified as a key, strategic vehicle in this transformation. An iconic manifestation of Statoil's ability to operate on the global scene is its ability to develop a resilient and flexible 'infrastructure that permits changes to the businesses without loss of time or quality for the customer . . . and be able to set up a new office site worldwide in five days', as stated in a 1997 internal strategy report. We describe and discuss the strategic efforts of Statoil to establish a Lotus Notes-based information infrastructure during the years 1992–8. This provides an instructive occasion to study how global business strategies are supported by IT in practice.

We conducted twenty semi- and unstructured interviews in the Winter and Spring of 1998, each lasting one and a half to two and a half hours. Our informants fell into the following categories: Involved in the Notes introduction: 3 (coded in the text as Intro1, Intro2, etc.); Managers and decision-makers: 7 (coded as Manager1, Manager2, etc.); Network managers: 1 (coded as Network1); Users: 9 (coded as User1, User2, etc.). In addition we had access to a rich set of written historical material such as reports, memos, and strategy documents as well as the Lotus Notes infrastructure which provided us with a rich source of information (e-mail discussions, memos and reports).

In the espoused version, the case of Statoil exemplifies the introduction and diffusion of Lotus Notes to meet the ambitions of strategic, communicative use of IT. Statoil in 1998 was seemingly an example of a highly successful introduction of Lotus Notes. With its 18,000 Lotus Notes users, Statoil in 1998 was among the world's largest user organizations. The number of Notes users in Statoil has grown rapidly: 1,017 (January 1994), 4,104 (January 1995), 8,210 (October 1995), 14,209 (October 1996), 18,300 (October 1997). Scratching below the surface, however, unravels a different picture. The 'diffusion' is but a convenient abbreviation for an ongoing socio-technical negotiation process. It took hard work—and luck—to mobilize sufficient support behind the Lotus Notes decision. Challenges had to be addressed, either by enrolling and aligning them with the existing infrastructure or by coexisting with them through a technological compromise (a kind of generalized 'gateway'). It was an ongoing effort that needed constantly to breathe to live. Establishing an information infrastructure is a long-term process; it does not simply unfold from a decision (Latour 1996).

This study is related to a body of previous research. In much of the MIS literature (Weill and Broadbent 1998), technology strategies are—like other plans—straightforwardly 'aligned' with the business strategy (see Chapter 2). There is a tendency, however, to emphasize the planned and controlled aspect of such efforts vis-à-vis the more opportunistic and improvised aspects (Ciborra 1997; Knights *et al.* 1997). This downplays to the level of non-existence the mutual negotiation as well as the improvisation between technology development and business strategies. Our analysis of strategic IS investments in Statoil in the 1990s is intended to shed some light on how strategic use of IT actually unfolds and how strategy development extends well beyond simplistic notions of 'alignment'. We employ an alternative notion of 'alignment' based on actor-network theory (ANT), as outlined in Chapter 5. Alignment, in the sense of ANT, underscores the bottom-up, heterogeneous, and performative aspects of strategy formation in action.

The emerging picture we paint comes close to a situation where decisions 'drift' (Ciborra 1996c; Berg 1997) or need to be 'improvised' (Orlikowski 1996a) to be defended. Our ambition, however, is to describe in some detail how an information infrastructure needs continuously to align new elements (user requirements, new information systems, new technological development, or new patterns of use) to the existing infrastructure (Monteiro 1998). Hence, the development of an information infrastructure only appears to 'drift' without direction. Although not planned, the continuous realignment of the infrastructure is anything but arbitrary. Not only is there agency underlying the 'drifting'; there is also a structure or pattern to it that we seek to unravel.

There exist a growing number of Lotus Notes studies in and around the field of computer supported cooperative work (CSCW) (Orlikowski 1992, 1996a; Korpela 1994; Ciborra 1996c; Essler 1998). The bulk of these, however, are focused around Lotus Notes as a fairly self-contained artefact. This misses out on one of our key concerns—namely, to recognize Lotus Notes as but one element of a larger, evolving infrastructure and its relation to the business strategy. Orlikowski (1996a) and

Ciborra (1996c) represent exceptions in the sense that they position the Lotus Notes introduction within the larger, organizational and business setting. What is lacking, and is of crucial importance in advancing our grasp on information infrastructure, is the description of exactly how Lotus Notes needed to be realigned to appropriate the sequence of challenges.

In what follows, we chronologically trace and analyse the unfolding process of constructing a strategic information infrastructure from the late 1980s to 1998. An outline of the background and history of Statoil is presented first and, by way of conclusion, we offer a critical assessment of the notion of 'strategic' information systems and the idea of 'aligning' business operations and IT.

Statoil

Statoil is a young company. Founded in 1972 with only one employee, it has since grown to an operations profit enterprise of NOK 5 billion. In 1998 there were over 17,000 employees in twenty-five countries, but the major activities were still located in Scandinavia and northern Europe. After Phillips found the substantial oilfield Ekofisk on the Norwegian continental shelf in 1969, there was an ongoing political debate in Norway about how to organize oil production. The decision to establish a new company, Statoil, with the Norwegian State as sole shareholder, was reached with a consensus voting in Parliament in 1972. It was anything but obvious. There was strong lobbying, also by the Prime Minister (Per Borten), to consider a takeover of the majority of Norsk Hydro's shares and let Norsk Hydro take charge. The argument for Norsk Hydro was that it would be better to build the future of Norway on a company that had already proved capable and competitive on energy production than to construct a new institution from scratch.

Immediately after Statoil had been established, the oil crisis struck. For Statoil, the crisis had two important consequences. First, it shifted power and control out of the hands of the 'seven sisters', the dominating oil companies, and into the hands of the oil producers, primarily OPEC, but also Statoil and Norway, who preferred to stay out of OPEC but with the status of an observer. Secondly, and of crucial importance, it paved the road for a significant rise in oil prices throughout the 1970s and into the 1980s. Without this rise, the development of the oilfields on the Norwegian shelf, deep under the turbulent Northern Sea, would simply not have been cost effective.

Statoil was the product of negotiations in Norwegian politics. From the outset, the company relied heavily on an array of different favourable encouragements and measurements aimed at tilting the competition. This reliance on political negotiations made Statoil particularly responsive and sensitive to signals in the political environment. The Statfjord field, the largest oilfield on the Norwegian shelf, was first discovered on the British continental shelf. Statoil was granted a licence for the astonishingly high share of 42.7 per cent of the field, with an option to take over the operational licence later from Mobil. This single stroke secured Statoil financially for more than two decades—and still accounted for a significant fraction of total incomes at the end of the 1990s.

The broad, political obligation in Norway systematically and aggressively to favour Statoil gradually faded away as the tide of liberalism rose. This forced Statoil step by step through a transition. It was transformed through a sequence of small steps into an internationally competitive oil and gas producer. The year 1984 marked an important year in this gradual transformation. In response to a growing fear in Parliament that Statoil would become too dominating, a new device was launched aimed at curbing Statoil's position by tapping directly into the generated surplus. This was an important impetus to develop Statoil's competitiveness further. There was one exception, however, to this new scheme—namely, the economical motor of Statoil, the Statfjord field.

The net profit after taxation was around NOK 5 billion in 1995–6, decreasing to NOK 4.3 billion in 1997. The operating profit before taxation increased from NOK 12.7 billion NOK in 1993 to an all-time high of NOK 18.3 billion in 1996 and a slight decrease to NOK 17 billion NOK in 1997. The largest part of Statoil is connected to exploration and production (E & P). In 1998 it contributed over NOK 15 billion of the result, leaving refining and marketing with NOK 1.3 billion and petrochemical with NOK 0.4 billion. Crude oil sales represented nearly 50 per cent of income but were decreasing. Natural gas accounted for around 10 per cent but was steadily growing and was expected to double by early in the twenty-first century. Refined products represented around 30 per cent, while transport (pipelines) and various smaller activities represented the rest. Statoil's money machine is Statfjord. Daily output from Statfjord hit a peak in January 1987, when it produced 850,204 barrels of oil in one day. After that, production dropped to 430,000 barrels, comparable to that of Gullfaks. The big difference lies in the shareholder percentage. While Statoil has 12 per cent ownership in the Gullfaks licence, it has 42.73 per cent ownership in the Statfjord licence.

A strategy document from the board of directors in 1997 argues that the results of the group in the years to come will rely on developments in the oil market. The build-up of global production is expected to continue, but the forecasted growth in demand is unlikely to alter fundamental market conditions. The document advocates a continued focus on cost-effective operation, development, and commercial progress to safeguard Statoil's competitiveness and earnings. Markets in petrochemicals and refining are expected to fluctuate and competition to be stiff. The Norwegian Continental shelf will still be the main operating theatre because of Statoil's operating experience and technical expertise.

Statoil's goal is to increase its daily oil and gas production to a million barrels of oil equivalent by 2005, including at least 300,000 barrels from areas outside Norway. Attaining these objectives will be demanding. The board was maintaining its goal of NOK 25 billion in operating profit for the year 2000. A number of improvement efforts were under way within the group to meet this target. CEO Norvik describes Statoil as moving from a pure oil and gas company to becoming an energy group. Gas will become more and more important for Statoil. Statoil will build up activities further into the value chain, such as gas power plants and production of electricity.

The Era of Cost-Cutting and Rationalizing: The Late 1980s–1993

The sequence of large reorganization efforts to streamline business

The post-Gulf War period after 1990 led to a recession in the oil industry, with falling oil prices and dollar rates. The average price of a barrel of oil in 1991 was $4 less than it had been in 1990. Large oil companies such as Shell and British Petroleum were restructuring their business and dismissed a large number of people, not only because of the recession but also because of substantial changes in the business itself because of the global market and increasing environmental pressure. In Statoil, exploration and production (E & P), the key contributor to company profits, painted a dark future prognosis in the philosophy of operations document for the 1990s. Work for a new strategy for operations in 1992 led to a diagnosis of the situation much along the same lines as their competitors. Statfjord, Statoil's money machine number one, had a shrinking reservoir and falling production rates. Oil analysts foresaw low oil prices in the future, comparable to conditions in the mid- and late 1980s. In addition, there was a political debate about further opening up the Norwegian Continental shelf to more competition, which meant that Statoil could lose its favourable position in the long run.

The assessment of the situation led to two projects called Operations 95 and Project 95, which came into effect from the autumn of 1992. The aim of the projects was to cut operational costs by NOK 2 billion by 1995. These projects had several long-term consequences. They were the first round of what turned out to be a sequence of similar projects that stressed the importance of internal customer–contractor relations as a way of streamlining business and developing internal pricing mechanisms and markets.

This streamlining of business led to a centralization of specialist knowledge, which up to now had been integrated or embedded within large operational divisions. Both technical-support and information-technology personnel were reallocated to centralized units to be able to track actual costs, expenditures, and profits more easily. This streamlining of business took place through a sequence of reorganizational projects like those outlined above. As described in later sections, it took several years and several similar projects to make the changes. They needed to be reiterated over and over again to have an impact, producing a gradual reorientation.

IT, yet another source of cost generation

The basic principles of these large reorganization efforts were mapped fairly straightforwardly onto the IT area as well. Investment in IT was viewed largely as just another source of cost generation and hence as a likely candidate for rationalization and cost cutting.

The choice of Lotus office tools was settled on price only. Lotus wanted the deal 'so badly they made Statoil an offer they couldn't refuse' (Intro2). Microsoft was so confident that it would win that it did not make a bid for 'fleeting' software licences, a type of contract that was largely unknown at the time—that is, a contract with restrictions only on the total number of licences, not on the identity of the users.

The choice of the Lotus suite of office tools as a corporate-wide standard followed a decision process in the central IT department and was fronted by its head in autumn 1992. It was not possible to ban other vendors such as Microsoft. But the implication was that people who wanted to buy non-Lotus tools had to make sure that they were compatible with Lotus—and that they paid themselves. As cost cutting was the basic rationale, this made the barrier to non-Lotus products considerable.

New work practices: ideas in search of an ally

Somewhat on the margins of the key concern for controlling and cutting IT costs were people trying to argue for a more strategic use of IT, for the potential for IT-based cooperation and distribution of documents. It took time before this effort picked up speed and became more widely accepted. Even as late as 1994, CEO Norvik made no reference to IT in his assessment of future challenges. At this time, the only way to communicate corporate-wide was with the use of Memo, an IBM-based e-mail system. It was purely text based and offered no support for attachment of electronic documents. Memo had been introduced in the 1980s and had a large community of users. Its functionality was poor, but 'the great thing about it was that everybody used it' (Manager3). Until 1991 Memo functioned only internally within Statoil. As Memo was developed in Sweden by Volvo, there exists a public network in Sweden based on Memo that connects industry and governmental institutions. Statoil in Sweden, and accordingly the rest of Statoil, had access to this public network, but it was never made use of systematically.

The maturing and growing awareness of using IT to support new work practices unfolded slowly over years. It drew on several, including external, sources, and seemingly 'drifted' along. On closer scrutiny, however, important elements of this implementation may be identified. We describe how the visions gain momentum from new oilfield discoveries and an international trend towards tighter cooperation within the oil industry. Really to take off, however, the visions about the strategic use of IT needed spokespersons or allies, a topic to which we shall return later.

For the diffusion of Notes to succeed, it was necessary to develop skills and competence in handling all aspects of Notes: developing applications, helping users, finding ways to coexist with existing systems, and providing maintenance and support. In order to gain further experience with Notes, it was introduced into the whole IT department, which consisted of about 200 people at that time. Rather than employing a stepwise strategy for deployment, the idea was 'breathe first', all at once. The manager of the IT department engaged forcefully in the introduction of Notes within the IT department. He signalled very clearly that he expected everyone to start using Notes. As an illustration, he stopped replying to e-mails using the old Memo system instead of Notes mail.

It was important for the IT department, in coalition with corporate IT (KIT), to stay ahead, to mobilize the impression that it was a competent, up-to-date, and responsive department, in order to strengthen its position in the turbulence and uncertainty surrounding all of E & P.

It was furthermore perceived as important to develop six standard applications. This was to avoid the impression that Notes was only an application framework, only 'an empty shell' (Intro3). These six applications were fairly general, administrative tools dealing with: meeting-room reservation, individual week plans, news, sick or absent leave recording, discussion bulletin board, and an answering service for users.

Centralization, the Flip Side of Standardization: 1993

The streamlining of E & P following Project 95 led to the centralization of the old decentralized IT units to form the new IT department dubbed Statoil Data (SData for short). Included in the challenges faced by this department was dealing with was the mistrust and frustration on the part of management relating to IT and with the need to justify both the investments in and the effects of IT. The technical rationalization and cost cutting through the standardization of office tools to the Lotus office suite were extended to include the organization of IT as well. In April 1993 the IT services were radically centralized, a move that was perceived to follow more or less from the efforts of strengthened control over IT investments and standardized tools, as 'the centralization of IT was as a direct outcome of Project 95' (Manager4).

In this sense, centralization was perceived as the flip side of standardization. The new, centralized IT department included the old IT department together with five of the local IT departments within E & P. This doubled the number of employees compared to the old IT department.

The key argument for the centralization was economies of scale—or, in the language of earlier days—to 'harvest the benefits of mainframes'. An additional, important argument was to solve the problems of fragmented and incompatible IT solutions. In other words, the task of cleaning up the office tools environment by settling for Lotus was regarded as a symptom of the more general problem of a too decentralized decision and budgeting responsibility for IT investments. Hence, the centralized SData was expected to function as an arena for broad consensus for IT investments, a consensus that had previously been unattainable because of the decentralized organizational structure, for, 'without the centralization of SData, it would be impossible to reach decisions' (Manager1).

This problem had been made painfully evident through two earlier projects, called VMS (dealing with maintenance and material flow, running from 1990 to 1995) and Sigma (for finance and economy), which had been expensive, ragbag solutions that needed numerous options in order to reach agreement. Hence, the lack of an effective forum for IT decision-making was acutely felt.

There was a well-developed sense that something drastic had to be done. The real challenge was to transform SData into a business- and market-oriented organization, to change from a 'planned economy to a market economy' (Manager2). This represented substantial changes along several dimensions: E & P's perception of SData, Sdata's perception of itself, Sdata's routines for handling customer enquiries, and the internal organization of SData. The implications of the reorganization within SData varied. The former IT department tended to view the establishment of SData as an expansion of its former organization, whereas the newcomers from the local IT departments tended to view it as a sign of radical reorientation, a confirmation that the old IT department was answering the needs of E & P (Manager2). In the process, 'middle management [from the old IT department] was massacred' (Manager1). In a sense, the new organizational structure was superimposed on, rather than a substitute for, the existing one (User3). This reshuffling created a deep sense of uncertainty about the future for SData employees. In this situation, it was of vital importance to construct trust between SData and its key customer, E & P, to 'avoid wasting all our energy on control measures' (Manager2). The central vehicle for establishing trust and security in the midst of this turbulence was a contract between SData and E & P. To work out and evaluate such a formal contract was unusual but signalled the commitment to go through with the changes. The core of the contract consisted of a two-way commitment. SData was to guarantee at least 30 per cent cost cutting of IT investments for E & P within two years while, on the other hand, E & P acknowledged SData as its preferred partner, a partner that represented 70 per cent of SData's revenues in 1993 (Manager1).

The establishment of trust was an effort; it could not simply be decided upon. It was top driven in the sense that the key ingredients were worked out by a handful of people from SData and E & P management, who spent a considerable time negotiating and discussing solutions (Manager2). In evaluating the contract after two years, the results were judged positively. The judgements were primarily concerned with the cost-containment side, the side which was the most easily put into operation. Although, in hindsight, one 'may ask whether the operationalizing of the goals was good enough, there is no doubt that SData satisfied them' (Manager1).

In sum, the major reorganizational efforts in Statoil were immediately translated into the simultaneous centralization, standardization, and market orientation of the IT services, the exact mirror image of the larger restructuring in E & P.

The Bundling of Notes: 1993–1994

The package

A striking aspect of Notes, closely linked to its infrastructural character, is the way it was not introduced in isolation. Notes partly makes up an infrastructure and partly is an element of one. In short, Notes was not introduced as a more or less isolated artefact; it was 'bundled', packaged, or aligned with existing and new elements. The establishment of an information infrastructure always requires this kind of careful alignment for adoption and diffusion to be feasible (see Chapters 4 and 5).

The Lotus Notes infrastructure that SData attempted to establish was packaged together with two other components—namely, the standardized suite of office tools from Lotus and a PC-based, wide area network (WAN) that allowed the PC to communicate across the geographical locations of Statoil in and outside Norway. This PC-based WAN was called I-net. I-net represented a massive investment for SData. In combination with Notes, I-net has been the gem of SData in the sense that it is a vital, corporate asset entirely under the control of SData. The control over I-net allows SData to act as a 'gatekeeper'. The continuous evolution of I-net is a resource-consuming endeavour but provides versatile and powerful network functionality. I-net included name directory services allowing logins independent of geographical location, a feature that was not standardly available in PC-based networks at the time. I-net was introduced piecemeal in Statoil as an upgrading of a PC. For instance, during one weekend in December 1994, twenty-five SData employees managed to upgrade 650 PCs at corporate headquarters to I-net. To upgrade all PCs to the first version of I-net took the best part of 1994.

I-net has since evolved in response to upgrading, in particular the upgrading from Windows 3.1x to Windows 95 during 1996 (see below). The fact that SData, 'rightly enough, is proud of its accomplishment with I-net' has made its gradual phasing-out and replacement by more standardized, off-the-shelf solutions rather cumbersome (Manager2). An illustration from March 1998 of the non-transparency of I-net and the increased pressure to substitute in-house-developed solutions with standardized ones was the breakdown of the 'home-made' fire wall against the Internet. One of the members of the Notes introduction team describes the lumping of Notes together with the office tools as 'in effect two parallel pro-jects—the introduction of SmartSuite [Lotus's office tools] and Notes' (Intro2). By the end of 1994 there were 10,390 Lotus users but only about 4,000 Notes users. It is easy to forget the novelty of allowing PCs to communicate beyond a purely local context. This had previously belonged to the world of mainframes and Unix; it was introduced as something really new in Statoil, something that the users were sup-posed to identify with Notes. In this sense, the fact that Statoil had previously lagged behind in offering communicative services to their PC users gave the Notes advocates an opportunity to take advantage of this to boost Notes, because 'remember—before Notes there was no wide area network [for PCs]' (Intro2)!

Given such a package and the functionality of Notes, a number of more ambi-tious changes would have been possible. But this was not the strategy pursued. Instead, the project group advocating Notes employed a more conservative approach, and focused primarily on a restricted aspect of Notes, the e-mail. E-mail, in itself, was not new to Statoil, as users had been accustomed to the IBM-based, text-only e-mail system called Memo. The fact that a significant number of users were already accustomed to the use of e-mail made it easier to introduce Notes mail as e-mail with a little bit extra. As one of the users recollects, 'the important thing about Memo was that we became accustomed to the use of e-mail' (User6).

Given the preparation accomplished through Memo, Notes was presented as Memo but with the additional feature to attach documents. In an actor-network vocabulary, this amounts to the alignment of e-mail and word processing. Hence, the real impetus for promoting Lotus Notes was its ability to attach documents to e-mails: 'the most important reason to use Lotus Notes . . . is the more effective distribution of documents', an internal report stated in 1994.

The role of e-mail

In the corporate folklore, Lotus Notes was to a large extent equated with e-mail. This impression seemed to be fairly widespread, despite the efforts to introduce Lotus Notes together with the six standard applications. This illustrates the difficulties of actually diffusing these six applications. It is instructive to enquire in more detail into the construction of Lotus Notes as e-mail, a conception quite distinct from the espoused theory on the use of Lotus Notes.

In the note issued in 1993 describing the functionality of Lotus Notes, the advantages of a more versatile e-mail system were presented up front. It was the very first thing about Lotus Notes that was described and clearly mirrored the belief that an improved e-mail service would facilitate a smoother introduction of Lotus Notes: 'Electronic message transfer (Notes mail) operates differently from what we are used to from Memo. A new and highly demanding function is introduced that makes it possible to attach all kinds of files to the message' (see the report mentioned above).

The introduction of the new e-mail service in Notes was made smoother by ensuring the coexistence with the older e-mail system, Memo, as a gateway between Notes and Memo was provided. Memo had a long history in Statoil (see above). In a twenty-four-hour logging in 1994 of e-mail traffic in Statoil, 12,821 out of a total of 14,977 e-mails were generated from Memo and the rest from Notes mail. The installed base of Memo was considerable. To the extent that Lotus Notes for e-mail was to spread, coexistence with Memo was essential; according to an internal report from 1995, 'today Memo is Statoil's main e-mail system and other systems need to be able to exchange messages with Memo'. The establishment of a gateway between Memo and Notes mail meant that users did not need to 'jump' to Notes—they could still communicate with the contacts they had e-mailed when they had still used Memo. And, conversely, from Memo, users could still communicate with users of Notes Mail. One reason, apart from the conservative nature of habits and acquired expertise, why users preferred to stick to Memo was that there was one function that was not reproduced in Notes mail—namely, an 'undo function that enabled you to discard an already sent message', inscribed through its centralized database solution (Intro1). The need to be able to communicate by e-mail with partners outside Statoil became increasingly important, resulting in the establishment in 1995 of a X.400 gateway accessible via Memo (and hence Notes mail via the already existing Notes/Memo gateway). This X.400 gateway was followed up by working out institutionalized routines for generating unique X.400 e-mail addresses formulated in the 1995 report. From 1996 a Lotus Notes server running SMTP made Internet e-mail directly available in Statoil, making e-mail communication with the outside world even more convenient.

This strategy of alignment—aligning Notes first with office tools (through attachment) and, secondly, with the simultaneous establishment of a PC-based WAN—was a key move for the diffusion of the infrastructure. It took the form that, as new requirements or 'incidents' occurred, the Notes proponents had to improvise in order to align these with the evolving Notes infrastructure. This pattern runs through any information infrastructure establishment; it is at the core of developing infrastructure. In this case, there were two additional, important illustrations of this process of alignment: address books and electronic archives. The repeatedly voiced need to have an electronically available address book for all employees of Statoil was translated and aligned with the Notes introduction in such a way that users were granted immediate access to the address book when filling in the headers of e-mails. As illustrated further below, the pressure for meeting the ISO 9001 quality standards was translated and aligned with the use of a Notes application for electronic achieving (Elark) that was perceived as a solution to the ISO 9001 requirements.

Diffusing Lotus Notes—or was it E-mail? 1994–1996

Redefining the road

Up to 1995 E & P had been the major area for large organizational change efforts in Statoil. A project called K-2000 tried to apply the same principles that had been behind the business orientation of E & P to the rest of the company. Here the same strategic thinking was implemented in this company-wide change effort: centralizing the expertise to business units; creating fifteen new streamlined business areas with decentralized profit responsibility and distinct profiles focusing on core competencies and defined products; reducing the numbers of layers in the organization; delineating the difference between staff and service functions. The main aim was to increase the teamwork and the exploitation of resources across the organization. New flexible collaborative work patterns were first developed in the Norne project and from 1995 also at a new methanol plant under construction at Tjeldbergodden site. Both these cases were used as examples of future practice. Even though it was not so evident in the argumentation for K-2000, IT was increasingly seen as a potential enabler in the implementation and development process of the new K-2000 organization from mid-1995 in order to establish the new company routines. This was reflected in the technology strategy of Statoil that was developed after K-2000 in 1995–6. Here information technology and coordination technology were embedded in the concept of holistic competence. K-2000 was the latest of a long sequence of reorganization efforts (called Project 95, BRU, PES, and so on), but it finally managed to break ground for more communicative use of IT.

Gaining momentum

The use of an improved e-mail (vis-à-vis the former Memo) as a spearhead for advocating Notes, combined with the growing acceptance (expressed through K-2000) of the need for a more communicative use of IT, meant that the evolving Notes infrastructure was picking up speed. To feed the process, it was necessary continuously to translate and align new requirements (as illustrated above with attachments, PC WAN, address books, and ISO 9001).

This created some leeway in the introduction of Notes; the project team pushing Notes was able to loosen up a bit. For instance, there was a clear policy that the users should be able to develop their own applications. The prime characteristic of Notes was undoubtedly e-mail, but in the background a more versatile use was prepared and encouraged, as 'we had a clear policy about allowing the users to develop their own Notes applications. This was the opposite strategy of Norsk Hydro' (Intro2). The Notes introduction project team had developed six standard applications that were made available in Statoil. These included applications for meeting room reservations, discussion bulletin boards, and frequently asked questions (FAQs). The intention was to 'show that Notes was more than e-mail', as one of the project team recollects (Intro3). The use, however, of these applications never became widespread.

The Notes introduction project team lobbied hard towards E & P for a wider diffusion of Notes. E & P kept a short list of core systems for which they paid well. The introduction of Notes was becoming increasingly important to SData, both in commercial terms and even more so in terms of a sign of acknowledgement. In a situation where SData was still working to acquire a sense of confidence (see above), this was vital, because, 'for SData, Lotus Notes was important, very important' (Intro2). After a succession of rejects, in September 1994 E & P finally agreed to include Lotus Notes in its core portfolio of systems, thus financially securing the situation of SData.

SData was then able to turn to the vast number of small details that were needed to glue Notes together, to facilitate further spreading. It needed to extend the Notes infrastructure with elements that 'Lotus had not focused on: they had emphasized network administration' (Intro2). What SData needed was support for the management of users—that is, creating, deleting, and moving users, changing names, and administration of the mailboxes. In addition, it was necessary to translate and align PINFO, the corporate database for personal information, with Notes.

Filling in the gaps, providing the invisible but necessary parts of the infrastructure, is a recurring pattern in the development of an infrastructure (Latour 1996; Monteiro 1998). We return to it further below. It may be recognized as a strategy of alignment, of making the infrastructure more robust by fleshing it out.

The institutionalization of patterns of use

As a result of these processes of alignment, the 'diffusion' of Notes unfolded. The use of Notes to a large amount boiled down to the use of e-mail, despite the six standard applications. In response to the more popular and 'free' use of Notes, SData started focusing on the institutionalization of patterns of use. A campaign late in 1995 illustrates this.

The campaign was dubbed 'Hunting for the Paper Clip'. The name made reference to what had initially been the key argument for Notes—namely, the ability to attach various documents to an e-mail. This is depicted graphically on the screen as a paper clip. The proliferation of e-mail with attachment was perceived as a growing problem. The ease of mass distribution and forwarding resulted in a growing number of e-mails with extensive attachments. Through the campaign in 1995, SData attempted to institutionalize a more disciplined use of attachments (and e-mail) by 'searching' for paper clips. The campaign was highly profiled internally through electronic and paper newsletters.

Balancing local variation and adaptation against uniformity

For a long time, Notes was basically equated with e-mail in Statoil. Despite the efforts to provide the users with standard applications (see above), serious use of non-e-mail applications of Notes started to pick up only around 1996. SData had used the six standard applications internally from 1994 and Elark, an application for electronic archiving, had been used in parts of E & P from 1995 as part of the ISO certification.

One of the core Notes applications that was developed by SData is ESOP, an application for supporting project management. It is instructive to look into how this was introduced. ESOP represents a serious use of Notes beyond e-mail. The key problem with ESOP, however, was to find a way to customize it to local needs rather than employ the strategy of 'one size fits all' that had traditionally dominated SData. The Notes project team functioned as an obligatory passage point, in the sense that it was delegated by E & P the role of approving the development of local variants of standard Notes applications, including the one for project management.

A member of the Troll project wanted to use Lotus Notes but not one of the six standard applications. Instead, he wanted to use a Notes application he knew about from colleagues working on a different project: 'We have assessed the Lotus Notes application used by the project Sleipner and found that, given a few modifications, it satisfies our requirements. We accordingly wish to be allowed to develop such a non-standard tool. We are already aware of the fact that the Statfjord project has applied for a similar tool.'

In its response to this enquiry, the Notes introduction team attempted to persuade the Troll project member to reconsider using the relevant, standard application. The team also pointed out that it kept track of related suggestions for tools and tried to coordinate and facilitate a cooperation among the different initiatives.

As I've already written . . . there is, in principle, nothing wrong with adopting the system [you refer to], but then the Troll project themselves must cover the expenses of this adoption. But as you now have 3 projects which all want to use the same application, would it not be a good idea to see if you, with a bit of joint effort, could make it available for all 3 of you? (internal e-mail message, 1995)

The introduction team was aware of the need to modify the existing collection of standard Notes application in response to user needs. There was accordingly a clear sense of the need to organize these modifications in such a way that new versions become available within reasonable time. Another message stated: 'Unless an outline for providing modified versions of the standard applications is worked out—quickly—local variants, despite the veto against them, will proliferate.'

Small or Big Changes? March 1996

By early 1996 the Notes infrastructure had acquired a certain robustness, a certain level of irreversibility. This, as we have illustrated above, did not unfold automatically as a result of the 'diffusion' of Notes. Rather, it was the pay-off of the continuous process of appropriating, or 'improvising' as a result of, the incidents that 'drifted' along. In short, it was a continuous process of alignment.

March 1996 marked a point in this process of alignment, this process of building up the robustness and strength of the Notes infrastructure. SData had decided to upgrade Notes from version 3 to version 4. The diffusion strategy of SData, as it had been all along, was one of alignment. More specifically, it framed this upgrading as one aimed at strengthening the position of Notes by making as few changes as possible. This strategy did not take advantage of the new, technical potential of the new version of Notes. The mechanisms to design clickable, graphic user interfaces mimicking the functionality of the Web were particularly interesting. But SData decided not to emphasize these and accordingly created space and opportunity for more proactive and fast-moving internal competitors. The group for coordination technology (KOT) was especially active in exploring the possibilities of Notes. In contrast to SData, KOT focused on developing Notes applications closer to the actual development and operation of oilfields, in particular the Norne field.

The way SData presented the upgrading as a means of strengthening the position of Notes was basically a way of making their own Notes administration more efficient. By March 1996 there were about 3,500 Notes databases in Statoil, which generated a considerable amount of administration for SData. These applications were poorly aligned with work practices. Along with the upgrading to version 4 of Notes, SData trimmed this jungle of databases by forcing owners of databases to identify the ones they wanted to migrate to the new version of Notes. SData simultaneously tightened the requirements connected to Notes applications by ensuring that all applications had an owner and a brief description of functionality (Intro1). This cleansing paid off. The number of Notes databases declined from 3,500 to about 1,200. Still, the proliferation of these independently developed Notes applications represented an important learning process that neither the use of Notes as e-mail nor the six standard applications captured.

In addition to this move towards rationalizing the administration of Notes, the changes related to the upgrading were bundled or packaged together with another and seemingly bigger change—the upgrading of Windows 3.11 to Windows 95. In this way, the Notes upgrading was made less visible by being only a (small?) part of what was perceived as the inevitable upgrading to Windows 95. In much the same way as the original introduction of Notes had been bundled with I-net in 1993–4, the upgrading to Notes 4 was packaged into a more invisible and 'inevitable' upgrading of I-net to Windows 95. Again, the non-transparency and almost unmanageable complexity of I-net created a lot of difficulties for the existing portfolio of applications: not all old applications were able to run smoothly on the upgraded I-net platform, so SData spent a considerable amount of its time extinguishing fires and acute problems (Manager3).

As an indication of the core importance of the e-mail function of Notes, SData also wanted to trim the mailboxes of the users to save some disk space. SData accordingly tried to encourage users to compress or delete parts of their mailbox in a similar way that Notes databases were trimmed. This, however, proved to be quite a different matter. 'The mailboxes were not to be touched' was the clear response from users, as 'it proved to be impossible to trim the mailboxes of the users—the mailboxes were important!' (Intro1). Around 1995–6, there was still a considerable installed base of the old e-mail system, Memo. There were an estimated 10,000 Lotus Notes users, while the number of Memo users was close to 12,000. The number of Memo users, however, is counted from the number of mailboxes at the time and does not necessary represent active Memo users. This might make the decision to 'phase out Memo in 1996' seem a bit more reasonable.

Enrolling the Outside World: April 1996–1997

Outside pressure

Establishing the Notes infrastructure in Statoil was never automatic. In the previous sections, we have illustrated how the momentum or irreversibility of an infrastructure—disguised by the potentially misleading term 'diffusion'—is the product of the hard work of continuous alignment.

We now turn to more serious threats to an evolving infrastructure, threats that obviously are not possible to translate and align into the existing infrastructure. If you cannot employ a strategy of alignment, what do you do then? Before returning to this question, let us first have a quick look at the sources of these threats.

In a number of ways, the pressure for opening up and orienting Statoil more towards the outside world was building up. Some of this thrust was of a fairly general nature. The rapid folklorization of the Internet and the Web in media was especially influential in Statoil. Additionally, the oil industry underwent important restructuring during this period. There was a growing awareness about the need to communicate with external partners and subcontractors. The development and introduction of NORSOK, in response to a British initiative (called CRINE), was a decisive move in focusing on external communication within the whole oil industry. Up to this point, Statoil had been characterized by a kind of self-centredness that was related to its remarkable achievements during its first years of existence. This was sustained by the fact that 'we are proud of what we have achieved. But we have probably been a bit self-centred, a bit reluctant to orient towards the external world' (Network1). Similarly, there was a growing focus on supporting industry communication—for instance, by establishing Oilnet (www.oilnet.com). The NORSOK work was supplemented by POSC, a standardization effort for facilitating a more efficient communication about technical components (pipes, platforms, ships, rigs, and so forth).

At the time of the research in 1998, in terms of technological infrastructure, the situation in Statoil was still characterized by multiple communication standards and platforms. There exists a FDDI fibre-optical network at the corporate headquarters. Between major sites, a number of different WAN communication solutions are used including leased lines, ISDN, Frame relay, and ATM. Communication with Statoil sites outside the Norwegian main land is by Frame relay or satellite. LAN communication is dominated by 10 or 100 Mbps Ethernet running Novell IPX, TCP/IP, and some Apple talk. There still exist Token ring segments in some locations.

Notes: a closed world?

With regards to the evolving Notes infrastructure, the overarching trends got translated into a simple question: was Notes an appropriate infrastructure to meet these challenges? There was at this time no obvious way to align these new requirements with the existing Notes infrastructure.

The initial strategy used by SData until about 1997 was one of marginalization. The proponents and arguments behind, for instance, the Internet and the Web were sidelined by presenting them as misguided. Hence, the proponents of Notes tended to downplay the significance and substance of the objections towards Notes because 'the advocates of the Internet are those who do not know how good Notes is with regards to the Internet' (Intro1). The heart of the problem, the accusation that Notes was a closed system and hence inappropriate when Statoil was to open up to the world, was defined as a misunderstanding, 'as Notes has tools for SQL queries together with the new Domino servers' (Intro1). And, as a consequence, 'the controversy died out' (Intro2). Further below, we study more closely how the introduction of a new version of Notes (version 4.5, called Domino) was framed as a compromise between the existing Notes infrastructure and the pressure from the outside world signalled through access to the Web. This is an instance not of alignment but rather of a kind of socio-technical compromise, a generalized 'gateway', preserving the two competing infrastructures.

Statoil has traditionally been fairly closed towards the outside world. Unix users have had access to e-mail communication with external partners from the early 1990s. Memo, the corporate-wide e-mail system introduced in Statoil in the 1980s, was only for internal communication. With the establishment of an X.400 gateway, Memo and Notes mail could be used for external communication from 1995. In 1996 a Notes-based SMTP server made Internet mail directly available from Notes. Non-e-mail communication with the outside world, however, arrived rather late in Statoil—that is, for PC users. Unix users had access to a broad range of services such as Archie, ftp, telnet, and Web. For this reason, Web was merely shrugged off as a Unix 'thing'. PC-based Web browsers were allowed only from late 1995, and only in response to a formal application. Only from January 1998 were users allowed to browse from a PC without special permission.

The Situation in 1998

The installed base of the Notes infrastructure

As a result of successfully aligning a rich set of elements, the Notes infrastructure has acquired a certain robustness, a certain level of irreversibility. Is it, then, finally 'introduced'; is it a stable, working infrastructure?

It is certainly the case that it is considered obligatory, that other decisions pre-suppose the existence of Notes, because 'we have to relate to the fact that Notes is per-vasive, to the already existing installed base of Notes' (Network1). The observation that the installed base of Notes is 'heavy' also gets reiterated in strategy documents of various kinds. Still, how sure is Statoil that it is not flogging a dying horse, that the future lies in the Web? The fact that Norsk Hydro is also a large Notes-user organiza-tion is used in Statoil to legitimize its own commitment, as '[Norsk] Hydro is also using Notes, so we cannot be completely off target' (Manager1).

There is a considerable installed base of Lotus Notes in terms of applications, routines, and delegation of roles. In addition to this, and a lot less visible, a set of institutionalized structures and arenas has developed over the years that contributes strongly to the argument for keeping Lotus Notes in place. Statoil and Hydro, the two largest user organizations of Lotus Notes in Norway, have established about ten different forums where representatives from the two companies meet on a reg-ular basis to discuss and evaluate each other's experiences. From a slow start, these have over the years turned into working institutions, not empty shells. Similarly, Notes-user forums, both in Scandinavia and internationally, meet regularly for formal cooperation and an exchange of experiences. In conjunction with the tech-nical side of Lotus Notes, this adds significantly to the purely physical aspect of the installed base of Notes in Statoil.

The level of confidence about Notes is a direct result of the successful definition of the Notes version 4.5, the Domino servers, as an acceptable compromise. Let us see in more detail how this took place.

The Internet and the Web: fiends or friends?

The threat to the Notes infrastructure from the Web was quite real. What the out-come would have been had Statoil not been saved by the bell by the introduction of the Domino servers is uncertain: 'Had Lotus not introduced their Domino servers, I think it would have been difficult to defend Notes [against Web proponents]' (Manager1).

The Internet had been of marginal importance to the company during the early 1990s. UNIX-based specialists and a few people at KOT or SData had used it regularly since 1993, but it was 1995 before the general potential of this new phenomenon was first realized via the media, with a steady increase in 1996 with the folklorization of the Internet. With this there was a general change of spirit, focusing on IT as an enabler.

The mobilization of the Web as an alternative to Notes was not merely in the form of 'pure' technology. Organizational actors also started to move in order to enrol the Web as an ally. The media and the information unit (INF) were especially active here. They were delegated a new role as Web editors. As is the case in many places, the most enthusiastic proponents of Web were initially found outside the traditional IT department. In a memo outlining a new project, a project manager of INF describes the situation as follows: 'Information sharing in Statoil will gradually shift from the basically Notes-based reality of today to a Web-based system.'

There were still distinct and conflicting views as to whether Domino represents a sufficient strategy to address the requirements on openness, as 'many are still very sceptical as to whether Domino is sufficient' (Manager1). The meshing of Notes and the Web through Domino has to a large extent erased this distinction. Few users have the knowledge or the interest to keep them apart.

The compromise in the form of Domino has since been justified by its use in several projects. KOT started using Notes Release 4, which it had had experience with from the Norne case, to develop the concepts from Norne further. After Norne, KOT had plans for reorienting its focus from operations to exploration within Statoil. A new pilot VISOK was launched from autumn 1996, together with SData, which had already had several people in the project from the start.

SAP: a new challenger

Lotus Notes repeatedly needs to fend off challengers. Over the years, there have been at least three challengers. The strategies have varied. Microsoft was fought down head on by arguing for standardization and cost cutting, as described earlier. The wave of interest for the Internet in general and the Web in particular was solved by way of a gateway solution—a migration strategy to Domino-based servers. The challenge of SAP, in the making through the so-called BRA project, is different yet again. The thrust behind SAP, backed by management right to the top, was tremendous. Hence, coexistence with Notes was the only viable option. This implies that, for Notes to keep its position, it was absolutely crucial to find solutions, technical as well as organizational, to integrate Notes with SAP. To do so has been anything but straightforward. Moreover, the introduction of SAP in Statoil is expected to replace about fifty out of a total of about 130 administrative, non-integrated systems (Manager7).

The new BRA-initiative from February 1996 to implement SAP also created a change in the role of the Human Resources unit (P & O). Key people in SData were interested in implementing SAP as the common administrative platform of the company and took an active part in the BRA-project from the start. P & O, which had been critical to SAP at the start, saw that it had to engage itself in the project, because the key idea was to improve all administrative work, including human resources. P & O employed its own personnel with IT skills and developed a closer relationship with SData. BRA marks the moment of truth when P & O and SData both accepted that they could not stick to their old separate functional responsibilities. They had to be integrated. This new policy appeared in the new IT strategy or Sdata from 1997, where it was more clearly stated that they should have an integrated approach of applying both information technology and organizational development.

There are basically two ways to integrate two or more information systems. The traditional one is that one of the systems is in control and the other(s) become(s) subordinate and has to comply. The alternative way is where none of the systems are in control; they are on the same level. This is the strategy of open systems. The relevance of this distinction is that SAP has clearly been adopting the former strategy towards integration—namely to allow other components to be included into the otherwise all-encompassing SAP system. In the opinion of one in the development team, this makes 'SAP self-centred . . . and old fashioned' (Intro3). SAP is highly restrictive in allowing other components to be integrated. It certifies those products that are allowed to contribute, and this tends to be uniform products with a large installed base, which meant that 'it is difficult to certify our Notes applications; we did not succeed' (Intro3).

Uniformity within administrative systems—signalled by the achievement to have only one mailbox, the Notes mailbox—was the result of many years of debates. The prospect of reintroducing fragmentation with SAP was not acceptable. As SAP comes equipped with its own mail system, there was a very real danger that the users would have to relate to two mail systems. The workflow functionality in SAP is message-driven by electronic mail. It was important, both symbolically and in terms of ease of use, that Statoil managed to integrate SAP's workflow module with Notes mail. Given the existing installed base of Notes, it was vital that 'none should be forced to use SAP; it should be possible to receive workflow actions through the existing Notes mail system' (Intro3). This requirement was possible to fulfil because SAP allows other modules, in this case Notes mail, to become subordinate to SAP. 'Had we not managed this, we would have lost the support and trust of top management' (Intro3).

The use of the existing Notes mail from SAP has been achieved because this is a 'product'-like component of Notes. For Notes applications, the situation is very different. A key Notes application in Statoil is the electronic document archive. To have an integrated, electronic document archive accessible by both Notes and SAP is not possible—for the existing documents. There are, however, SAP-certified products on the market that are also accessible from Notes (for instance,

Archivelink, an IBM product). New documents will accordingly be accessible across both Notes and SAP.

Conclusion: 'Alignment' Revisited

According to one strand of MIS literature, the relationship between business strategies and technology development is straightforwardly conceived of as strategic 'alignment' of the one to the other (Weill and Broadbent 1998; see also Ciborra 1997 and Knights *et al.* 1997 for a critique; see also Chapter 2 above). The picture emerging from our study in Statoil, however, diverges substantially from this. It is not so much a question of alignment as a process of mutually constructing each other. Strategic intentions behind Lotus Notes developed fairly independently of business strategies, but met or coincided in punctuated situations. We analyse how the business strategies of Statoil and the diffusion of Lotus Notes co-evolved over the years 1992–8.

The prevailing and general attitude towards IT use and investments in Statoil throughout the early 1990s was that of IT as an expense. Within relatively few years, say by the mid-1990s, there had been a substantial change in attitude towards IT in general and Notes in particular. To understand how the further diffusion of Notes took place in Statoil it is necessary to enquire into the role of these new visions and images of IT, the work they do, how they are constructed, and how they become productive through circulation and distribution. In short, Lotus Notes was not simply 'introduced' and later spread in Statoil. It was, in essential ways, redefined and improvised in order to gain benefits from the more general redefinition in Statoil's attitude towards IT. This redefinition was partly a result of trends in the outside world. Still, it needed spokespeople and allies within Statoil to gain momentum.

The general pressure for cost containment during the early 1990s was straightforwardly translated into the need to standardize office tools (ending up with the Lotus office suite) and the centralization of IS resources (leading to the establishment of the central IT department, SData). The strategic role of Lotus Notes at this time was modest if any. Notes was subordinate to the business goal of cost reduction and was basically an unplanned surprise.

The fact that attention was directed exclusively towards traditional rationalizing does not imply that no one tried to interpret Lotus Notes differently. It simply implies that these alternative interpretations did not mobilize sufficient support. They remained at the margins. To illustrate, in a meeting in 1993 the Notes introduction team in the IT department emphasized the need to do 'at least a minimum of BPR analysis'. Consultants from McKinsey were involved in providing this analysis. Still, these attempts to align Notes with a broader BPR effort in E & P very quickly faded out with no apparent impact.

As late as the summer of 1994, there was still a profound sense of urgency in Statoil, of a need to rationalize, economize, and improve in order to stay competitive. Even though the price of oil was rising, the sense of hardship was kept vivid in Statoil. A telling example is CEO Norvik's address to corporate management about the challenges facing Statoil. He explicitly stated that he found the employees' worries over possible downsizing 'natural', and that, if the necessary efforts to reorganize Statoil's operations did not succeed, then 'lay-offs may be inevitable' (ibid.). In the context of Norwegian working life, with a rich set of rules regulating employees' rights, and in conjunction with the fact that Statoil had been a steadily growing, state-owned enterprise for two decades, this message represents tough talk. In Mr Norvik's address, there is no role for IT as anything but a vehicle for rationalization. IT in general, Notes being no exception, was accordingly not perceived to have a strategic role.

This relatively well-developed sense of crises changed markedly throughout 1994 and 1995. The resulting, more relaxed working atmosphere paved the road for other—or 'strategic'—patterns of IT use. The single most influential factor contributing to this change was that the revenue surplus in 1994 reached an all-time high; it almost doubled from 1993. The principal reason for this was the increase in production volume and reduced costs for the running operations. It is likely that, had the profit margins in Statoil not improved as dramatically as they did during this period, then it would have been very difficult to lobby for the strategic use of IT in general and for continued and extended emphasis on Lotus Notes. At the end of the 1990s, with a newly gained space for action, the actors lobbying for the communicative abilities of IT as illustrated by Notes were listened to more carefully, were more visible, and made the headlines more often. In this sense, the strategic contents of Notes were perceived as a 'luxury' concern that Statoil could not afford during the years of (relative) economic hardship in the early 1990s. Only with the more comfortable profit margins of the mid-1990s did 'luxury goods' become legitimate and acceptable.

Slowly, originating from the IT department, Lotus Notes was explored. Advocates of a more strategic, communicative use of Notes existed in isolated pockets of Statoil but were unable to mobilize a concerted impact. In the absence of widely accepted scenarios for the use of Lotus Notes, a collection of six fairly generic Notes applications were packaged alongside the introduction of Notes in E & P during 1994–5. These six applications were geared not towards core business processes but rather towards more administrative routines (meeting room reservations, weekly plans, sick or absence notifications, discussion bulletin boards, newsletters, and answering service). Beyond their immediate usefulness (or lack thereof), they were intended to sow seeds to spawn further curiosity from the users to explore the possibilities of Notes. The six applications were intended to give users a handle on the potential of Notes (Intro3).

From the mid-1990s and onwards, there was a growing awareness and accumulating pressure to use IT in a more communicative and strategic manner. As outlined earlier, this pressure had sources that were both internal (the exploration of the Norne oilfield; the internal manoeuvring of KOT) and external (focus on industry cooperation as formulated in NORSOK; folklorization of Web technology). To an increasing degree, business strategy documents emphasized how 'IS/IT should support information exchange and sharing . . . by focusing on cooperation with customers, partners, vendors and governmental agencies'. Despite this attention to business orientation, it takes an effort and quite some time for everybody to internalize the new concepts, to appropriate them in a meaningful way. As one employee of the IT department complained, 'we struggle to learn new words and concepts such as process management, customer orientation, market thinking . . . none of which are difficult to pronounce . . except that they now, shrewdly enough, are endowed with a completely different meaning!'

In terms of Lotus Notes applications, there have been three efforts during these years to support the business strategy that we describe: ESOP (project documentation and workflow management), Elark (electronic archiving), and SAREPTA/Delphi (experience transfer).

ESOP is a Lotus Notes application developed within Statoil primarily aimed at facilitating administration of project documentation, such as meeting summaries, memos, budgets, and plans. In addition, there are some functions aimed at workflow management, including delegation of work tasks and overview of the status of work tasks, that have so far not been much used outside the IT department's own use of ESOP. The ESOP product itself covers functions that are demanded in a project-oriented, high-risk environment like the one Statoil operates in. This has lead to a contract with IBM for the further product development and international marketing of ESOP by IBM (under the name of SAREPTA). ESOP is a 'one-size-fits-all' application, in the sense that it is not sensitive to the type, duration, or size of the projects. This lack of support for local adaptation has been criticized by the management in the IT department. ESOP has been introduced systematically, three years after the first versions (User3).

The Elark application was closely aligned with the ISO 9001 quality improvement effort. Even if it is 'never used' by the users themselves, it serves the (management's) needs in relation to documentation requirements for ISO 9001 certification (User4). Elark seems to have played only a modest role in influencing the work processes themselves involved in the finding and production of oil.

The first and most goal-directed use of Lotus Notes aimed at solving what was perceived as a strategically important problem in Statoil—experience transfer. Lessons learned in the design of past installations were not being reused and implemented in the design of new installations. In 1992 KOT had started to use Lotus Notes in the development of a Notes database that supported the experience transfer of materials (steel quality, corrosion, etc.). Experiences from the Gullfaks field and Kårstø process plant were collected by KOT and delivered as input to the detail engineering of the new Troll installation (Borstad *et al.* 1993). The same year KOT also developed a prototype to support the experience transfer process by using Lotus Notes as a tool in the elicitation and discussion of experiences. At this point, it was impossible to implement these elicitation processes into groupware functionality, since there was no Lotus Notes infrastructure that made it possible to use the databases in daily operations. This was, however, the first attempt to develop

Notes applications that supported core business processes and this work was a vital input in the development of DELPHI that started in 1994.

KOT had plans for developing experience transfer to be much more than transfer of experiences with company documents, but was forced by E & P management to narrow its scope in 1994. DELPHI then became one of the first core business Notes applications to be used in Statoil in 1995 (Hepsø *et al.* 1997). The functional difference between DELPHI and the competing alternative could be described in terms of push and pull interfaces. DELPHI had a simple pull user interface. It was possible to find various kinds of business documents sorted by different categories, all documents being instantly accessible from the same database. It also had functions for rerouting documents and a module to support work in organizational networks— that is, a discussion database that made it possible to give comments to these company documents and support an elicitation or experience transfer process. It had a strong collaborative group-ware functionality. The competing alternative was based on push technology. Documents were situated in the electronic archive (Elark) and this document was sent to the user. It lacked functionality for experience transfer and had less group-ware functionality. Functionality from both applications melted together in the DELTA application from 1996, a core business application. The group-ware functionality of DELPHI and DELTA has never been a success, but the information sharing of best practice document has been successful.

The outcries for using IT to promote the reorganization of work became more pronounced from around the mid-1990s onwards. As outlined, the installed base of Lotus Notes was able to forge a compromise with the Web challenge through the use of Domino servers. Still, this compromise simultaneously delegated a less strategic role to Lotus Notes vis-à-vis the Web. Notes is, according to the IT director in Statoil, 'best suited to internal' (and hence non-strategic) communication, while the Web is 'the only sensible option' for external communication. Similarly, the SAP introduction also carved out a niche for itself, leaving the existing Notes applications with less responsibility. After an initial and ritualistic focus on BPR, the SAP introduction was transformed into a much more mundane implementation project. As one of the members of the SAP introduction team explained, 'SAP is not aimed at strategic or core business processes. We simply aim at rationalizing administration—an administration layer which is very thick in Statoil' (Manager7). Through the assaults of the Web and SAP, Lotus Notes together with its proponents has been delegated a more restricted, internal (hence non-strategic), and less visible role in Statoil's strategy.

On the other hand, the I-net that the IT department developed in tandem with, and bundled together with, the Lotus Notes introduction has become the witness of the successful globalization of Statoil. For instance, the establishment of a Notes client in Statoil's new Nigeria office signals this, as does the hooking-up of the Azerbaijan office with an ESOP access in 1996. Hence, by the late 1990s, the strategic role of Lotus Notes in Statoil was not so much related to supporting core business processes as functioning as an icon of Statoil's globalizing ability, its ability to 'set up a new office site world-wide in five days'.

At the end of the 1990s the overall ambition for the use of IT was, in the words of CEO Norvik, to 'change working processes in a company and thereby strengthen competitiveness and value creation even further'. Lotus Notes plays but a modest role in this. One effort, which caught quite a bit of media attention in Norway, was dubbed the IT step. It involves offering all Statoil employees an ISDN networked, multimedia PC for free at home—provided they give a commitment to spend some time learning how to use it. At the time of writing, the current strategy towards 'flatter organizational structures, new and simplified ways of working and opportunities for decentralized entities' is sought not so much by the use of Lotus Notes (or the Web) as as a result of the broadening and deepening of the experience with IT—that is, the internalization of the use of PCs.

10

Global and Local Dynamics in Infrastructure Deployment: The Astra Hässle Experience

ANTONIO CORDELLA AND KAI A. SIMON

The end of the millennium has represented a period of substantial change in the pharmaceutical industry. The wave of mergers and acquisitions is an obvious indicator of a changing sector. The creations of Novartis, Pharmacia & Upjohn, and AstraZeneca have emphasized the fact that business in the pharma-industry is no longer what it used to be. The industry has faced a radically shifting client base and revised business economics that have squeezed profits. As a result, drug-makers have had to downsize, consolidate, and reorganize. In an industry where a product's life cycle rarely lasts more than a dozen years, and profits are no longer guaranteed, efficiency has taken on a new urgency.

In their striving for increased productivity and an accelerated pace of innovation, many pharmaceutical companies have initiated large-scale changes in order to implement new organizational and technical infrastructures. The integration of functional activities and the removal of departmental barriers in the chain from pre-clinical research to clinical testing, production, and marketing are measures that are frequently used. New technology for remote data collection, study management, and bio-informatics has been put in place, and, as a result of these combined efforts, many companies have achieved significant cycle-time reduction in R & D.

However, the case study reported in this chapter indicates that implementing and deploying an infrastructure are not just organizational and technological matters. An important role is also played by the dynamics between these factors—dynamics resulting in tension between global and local aspects of the infrastructure in use. Consequently, we have chosen to focus our analysis on this tension between organizational procedures and technological flexibility. As the evidence presented here shows, the infrastructure in use is the result of the interaction between these endogenous factors, and not simply the implementation of the ex-ante design. The

The case study on which this chapter is based was conducted over a period of six months during 1998. Interviews were held with study monitors in Sweden, Germany, Spain, and the USA. In addition, other personnel involved in the project at Astra Hässle were questioned and multiple discussions with managers at various levels took place. The research was sponsored by the Swedish Board for Industrial and Technical Development (NUTEK) and Astra Hässle (now AstraZeneca Mölndal). The authors would like to thank the interviewees and other Astra staff for their time and effort.

case study also shows that the design and introduction of global standardized processes and technologies certainly contain potential for significant improvement, but that disregarding the aspect of local adaptation limits the understanding and deployment of the infrastructure in use.

New Challenges for the Industry

Historically, after the Second World War, the pharmaceutical industry developed into one of the most profitable business sectors. The discovery of new drugs against so-far intractable diseases, with about 1,000 new products in the 1950s alone, resulted in the emergence of large-scale pharmaceutical companies, often with a heritage in the chemical industry. The industry has been characterized by its dependency on blockbuster products and their patent-depending life cycles, a strong vertical integration from basic research to marketing, and sales-driven market behaviour with low participation in the health-care system it is supplying.

The pharmaceutical market structure is also very different from consumer-goods markets. It has been a highly regulated oligopoly with high profits due to branding and patent protection. In addition, the huge investments in R & D required for developing and testing new drugs could be passed on to patients, government health-care programmes, and insurance companies. At the same time, dependency on a small number of high-volume selling products made it difficult to sustain long-term competitive advantage, and patent expirations could reverse the situation even for highly successful companies. The conflict between the investments required in long-term research programmes and the demand for increased short-term profits and shareholder value has been another factor creating tension, as expectations from investors have been high after a period in the 1990s when the pharma-industry delivered an average of more than 11 per cent in annual earnings, outperforming the S & P 500 index by 90 per cent.

During the 1990s, significant changes took place in the pharmaceutical industry and the future is expected to require even more radical adaptation, breaking with the pre-existing paradigm. This means leaving the concept of organizational integration from basic R & D to marketing and creating alliances with small and medium-sized specialized companies; reducing the development of drugs for large populations and instead focusing on specialized drugs for smaller communities; and embracing new information technology for managing bio-informatics and high-throughput screening.

Also, new drug indications and niche products, in combination with higher demands for documentation and drug safety[1] by regulatory organizations (the US Food and Drug Administration (FDA) and the corresponding bodies in other countries), have increased development costs and resulted in longer development

[1] The sleeping pill Thalidomide, developed by Merrill in 1962, caused serious side effects such as birth deformities resulting from women taking the drug during pregnancy. This event was the starting point for increasing documentation requests, and resulted in drug safety becoming a priority among customers as well as drug approval authorities.

cycles. The increasing costs of health care, in many countries consuming 12–15 per cent of national spending, and the consequent governmental regulations regarding price setting and drug prescription, have further reduced profitability. Despite the fact that profits are still high, these developments have forced pharmaceutical companies to rethink their business and to redesign their way of developing, testing, and marketing products.

Similarly, industry studies conducted by consulting firms[2] urge pharmaceutical companies to overhaul their competitive focus. They commonly identify the following factors as driving forces in the industry in the immediate future:

- declining overall R & D returns in the industry, caused by managed care programmes, cannibalizing generic products, and extra costs for new product development;
- the need for new drugs, focusing on new indications and smaller patient communities as a result of genomics and an increased understanding of molecular intervention;
- the capability to exploit bio-informatics and new information technology for increased efficiency in clinical research.

Company Setting

At the time of study, Astra Hässle was a research company within the Swedish Astra group, focusing on the development of pharmaceuticals for cardiovascular and gastrointestinal diseases. The company employed about 1,400 people at three sites: Mölndal and Umeå in Sweden, and Boston (Mass.) in the USA. The company had a line/staff organizational structure, consisting of four operational and four staff units. The organizational structure derived from a restructuring project conducted in 1994 (see Fig. 10.1).

In 1997 the Astra group achieved a total sales volume of 44.9 billion SEK. For 1998 a 27 per cent increase was reported, raising the total to 57.2 billion SEK. Products originating from Astra Hässle accounted for more than 80 per cent of total sales. The Astra group's main product, Omeprazole (Losec©), accounted for about half of the group's sales, including licensed products, thus making it the best-selling drug worldwide, but also creating a significant dependency on a single product.

The core competencies of Astra Hässle have traditionally been developed and sustained in four areas—medicine, biology, pharmacology, and chemistry—with a focus on technical knowledge within these disciplines. These four core areas are spread over a wide variety of sub-disciplines, and new competencies have been added as a result of technical development, extended research, documentation requirements, and social trend. The use of information technology (IT), in particular, has come to play a major role in pharmaceutical research, being used for the communication of research results, for data collection and the analysis of data in

---

[2] Industry reports from the following consulting firms have been investigated: The Boston Consulting Group, McKinsey & Co., PriceWaterhouseCoopers, Andersen Consulting.

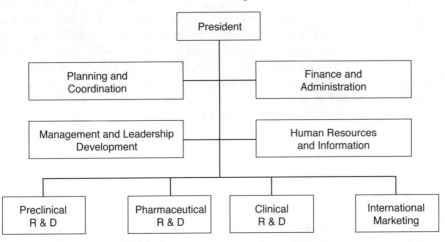

FIG. 10.1. Astra Hässle organization

clinical trials, and for cooperation and coordination purposes within and between research groups. Throughout the industry, the employment of IT is also considered to be a major enabling factor for successfully elevating performance and finding new indications and more efficient ways of conducting clinical trials, thus reducing the time and resources required for testing new drugs and contributing to an increased return-on-investment (ROI) and shareholder value.

In order to sustain their competitive position, virtually all pharmaceutical companies have embarked on large-scale improvement projects. Astra Hässle has also found itself in the position of needing to elevate its organizational processes and to find new ways of employing IT. The company has a strong record; the products developed at Astra Hässle include the blockbuster substances Selocen and Omeprazole. Nevertheless, a considerable number of projects for improvement have been initiated and conducted since the early 1990s.

After several limited structural modifications, a large-scale reorganization took place in 1994, resulting in a new organizational structure, consisting of four major operational units and four support areas. This new structure succeeded in delivering some operational improvement and a more efficient functional organization, but was considered as inappropriate for achieving the radical improvements the company was aiming at. Management became increasingly aware that a general overhaul of the company's business processes would be required in order to meet the goals being set in terms of cycle-time reduction, quality improvement, and cost reduction. Consequently, a large-scale re-engineering-style project was initiated in 1995 under the name of FASTRAC (Fastest and Smartest to Registration and Commercialization). The project was also considered as a major leap forward towards achieving the strategic goals that the company was to realize by the year 2000. These comprised three new, original drugs, a total of twenty new registration applications, the establishment of a new research area, and the establishment of a research unit outside Sweden. Accordingly, the new research area, biochemistry, was established and a research facility in Boston was opened. However, the ambitious goal for product development and registration could not be achieved with the organizational and technical infrastructure that was in place and the FASTRAC project was seen as the most important effort to bring the company forward in its striving for improved efficiency and effectiveness in clinical R & D.

Product development in the pharmaceutical industry

The conduct of clinical trials, used for investigating the effect of a drug on humans, is the final stage in the product-development process. The development process as a whole consists of three sequential sub-processes (Fig. 10.2). Traditionally, the three phases within the clinical-trial period have always been conducted in sequence, and a major aim of the current change initiatives is to parallel the planning, conduct, and analysis of multiple trials within the same study.

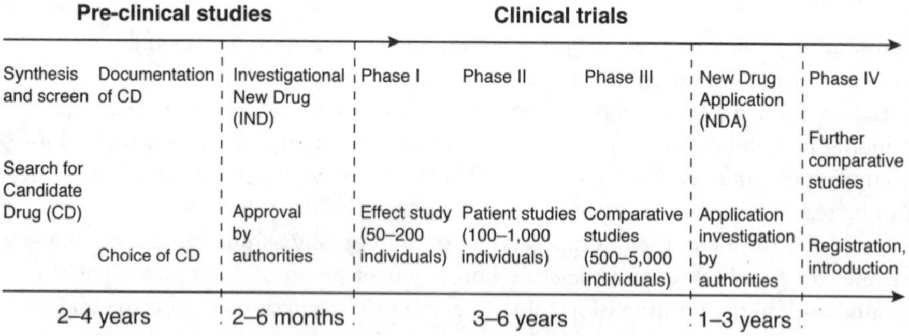

Pre-clinical studies			Clinical trials				
Synthesis and screen	Documentation of CD	Investigational New Drug (IND)	Phase I	Phase II	Phase III	New Drug Application (NDA)	Phase IV
Search for Candidate Drug (CD)							Further comparative studies
	Choice of CD	Approval by authorities	Effect study (50–200 individuals)	Patient studies (100–1,000 individuals)	Comparative studies (500–5,000 individuals)	Application investigation by authorities	Registration, introduction
2–4 years		2–6 months		3–6 years		1–3 years	

FIG. 10.2. The drug development process

During chemical synthesis, different chemical substances are produced with regard to their usability as components in drugs. The biological testing and evaluation result in a number of substances being presented as possible drug components. These 'candidate drugs' are further investigated through scientific and patent literature studies. For prospective candidate drugs, a patent application is submitted. The patent protection for a new drug begins after patent protection has been approved. Therefore, all further activities reduce the patent protection time, thus reducing the ROI.

The pharmaceutical research process investigates various delivery mechanisms for candidate drugs (pill, injection, aerosol, and so on). The delivery mechanism promising the most effective absorption of the drug in the human body is developed and tested. Clinical trials comprise a series of steps, where a new drug is tested on different patient groups. The purpose of these studies is to find the optimum dose, detect side effects, and evaluate the drugs' therapeutic effect. These investigations are conducted at different clinics in various countries. The results of the clinical-trial phase are extensively documented and analysed, and these form the basis for the application for approval that is made to the respective authorities in different countries. After approval, the product is handed over to a production unit within the Astra group, and marketed by local organizations in various countries. In addition, further comparative studies are conducted and the use and results of the drug are monitored for control and further improvement.

FASTRAC: Re-engineering *à la* Astra Hässle

The FASTRAC project was inspired by successful projects in other pharmaceutical companies, which introduced organizational and technical infrastructures allowing them to reduce time-to-market significantly. The FASTRAC project took off by identifying three major processes to be scrutinized: drug acquisition, clinical trials, and market support and safety. Of these, the clinical-trial process attracted most attention, since it was considered to be the most resource consuming, but also to contain the highest improvement potential because of its major impact on overall R & D cycle time. The objective and strategic intent of the initiative was clearly defined: the reduction of cycle time from *Investigational New Drug* to *New Drug Application* by 50 per cent, from an average of eight to four years. Since drug development is not only a lengthy, but also a very expensive process, with an estimated cost of between $60 million and $250 million, financial aspects also played an important role, and the achievable benefits of cutting time and cost in clinical trials were considered to be significant in terms of competitive advantage.

The analysis of the clinical-trial process focused on three major areas: planning and reporting, data handling, and operating values. For each of these areas a project group with members from the involved units was assembled. Membership in the project groups was voluntary, since it was considered important that all members of the project team should be highly committed to the project. Of the more than 100 organizational members volunteering for participation in the project, about thirty were chosen and assigned to the three groups. To support the groups in their work, third-party assistance was contracted. A team of five consultants of an international management consulting firm was assigned to the project. The FASTRAC project was prepared during spring 1995 and presented to the members of the unit during June. The three main project groups, now broken up into nine smaller groups, started their work during the summer and were supposed to deliver their analysis of the current process and their conclusions and recommendations by the beginning of 1996.

The project group members were assigned to the project with 20 per cent of their working time, while group leaders were assigned with 50 per cent. Despite the intention of reducing their day-to-day workload, many project participants, especially group leaders, found themselves overwhelmed with additional tasks. Because of the overall time frame and the request to deliver feasible proposals after six months, group leaders were allowed to dedicate 100 per cent of their time to the project after November 1995. The reporting date was followed by a ten-week period dedicated to developing an implementation plan to be realized by autumn 1997. A group called FIST (Fastrac Implementation Steering Team) was formed to conduct these final stages.

Summary of the FASTRAC outcome

The project group delivered its report on time in February 1996. In accordance with the project directives, the report contained a description and analysis of the current clinical-trial processes, a new process design proposal, and recommendations for infrastructure deployment. The report indicated nine areas for potential improvement of the clinical-trial process, falling into three main categories: managerial, organizational, and cultural. In addition, a set of actions for achieving the change was defined. The use of IT infrastructure, especially for data collection, was identified as one of the major enablers for improvement, but no direct suggestions were made regarding specific technologies.

Management and control.   In order to focus the available, yet limited, R & D resources on the most promising areas, adequate mechanisms for project planning, assessment, and prioritization were considered critical and had to be developed and adopted. So far, too many projects had been conducted with high priority, resulting in internal competition for resources. Another important issue was the management of documents throughout the clinical process. While clinical R & D is very often perceived as a primarily research-oriented process, document management is, in fact, critical to its efficiency. In order to shorten the drug approval time required by regulatory authorities, the preparation, compilation, and management of drug documentation can be an important area for focusing improvement efforts. A third aspect that was conceived as crucial was the application of common standards and coordination mechanisms. Because of the highly decentralized structure of the Astra group, a wide variety of terms, systems, standards, and protocols were in use for different purposes. The coordination of different activities and processes enabled and facilitated by the use of common standards and terminology could contribute to a more efficient coordination within and among different parts of the organization.

Structures and processes.   The clinical-trial process, with its average cycle time of more than eight years, was generally considered as being too time intensive. Parallel work, improving coordination, and cooperation between line and project were identified as the major organizational factors for time reduction, optimized resource allocation, and training and competence development for study participants. Moreover, the conduct of various work processes, especially Phases I–III studies (see Fig. 10.2), was primarily sequential, awaiting completed results before initiating the subsequent process. Using a parallel approach to planning and conduct would allow non-critical activities to overlap and thus reduce wait-states in the process. The implementation and deployment of a new IT infrastructure were considered to be prerequisites for achieving the targeted improvements of processes and the underlying organization.

Culture and values. The spirit and the informal ways of doing things, considered as an important part of the organizational culture, play an important role as informal guidelines. They can be used effectively as replacements for formalized chains of commands and bureaucratic structures, and thus reduce the need for managerial control. The re-establishment of Astra Hässle's operating values, which had become less prominent during the period of rapid growth, was therefore seen as an important instrument for facilitating direct communication and an information-sharing environment. These values and beliefs, which had played a significant part in establishing Astra Hässle as a successful R & D company, should also be shared by temporary employees and consultants, who are used in a variety of areas, from medical research to systems development, help desk, and systems maintenance. Incorporating temporary members of the organization into the social context of work can improve work satisfaction as well as enhance cooperation between permanent and temporary staff.

Action for change. Within the areas that were targeted for improvement, a set of measures was identified in order to assess their potential and define concrete actions that could be initiated and performed under the coordination of the implementation steering committee. These actions comprised technical solutions, operational process improvements, and structural changes, as well as guidelines for the re-engineering of the organizational value system. Following the steps of the clinical-trial process, project planning and documentation were the first areas to be changed. The action to be taken included the introduction of clear targets for project prioritization, funding, and resource allocation, as well as the development of a master plan for all activities from the investigational new drug (IND) to the final product. Additional steps were to be taken to align project documentation with requirements imposed by regulatory authorities. To make internal and external document and data management as efficient as possible, new IT infrastructures were to be explored and introduced. Special attention was paid to remote data capture (RDC)—that is, the collection, analysis, and management of the results of drug tests on patients—within clinical trials, and all projects were urged to initiate RDC.

Instead of running project activities in sequence, sub-processes were to be conducted in parallel, thus reducing wait-states and waste of time between different activities. This measure was considered to be an integrated part of the overall redesign of business processes in the clinical unit. In addition, all clinical projects were to be concentrated within clinical research projects. Instead of there being small-scale clinical studies, comparable to Phase I clinical studies, in pre-clinical research projects, all field trials were to be moved into the clinical phase and conducted in accordance with the new process design. Alongside the new process, the process of cultural re-establishment was to be initiated. It included respect for each others' competence and work, clear goals, and leadership that facilitated the implementation and acceptance of the process.

The FASTRAC project also proposed that a complete overhaul of the clinical trial process should be initiated as soon as possible, to include the introduction of a new set of business processes as the basis for the future organizational and technical infrastructure (see Fig. 10.3). In the spirit of Business Process Re-engineering, which was the encompassing approach for the FASTRAC project, a strict focus on processes, cycle-time reduction, and radical change was applied. Consequently, in order to monitor projects' performance and their impact on overall R & D efficiency, a set of quantitative measures, aligned with the new process, was introduced. The continuous evaluation of projects conducted in accordance with the new process design was used to inform the change team and prepare for further improvement.

As mentioned above, IT was conceived as one of the major enablers of the new, streamlined, and time-compressed clinical-trial process. Special attention was paid to RDC as a technological infrastructure component that would allow faster, more accurate handling of clinical trials. The target of twenty-four hours was set for the data flow from patient to the national project coordinators in each country. At the same time, each department was urged to initiate an IT project for developing a technical infrastructure for RDC and six projects were started, employing different technologies.

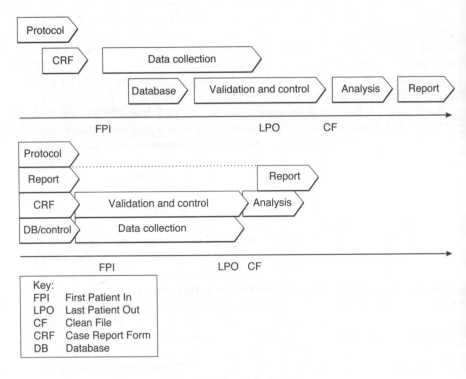

FIG. 10.3. Old and new process design for clinical studies

Six IT-infrastructure projects

It was obvious to the FASTRAC team that the employment of up-to-date and relevant IT could make a major impact on the implementation of the agenda for proposed change. Consequently, serious efforts were made to investigate possible IT infrastructures that might provide support for the clinical-trial projects. As a means of improving performance in clinical data handling, special attention was put on RDC—that is, the collection and transfer of clinical data by means of technology. The use of RDC-based technological infrastructures was seen as a way of satisfying the organizational and technological needs of the new process design. As a result of identifying the need to improve data collection and management, six projects employing different technologies were initiated.

- *Apple Newton*. For a patient quality-of-life study, a system for data entry by patients was developed and implemented on 130 Newton PDAs. The system was based on multiple-choice lists and ticking boxes and was accepted by people with a wide age variety.
- *Internet*. The possibility of using the Internet as a carrier for remotely collected data is under exploration and a first trial application has been in use since April 1998 with promising results. Medical personnel at the test centre enter the clinical data directly into the central database at Astra Hässle through a Web interface.
- *Bedside continuous data collection*. Collecting data directly from bedside medical equipment is a way of collecting highly accurate patient data without interfering with the treatment of the patient. It also makes the manual collection and transfer of data obsolete.
- *Datafax/OCR*. For studies with low reporting frequency and standardized measures, where handwritten notes are not used, the transfer of data via fax with subsequent optical character recognition is considered as a cost-effective technology.
- *SCODA: Semi-RDC*. Instead of employing direct data entry, the SCODA system consists of a data entry client and a server module. The transfer between client and server application is achieved through a modem connection through a private network.
- *AMOS C/S on WAN*. AMOS is a study and data management system developed internally by Astra. In its client/server version it consists of a proprietary client for data entry and access and a database.

The tested solutions range from traditional forms of data capture, over client/server-based architectures, to Internet-based RDC. The further analysis of this case is taking its departure from one of the six RDC implementation projects that were initiated to provide a technological infrastructure for clinical studies. It shows that the actual implementation and use of the IT infrastructure have not been fully aligned with the strategic intent of the FASTRAC re-engineering initiative. The local implementation of organization procedures and the technology for supporting them have been influenced by the tension between local and global dynamics that were not considered in advance.

The SCODA Project: An Example of Rigid Technology

SCODA is a data-capture application. It was tried out in a drug-testing phase, a so-called clinical project, conducted at 500 centres in twelve countries, and comprising 4,000 patients. The technical solution is based on a client/server system, consisting of a data-entry support application running on a laptop computer, and a central server component for data aggregation and analysis. The connections between clients and servers are established through modem links over a commercial global network.

The SCODA application interface represents a digital version of the traditional paper-based case report form (CRF). The study monitors, being responsible for data entry, use this electronic CRF for transferring patient data, which are collected by the investigators during the study. Most of the collected data consist of numbers, describing the status of various medical variables, such as blood pressure, and so on. If additional information regarding the patient or the treatment is annotated by the doctor, the monitor can open hidden fields in the electronic form with a simple mouse click and enter the supporting information. At a first glance, the interface gives a user-friendly impression, but it lacks some fundamental functions. It is basically the reproduction of the paper folders and as such it does not provide support for study management, which is the monitors' other important task. The monitors cannot easily access the state of work, nor the status of patients' recruitment for the study and for individual study centres. The study management capability is basically limited to individual patient records, but does not include the collation of results. Editing and monitoring are limited to one patient record at a time. When the CRFs are submitted via a modem to Astra Hässle, requests for further specifications or error notifications can be received in return. In such a case, the problem is checked locally by the monitor, eventually corrected, and the record re-submitted to the central database. The work process for using the system is strictly sequentia—data entry cannot disregard the structure and sequence of data-entry fields prescribed by the folder—and empty fields are not accepted by the system. For data handling at Astra Hässle, the AMOS database system, which was developed in-house, is used.

The choice of the new organizational and technological infrastructure was based on the rationale of supporting clinical studies with a time-saving tool for data collection and transfer into the central database (see Fig. 10.4). It was also anticipated that data quality would increase because of the shorter feedback cycles between the study monitor and the investigating personnel at the study centres.

The new process was aimed at bringing data collection and quality control together at the study centre. Data entry was moved from a central facility to the study monitors in each country and data cleaning and entry were supposed to take place on-site, involving cooperation between the monitor and the investigators. The new process design also changed the work content of the study monitors to a

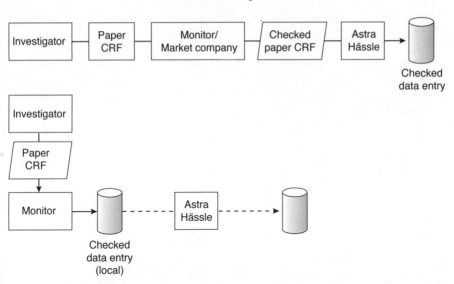

FIG. 10.4. Old and new data-collection processes

large extent. From being primarily concerned with data cleaning and local study management, their work now spanned a much wider part of the process, including the entering of actual data into the computer system, which is very time-consuming.

SCODA case analysis

The report resulting from the FASTRAC project contained an analysis of the existing clinical-trial infrastructure and recommendations for a new process design and other areas for improvement. However, it did not include a specific recommendation with regard to technological solutions or implementation strategies for the new organizational and technological infrastructures. The decision to use RDC, and the consequent introduction of new project-specific infrastructure, was delegated to the clinical project leaders.

The technology to be used for improving data collection was thus chosen locally and the choice was based on the knowledge about available systems in the Clinical IT department. In the SCODA project, the system selection followed the same rationale. The system that was chosen had been developed by a small development company that specializes in systems supporting RDC. Moreover, it had been recently purchased and implemented on a large scale by another pharmaceutical company, Glaxo Wellcome. However, the system was originally developed not for use by study monitors, the pharmaceutical marketing people who manage the clinical projects, but for data entry by investigators, the doctors testing the drug on the patient, and the data-entry process embedded in the system followed this rationale.

Accordingly, the system was highly functional for data collection, but lacked substantial functionality for the monitors' main task: study management.

System implementation and training.   The SCODA system was used for a study of considerable size. Implementing organizational and technological infrastructures for large-scale studies on a global basis is neither simple nor intuitive. Consequently, the SCODA implementation process was planned thoroughly. The experience from the implementation process also revealed several critical aspects to be considered in the context of introducing the new infrastructure.

The RDC software, used as the technological component of the new infrastructure, had not been used previously within Astra Hässle. It was also the first time that it had been employed for use by study monitors, rather than investigators. Because of the limited experience with the software within Astra Hässle and its intended use by study monitors, training was considered as an important issue for the successful deployment of the new technology. All study monitors received a two-day hands-on training. Despite these efforts, the training period was considered insufficient for several reasons. The training was actually based on a version of the product that was not fully functional. Some specific new functions, required by Hässle in order to adapt the system for use by monitors instead of investigators, were not part of the version used for training. When the system was delivered in its final version, the monitors had to adapt to this version before it could be put into production.

Work procedures.   Together with the new IT infrastructure, the organizational procedures for clinical trials were overhauled in order to fit into the new way of technology deployment. Instead of collecting paper copies of medical records, which would then be shipped to Astra Hässle for data entry, monitors were supposed to stay at the test site and enter the cleaned medical data into the SCODA system. According to the new process, the monitor was supposed to discuss unclear data on the paper CRF (Case Report Form) and other problems with the doctor on site, and then transcribe the data into the SCODA system for transfer into the central AMOS database at Astra Hässle. The case study revealed that the actual process used deviated from the intended one, for several reasons.

- *Time limitation.* Depending on the number of test centres used for monitoring, their geographical distribution throughout the country, and the time required for study management and data entry, excessive travel could be required in order to follow the procedure.
- *Budget constraints.* The project budget was negotiated between Astra Hässle and the local market companies in each country in advance of the project. Consequently, when more travelling than anticipated was required, the result was a conflict between the requirements imposed by the global process design and the budget constraints.
- *Space restrictions.* The study centres were not considered during the process design and were often unprepared for hosting monitors. They were often

unable to provide the necessary physical office space and investigators were not prepared to spend the necessary time with the monitors.

As a result of these tensions between the global and the local expectations, several instances were found where monitors had tinkered with the process in order to manage the contingent requirements. A typical situation would be monitors obtaining a copy of the paper-based CRF and entering the data at home, rather than spending time at the study centre. In one case, the monitor introduced extra pages into the CRF, using carbon copies. Once the CRF was completed, the monitor collected the carbon copies and then paid external people to enter the data.

Project management and 'serious adverse events'. As mentioned, the IT system was originally designed to support investigators with their data entry in local study centres. The main focus of the system was, therefore, to enable a structured and sequential data-entry process. When we consider the work of study monitors, we find that the process and content are rather different. Data are entered at different times and in varying sequences, and data entry and study management are interwoven activities. However, the monitors were expected to comply with the rather strict and sequential process design developed around the use of the SCODA system.

In order to reduce the time required for data entry and cleaning—that is, checking the data for consistency and completeness—the procedure requires the monitors to stay at the study centres. The rationale behind this design is so that the monitor has the opportunity to discuss any problems directly and immediately with the responsible investigator. However, in practice it is impossible to interrupt the investigator's ordinary work for every occurring question. Alternatively, the monitor might enter all data without interruption and then discuss deviations and problems with the doctor. This alternative procedure is not facilitated by the system.

Study monitors also maintain responsibility for study management at a local level. In order to facilitate effective study management, a computer system would need to contain additional functionality, such as accumulated recruitment figures and patient status information. The system does not fulfil these requirements and monitors had to use an inductive procedure through the CRFs to obtain study management information.

An important aspect of clinical studies is the handling of so-called serious adverse events—for example, the side effects of the investigated drug or other unexpected events. Should they occur, regulatory authorities require that they are reported to Astra Hässle within twenty-four hours. Because of the asynchronicity of the system—that is, the fact that there is a delay between collection and delivery of data—it is impossible to introduce the handling of serious events into the system. As a consequence, a manual procedure to support these unexpected events, based on phone and fax communication, is used in parallel with the computer-based data-collection process.

A second aspect related to system asynchronicity, and common for all client/server systems, is that information is not available centrally before it has been transferred from the client application to the server. Considering the complexity of the architecture, together with the movement of the client system—the monitor's laptop—between different sites, it is obviously difficult to ensure a smooth and continuous data flow. Also, data may be stocked in client applications—for example, as a result of technical problems. Consequently, central study management and data analysis at Astra Hässle are heavily depending on the functioning of local client systems.

System choice and implementation. During the clinical project investigated in this case study, a considerable discrepancy emerged between the needs of the monitors and the organizational and technological support that they were given. The task of monitors is not limited to data collection. It includes study management and it is characterized by different constraints of time and space. Obviously, the objectives and performance of these tasks can conflict with each other and this tension affects the infrastructure in use. The infrastructure deployed in the SCODA project was chosen to support and increase performance in data collection. The rationale and design idea were that the use of a common computerized platform, used for data cleaning with the help of the investigators and digital transmission, would enable a faster, more accurate collection of all data required for analysis and the subsequent drug registration. Following the intentions of the BPR-style FASTRAC project, time reduction was the dominant justification for choosing the SCODA system, as time consumption in clinical trials was identified as one of the most important factors for long time-to-market.

As a result of this strict time focus, other aspects of data collection and study management had to stand back. The need to support effective local study management by the monitors, their time constraints, and the lack of space at study centres were considered as subordinated factors. As a result, the tension between the different rationales governing the SCODA project at different levels had a considerable impact on the deployment of the infrastructure—that is, how to use the system and how to comply with the organizational procedures designed around it. Understanding the rationales and intentions of the project and the tension that was resulting from them is therefore imperative to improve the performance of future projects.

Looking back at the outcome of FASTRAC, it was obvious that momentum was too important to be lost in long-term evaluations of different options. Four years had been spent on analysis and project advertisement, and visible results were needed to justify the project and maintain confidence in the capabilities of the company and the change-team. The initiation of the six RDC projects can, at least partly, be seen as the consequence of this requirement. Clinical project leaders encountered situations where they felt obliged to choose FASTRAC-compliant technological and organizational infrastructures for their projects, but also to conduct the clinical tests within given time and budget frames. Since FASTRAC did not include detailed implementation guidelines, the systems were chosen and implemented in accordance with decisions taken by clinical project leaders or the technical staff responsible for the projects. In the case of SCODA, the system was purchased from an external software company, which undertook the implementation of the software as well as system maintenance. The system provider also furnished the network supporting the data transfer. Consequently, there was a division of responsibility in the support offered to the monitors. Technical aspects were taken care of by the software company, and content or study-related problems by Astra Hässle. Several monitors, however, expressed doubts about this division, since the borderline between technical and content-related problems was not clear to them, or to the help desk staff. Before contacting the help desk, the monitor had to determine whether the encountered problem was related to the study itself or to the technology employed, a question that was often not clear. Moreover, simple technical problems, that could easily be fixed by the local IT support staff, had to be solved by the system provider in the Netherlands. This proceeding was part of the contractual agreement between Hässle and the software provider and relates to warranty issues. But the monitors found this situation time-consuming and frustrating.

To summarize the results of the analysis, the SCODA deployment reveals the presence of different, and partially conflicting, rationales behind the decisions governing the project. On the one hand, providing an appropriate infrastructure to support the monitors' work was considered important to improve the overall performance in the clinical-trial process. On the other hand, the chosen solutions had simultaneously to be compliant with the FASTRAC recommendations—that is, they had to reduce cycle time in the clinical-trial process—and this caused a dilemma when systems had to be selected. The monitors' working situation and the problems that they experienced, which related to local conditions in the countries participating in the study, highlighted issues that could not be solved by implementing a system and process that primarily followed the rationale of cutting time without taking into account the local circumstances under which they were to be used. Considering the solutions that were implemented for all the projects, and the different rationales that governed the underlying decisions, one can conclude that there was a significant amount of patchwork in the system selection and implementation process. The system was chosen and implemented to reduce cycle time in data collection, while monitors' expectations included functionality for study management. In addition, the system came bundled with process design and organizational procedures—that is, the project infrastructure for SCODA was a combination of information technology and organizational elements, partly conflicting with local objectives and environmental constraints. Consequently, the monitors were tinkering with the infrastructure with which they had been provided in order to adapt it to their local conditions, while still complying with the objectives of the SCODA project.

Discussion

Recall the Webster's *New World Dictionary* (1988) definition of infrastructure mentioned in Chapter 4: 'A sub-structure or underlying foundation; esp., the basic installations and facilities on which the continuance and growth of a community, state, etc. depend, as roads, schools, power plants, transportation and communication system etc.'

In the SCODA project, the underlying foundation is the design of a global business process, supported by high-end, standardized technology. The aim of this infrastructure, which is actually a bundle of a computerized system and organizational procedures, is to achieve compliance with the strategic intent of the FASTRAC project. Consequently, the selection of the SCODA infrastructure is not the result of cultivation (Dahlbom and Janlert 1996) or evolutionary processes in the organization, but stems from a single point of reference: the FASTRAC recommendations. Considering the span of FASTRAC, including new business process design and organizational change as well as cultural aspects, the SCODA project not only concerns the implementation of a computer system, but implicitly addresses the problem of interaction between technology and organization. When analysing infrastructure redesign processes, the understanding of global and local dynamics and the occurring tensions is crucial. Distinguishing these two levels of change, we can refer to the depth and magnitude of the change process. Changing infrastructure means to redefine the underlying foundation, the skeleton around which operational activities are built.

The FASTRAC project at Astra Hässle was conceptually based on the idea of radical and disruptive change, as promoted in the literature addressing Business Process Re-engineering and also used in the Strategic Alignment Model (SAM). The SAM is pushing the idea of matching organizational structure and IT to achieve an inherently dynamic fit between external and internal domains, comprising business strategy, IT strategy, organizational infrastructure and processes, and IT infrastructure and processes (Henderson and Venkatraman 1993). The role of infrastructure is generally regarded as being an enabler for new predefined organizational forms and procedures, rather than being a non-separable element of a dynamic and not fully predictable change process. Accordingly, the use of simplified assumptions—for example, that introducing new IT in institutionalized organizational procedures will enable strategically defined positive externalities—is a common conclusion in the infrastructure-related literature (see e.g. Broadbent *et al.* 1995). Moreover, IT infrastructure is conceived of as an engine for business globalization and standardization of procedures throughout the global enterprise, as discussed in Chapter 3.

The analytical model normally employed in projects aiming at strategic change and following the re-engineering and alignment philosophy is based on a description of business processes, the rational evaluation of change options, and the identification and implementation of the best innovative technologies and procedures to improve organizational performance from a given and well-defined point of departure. The role of infrastructure in this context is to enable and accelerate the defined business processes on a global level, where it is implicit that global means uniform. Shared databases and common sets of organizational procedures, often combined with workflow technology, are frequently proposed as measures to cope with diversity, which is considered as a disturbing factor in the process of creating a global organization. Consequently, the infrastructure becomes an engine for reducing variation and diversity in organizational processes. As Lévy (1996) puts it, the organization is striving for 'universality with totality'. Following this argument, globalization is perceived not as the process of organizing and doing business worldwide, but as a way of constituting a global institution, and thus to a large extent a process of *standardization*. Through standardization, local characteristics are homogenized to the global, predefined ones. The result is thus uniformity rather then globalization (see also Chapter 4).

A major imperative for the implementation of change based on the concept of standardization is the alignment of organizational structure and processes, on one hand, and IT infrastructure and its deployment, on the other hand. Each form of misalignment or variation in the adoption process is considered as an organizational pathology, rather than an effect of local adaptation in the implementation process, and must consequently be removed or realigned in accordance to the predefined business process or action plan (see Chapter 2). Our case reveals that local adaptation of globally defined infrastructure, variations in organizational procedures, and differences in the use of IT are characteristic elements of infrastructure implementation and deployment processes. Otherwise, globalization would be nothing more than the upscale of a local implementation process, and the global organization a larger extension of the local one. To organize worldwide, however, means to deal with local circumstances and dynamics, without losing a perspective on the common goals of the global organization.

Summarizing the result of the case study, we can conclude that infrastructure implementation and deployment are highly situated. 'Situatedness' derives from specific organizational needs, but is also strongly influenced by the dynamics of the change process, such as global and local organizational politics and power games. Instead of creating a single infrastructure, alternative systems were implemented to comply with the FASTRAC recommendations, partly to enable investigation of different technological threads, partly because of a heterogeneous image of the planned change. Analysing the specific infrastructure used in the SCODA project, we have found an approach to change based on different levels of tinkering and improvisation, rather than re-engineering and strategic alignment (Ciborra 1997).

Organization and technology: reciprocal inscriptions

The relation between global and local aspects of an infrastructure, which we have found to be an endogenous element of its implementation and deployment process, can be analysed through the concept of inscription (Akrich 1992; see also Chapter 5 above). Using this approach, we can describe the world as being defined by the reciprocal interaction between objects and subjects. 'Objects are defined by subjects and subjects by objects' (ibid. 222)—that is, the world is inscribed in the object and the object is described in its placement. This concept of reciprocity in the relationship between two phenomena lies at the core of our analysis of the relation between technological and organizational inscription with regard to local and global dynamics in infrastructure implementation.

We define *Technology inscription* as the rigidity of the technology in constraining the users in the way they are related to the technical object. *Organizational inscription*, on the other hand, reflects the level of freedom or rigidity in organizational procedures or, in other words, the extent to which organizational agents are allowed to reshape the ways in which the technical objects are used with respect to organizational rules. As a consequence of this relationship, organization and technology interact and reciprocally shape the organizational context that results from their interaction. Technology provides a platform for performing organizational activities, and the way of using the technology in the organization 'situates' technology itself.

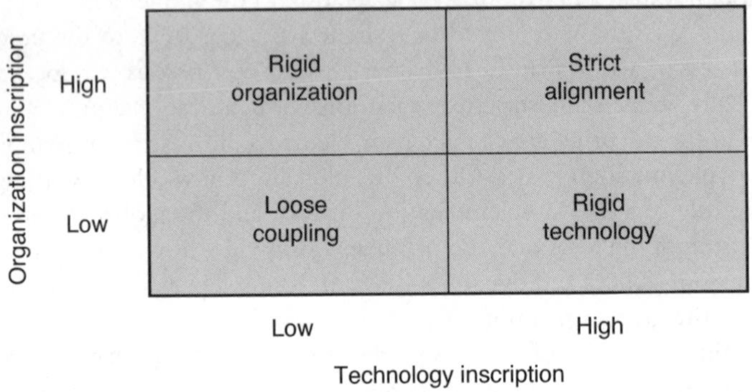

FIG. 10.5. The framework for analysis

The double-entry matrix in Fig. 10.5 provides a combination of alternative scenarios based on different inscription levels in its two dimensions, and allows us to characterize different ways of conceiving infrastructure and its deployment. The entries in the figure represent four alternative infrastructure implementation contexts.

- *Strict alignment.* In this case, the design of organizational procedures leaves no room for local adaptation. At the same time, technology is rigid. There is no option for use outside the defined context. Standardization of technology and organizational procedures and strict alignment between these elements typically characterize the infrastructure.
- *Rigid organization.* Organizational procedures are strictly defined at global level, while technology is open to modifications. The infrastructure is characterized by tensions between different technologies adopted at local level.
- *Rigid technology.* Organizational procedures are open for local adaptation, while technology does not permit changes in use. Infrastructure is characterized by tensions between global and local organization procedures, which may aim to satisfy the same objectives, but differ in the means for their achievement. The case study presented here falls into this context.

- *Loose coupling.* Organizational procedures and technology use can be redefined and adapted locally. The infrastructure allows adaptation to internal and environmental dynamics and is typical of knowledge-intensive organizations.

Obviously, the four contexts presented here cannot serve as a prescriptive model for selecting the best possible infrastructure for a given organizational setting, or for optimizing an organization using a specific technology. Rather, they can be considered as an explanatory model to understand possible interactions between organization and technology and to outline the characteristics of the infrastructure in use in these two dimensions.

The SCODA project: a rigid infrastructure example

The adoption process at local level can define or redefine the infrastructure in use. In the case of Astra Hässle, the infrastructure in use in the SCODA project has resulted from different local organizational adaptations due to the low organization inscription. The monitors use different procedures, developed on the basis of a local organizational context, to fulfil their task; so, for example, data entry is not always done on-site in the study centre, as prescribed in the global process design. At the same time, technology inscription is high, for the IT system does not allow local customization.

While standardized technology can be used to achieve a high inscription in the technology dimension, local factors can have a considerable influence on the implementation of organizational procedures and therefore, subsequently, on the use of the infrastructure. In the Astra Hässle case, the different local adaptations of the global organizational process are affecting and reshaping the global infrastructure and the way globalization is achieved. In fact, the infrastructure is not only constituted by technology itself and its highly inscribed characteristics, but is a result of the reciprocal relation and interaction between two dimensions, the organizational and technological. Limiting the analysis of infrastructure to either one of these dimensions would provide an image of reality considerably different from what we have found in our case study. The analysis of the technological dimension alone would lead to the conclusion that the infrastructure is, in fact, standardizing organizational procedures and resulting in globalization in terms of uniformity. Looking solely at the organizational dimension, we would find a non-articulated and uncoordinated puzzle of locally defined activities. In order to understand the scenario in which the organization is situated, as well as its implications for the use of the infrastructure, it is thus important to take into account the organizational and technological dimensions and their level of inscription.

Conclusion

The analysis of the case study at Astra Hässle has allowed us to identify some critical factors for the introduction and implementation of a new infrastructure for the clinical-trial process. Even though the lessons learned stem from a specific case, they can be applied to a wide variety of organizations.

It was observed that there is a divergence between the way of working as originally designed and anticipated and the actual local work procedures being applied in the project. At the same time, the study of the technological infrastructure being employed for data collection and entry has revealed two major shortcomings. First, the technology supports only a subset of the tasks to be conducted by monitors in the project. Secondly, the technology does not facilitate organizational processes to be fully compliant with the recommendations of the FASTRAC change initiative. The infrastructure in use is thus the result of a deliberate planning process regarding the design of organizational procedures and the selection, implementation, and use of IT, intertwined with dynamic and unpredictable elements due to non-anticipated local adaptations (see also the notion of infrastructure side effects in Chapter 3).

In order to comply with legal and other requirements, clinical-trial processes require a certain rigidity, and thus a minimal general level of specification. As shown in the case study, a process definition and general rules for IT use were introduced through the FASTRAC framework: the global level of organizational inscription. However, IT use was characterized by adaptation in its local organizational context: users' actions took place at local level. Consequently, global design and inscription were only one element in the infrastructure adoption processes. Local adaptation and the unfolding of local inscription are other factors that influence the emerging work process and infrastructure use. In this case, the traditional managerial approach to study infrastructure deployment is not fully sufficient to describe and understand the *infrastructure in use* and the global and local dynamics influencing it, for it disregards the phenomena of drifting and side effects that we have observed.

Infrastructure deployment has to be considered as the outcome of the interaction between global design and inscription and local adoption, rather than as the result of a deliberate and straightforward planning and implementation process. Local adoption processes regularly result in adaptation of global specifications and the development of locally situated technological use and organizational procedures. Different contexts of interaction can be identified, depending on the selected organizational and technological approach: strict alignment, rigid organization, rigid technology, loose coupling.

I I

From Alignment to Loose Coupling: From MedNet to www.roche.com

CLAUDIO U. CIBORRA

The previous chapter has already described the pharmaceutical industry as characterized more than ever by alliances, mergers, and acquisitions, followed by cost-cutting exercises and externalization of different activities at an increasing pace. The big pharmaceutical companies are struggling to increase their size in certain functions, by seeking economies of scale. Moreover, they are seeking further economies by combining traditional pharmaceutical R & D, production, and distribution with the acquisition of complementary technologies such as diagnostics and new R & D biotechnology firms. The deployment of IT and process infrastructures takes place in such turbulent industrial and organizational contexts that it cannot be considered in isolation from them. In general, the strategic intent of the major industry players is to further enhance globalization, recombination, and consolidation of activities.

Using redesign and standardization to achieve higher levels of globalization involves various infrastructural issues (see Chapter 3).

- Do the respective installed bases interfere with the merger of previously independent companies ?
- How can new joint functions be reinforced by an IT infrastructure?
- What is the nature of the infrastructure supporting the centralized, unified functions, and how can it be effectively managed ?

The answers being given to these design and implementation questions are, if possible, less linear than those that were examined when the deployment of groupware in the R & D and marketing functions of Hoffmann-La Roche (Roche) was considered (see Ciborra 1996*b*). Despite the increasing scope for IT and process

The field study at Roche was carried out in Switzerland, Sweden, the UK, France, and Italy. It involved about thirty interviews with the Marketing Managers of four main Therapeutic Units; those responsible for various web sites and local IT managers; the Head of Strategic Marketing and the IT and Web resources managers for Strategic Marketing. Interviews lasted for about two hours, and frequently included the guided navigation of relevant Internet and Intranet sites. The author wishes to thank Hoffmann la Roche for its generous logistical support, Kristiina Saeilae and Yves Goulnik for having suggested the study in the first place, Antonio Cordella and Andrea Resca for the handling of some of the interviews, and last but not least all Roche personnel involved in the study.

platforms to be developed and installed, no coherent infrastructure seems to emerge. Centrifugal forces shake existing and new infrastructures, while the emerging ones carry the imprint left by conflictual forces during implementation. The following instances, which emerged during the case study, are typical.

- Some infrastructures (like SAP packages) of individual firms that are being merged do not match, either by generation or by parameters. Their 'alignment' is so difficult in certain cases that a company merger has to be postponed or severely limited in operational terms.
- The diffusion of multiple approaches to IT (from mainframe to Internet) can lead to fragmented feuds within the organization. Corporate IT has many problems in establishing its role and enforcing policies and standards. The autonomy of the units (divisions, functions, and regions) prevails.
- The spreading of the Internet, and Internet-like platforms, within and across the boundaries of the firm has far from reached its potential. Thus, the stage is one of exponential growth and variety of applications. The diffusion process keeps accelerating and cannot be governed by traditional, top-down management tools.
- The applications are more and more knowledge based, since this is the nature of the business that drives them. However, knowledge in a pharmaceutical company tends to be multifaceted and decentralized and changes rapidly. This is not an easy terrain for the development of an orderly and aligned knowledge-supporting infrastructure.

The Roche case illustrates the practical implications of an infrastructure being developed within an organization context torn by all the forces and events just mentioned. The infrastructure being considered is the new 'backbone' for the Strategic Marketing applications of the Swiss multinational, which ranks among the first ten in the world pharmaceutical industry. The infrastructure is based on the Internet protocol and at the end of the 1990s does not contemplate any tightly defined business process support. The case also reveals the following interesting features.

- The infrastructure succeeds MedNet, one based on a different philosophy and set of applications, which has been documented elsewhere (Ciborra 1996*b*). This allows a comparison between successive applications of two distinct infrastructures to the same business function.
- Some features of deployment of the Internet and Intranets, such as their highly decentralized nature and their permeability to outside forces and pressures, seem to be in stark contrast to the vision of carefully aligned infrastructures and processes advocated by the current managerial literature (see Chapter 2).
- The company's management agenda, centred around an attitude of 'releasement'[1] (Ciborra and Hanseth 1998*a*), or loose coupling (Weick 1976) is in

---

[1] The term 'releasement' has been borrowed from Heidegger's discussions about modern technology: a comportment toward technology which expresses a 'yes' and a 'no' simultaneously. 'We let technical devices enter our daily life, and at the same time leave them outside' (Heidegger 1959).

contrast to the top-down, highly control-oriented managerial narratives on how best to best strategy and infrastructure in modern corporations (Weill and Broadbent 1998).

The emerging picture is one of structures, processes, business, people, and systems in transition. Transition, or multiple forms of it, seems to be the permanent state of the industry and the firms that populate it. Thus, the case offers evidence of how an infrastructure for large, transient, nomadic, and knowledge-intensive organizations may appear, and how it can be 'managed' (if, in fact, that is not too strong a word).

Strategic Marketing at Roche

In 1998 the Strategic Marketing function comprised a couple of hundred people. It was at the crossroads of the various market and industry forces that influenced the pharmaceutical industry worldwide. More specifically, it reflected some of the multiple restructurings that Roche had implemented in response to such forces. This function was created in the 1980s to centralize and globalize Roche's marketing. At the same time, the headquarters had to operate with national companies (affiliates) that still had a strong power and autonomy in the local markets. By 1998 there was still no new process of re-engineering aimed at streamlining and unifying marketing worldwide. Adaptation to local markets, and especially national regulations, was still of paramount importance, which was impeding the enactment of fully global processes. (Remember that the pharmaceutical industry belongs to the class of heavily (locally) regulated industries.)

Marketing a drug is 'knowledge intensive', as are most other activities in a pharmaceutical company. Knowledge is created in developing a new product; knowledge emerges from the clinical trials and is consolidated in the New Drug Application; new knowledge is acquired and processed once the product is in use. Knowledge comes from various sources, inside and outside the company, and is continually gathered, processed, and communicated throughout the product life cycle. Strategic Marketing sifts, filters, accumulates, and distributes the knowledge that is necessary to market a global product. Strategic Marketing can intervene in and influence the local marketing activities only indirectly—namely, by providing the background knowledge that is essential to carry out marketing in each country. Such knowledge has many forms and supports: training on the product features; information from clinical tests, both before the launch of the product and after; prescription strategies, and so on. Most of the knowledge consists of 'template' contents that have to be adapted, enriched, and modified locally.

While this is valid in general, particular circumstances make the task of Strategic Marketing complex and turbulent. First of all, the new orientation to transform large pharmaceutical companies into 'efficient machines' for the development, marketing, and distribution of new drugs makes functions such as marketing more crucial. Secondly, the increased emphasis on efficiency and speed reduces the reaction times dramatically. Thus, marketing has to collect, process, and distribute knowledge quite early in the development process (hence its early involvement in the so-called International Product Teams (see Ciborra 1996*b*)).

Finally, at the time of the study, two specific events characterized Roche's growth: first, the launch of five new drugs dedicated to major diseases, creating potentially huge new markets and revenues; and, secondly, the acquisition of new companies such as Boehringer in diagnostics, which required the integration of multiple business functions, including marketing. These latter moves meant that the operating context was turbulent, composite, and in continuous evolution, which limited the actual possibilities for control based on stable rules, standards, and procedures. Obviously, this affected the style of infrastructure deployment.

Phasing Out MedNet

In the second half of the 1980s Strategic Marketing championed a major innovation within Roche: the establishment of the first corporate network, supporting a variety of applications. The purpose of the network and its applications, which went under the name of MedNet, was to support the new, centralized function of marketing, aimed at unifying the various national Roche affiliates. MedNet was established further to increase the levels of globalization and integration through standardization.

As mentioned elsewhere (Ciborra 1996*b*), marketing developed the infrastructure outside corporate IT at the price of a duplication of efforts and a severe competence shortage. Moreover, standard solutions were not yet available off the shelf and the applications had to be programmed before the Windows environment became available on the market. This slowed down the development time and increased costs. This was also the cause of the uneven level of adoption in the thirty-five affiliates, for an affiliate had to face relatively high costs up front to access and use the system (including training costs). After eight years of development, the use of MedNet for consulting literature, accessing clinical trials' data; enabling office automation, and so on was low. This generated considerable top-management frustration ('we would never do it again, had we to start it today') and caused the deployment of an intense internal marketing and education effort—with mixed results. Some affiliates went so far as to develop systems of their own, like Roche France, which decided more or less officially to adopt an alternative platform, Medtel, based on the public Videotex network: the Minitel.

On the whole, MedNet was a breakthrough for Roche, not for its results, but for its side effects. It heralded a cultural revolution: IT could be regarded as a key tool for networking and not just for data processing. MedNet introduced the ubiquitous use of e-mail in marketing and increased the general IT culture of the users in the headquarters and affiliates.

Despite these positive impacts, MedNet was discontinued. Its negative outcomes, especially the costs compared to the low level of use, dictated its end. However, the corporate network remained as a purely technical infrastructure: the large investments were not completely lost. What was phased out, or superseded (see below), was the application portfolio. After that new Internet and Intranet applications took the place of MedNet.

The use of the Internet and Intranets in Roche, however, has not only brought about a different infrastructure; it has also introduced a newer style of networking and IT use. Some of these modern features are rooted in MedNet; some have been brought in by the possibilities offered by the Internet. Perhaps most important, though this is still only emerging, the later infrastructure is the carrier of a new vision: how to look at the business, at technology, and, more generally, at the customers and the outside environment.

Schematically, one can consider the succession of the two infrastructures as the non-linear and still unfinished sequence of various 'formative contexts' (FC) (that is, cognitive frames and institutional/technological arrangements) (Ciborra and Lanzara 1994). As shown in Fig. 11.1, first of all MedNet was supposed to enact and support a new formative context (FC 2)—one of global networking in the place of autonomous national feuds (FC 1). The transition failed. This was partly because the introduction of the infrastructure revealed an old, headquarters-based formative context—one of a centralizing bureaucracy wanting to use IT to standardize local behaviour; this was resented by the affiliates. The very high costs accounted for the rest.

In the vacuum created by the failure of MedNet, the Internet provided an emerging formative context (FC 3)—one of *decentralization, autonomy*, and *loose coupling*. Headquarters used a 'releasing' attitude to accompany the unfolding of this context, and so far not have not impeded or slowed it down, as shown by the case study of the use of the Internet and Intranet by the Therapeutic Units (TUs) and affiliates (see below).

Paradoxically, in this highly uncertain situation, the most favourable approach seems to be no plan/no strategy—just let the Web use unfold. The process is not mature enough to be managed; it is still in a 'discovery' stage, and as such is nurtured and 'cultivated' by marketing top management. The fact that the Internet and Intranets cost less, or at least much less than MedNet, favours the hands-off, releasing attitude of top management. In the new practice, while a new context for doing business is possibly emerging, terms such as alignment or BPR simply have no meaning: they lack a relevant management context. Words such as drifting, bricolage, and cultivation (Ciborra and Hanseth 1998a) seem better to capture what was going on at the time of study, not only in the affiliates, but also in the very headquarters among the various TUs.

Headquarters: Web Practices within the Therapeutic Units

While MedNet was envisioned as a common infrastructure and a portfolio of common applications, the new external and internal web sites belong to, and are conceived and developed within the TUs. (Actually, some sites are designed and managed by outside agencies, but this is a technical outsourcing decision that does

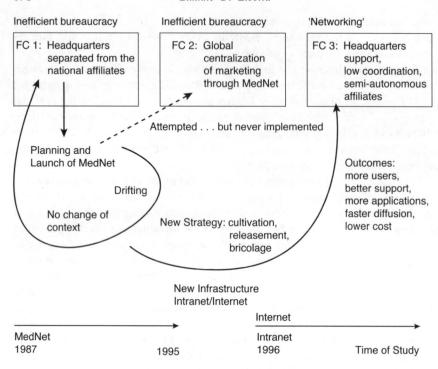

FIG. 11.1. Phases in the implementation of MedNet and the Internet

not infringe the full ownership by a TU.) TUs are the Strategic Marketing units in which headquarters marketing is organized. A TU is autonomous and composed of a team of managers and a lean support staff (as is often the case, in Roche they are mostly MDs who now work in marketing). Their responsibility is to craft the global marketing policies for the Roche products, and provide the national affiliates with a template of advice, knowledge, and training material. They also represent Roche in international events such as international medical conferences.

Internet technology fits well the autonomy of the TUs. With little coordinating effort, each TU has developed or is developing web sites for internal and external communication. Style, approach, and content may vary sharply. Thus, for example, the Parkinson's disease TU opted for an interactive site, but not so the AIDS TU.

One striking feature of these two TUs (but not of others such as rheumatic or cardiovascular diseases) is their interaction with constituencies outside Roche. For both diseases, external bodies such as associations, lobbies, pressure groups, doctors, even individual patients are able to express opinions, and they have a relatively high degree of horizontal communication and organization among them. For example, these constituencies are particularly visible and vociferous at international meetings and conferences. And they are very active on the Net. All this has pushed the two

TUs to set up Internet sites directed at the public at large, apart from the internal web site for the corporate Intranet. For the AIDS TU at least, this has been done with some reluctance because of the legal considerations (in some countries, like Italy, a pharmaceutical firm cannot communicate about its products directly to its potential customers), as well as more general policy considerations. However, the outside bodies are so active and influential that having a web site becomes part of the marketing-mix and general communication policy of Roche. Since any news about advancements or side effects of a particular drug may travel at the speed of light on the Internet, it was felt necessary to be present and in a position to provide factual information about Roche products. Also, new results of therapies are put on the Web to meet the expectations of customers and associations: publication in a scientific journal is not fast enough. In a way, then, such Internet sites have been developed to align marketing with external stakeholders' needs, rather than to obey any internal strategy coming from the top.

In fact, as mentioned above, there is no strategy or plan connecting the Intranet initiatives of the various TUs. There are only pooled resources within Strategic Marketing that provide expertise and advice (through the role of a common internal Webmaster in Marketing Resources Services) and impose minimum standards (such as the Roche logo to be put on the top right corner of every web page). The Marketing Resources Services are responsible for supervising and 'cultivating' the initiatives using the Internet and the Intranets within the headquarters and at the level of the affiliates. But variety rules. For example, the Parkinson's disease web site has an interactive area ('Awakening') to establish a dialogue with any Internet user who visits the site and asks a question. It is envisaged that one person in an external agency will be dealing on a full-time basis with requests reaching the interactive site. Other TUs can learn from that experiment, and imitate it or not, on the basis of their own autonomous evaluation.

Next, the Intranet functions as a marketing production tool. A marketing manager in one of the affiliates can download a presentation, or material that can be cut and pasted to elaborate local presentations, or informative and training material. This is part of the template function that Strategic Marketing fulfils towards the affiliates, and that is well enabled by Internet technology.

The Internet and the local Intranets also multiply the capacity of each TU for communication and knowledge management. Since each unit is composed of very few individuals, usually less than ten people, the Web technology amplifies the power of collecting, packaging, and delivering the vast amounts of preformatted knowledge that are available inside and outside Roche in a focused way.

The limits of the current mushrooming of initiatives are not due to money, people, or skills. The applications are sufficiently cheap to disappear in the wrinkles of the TU budgets (that is, they are relatively easy to justify). And development or management work can easily be outsourced. On the other hand, it is still unclear just what will be the impact of the initiatives emerging from the marketing IT service to enter the picture and take over the management, and especially the standardization, of the sites.

This is not just a matter of technical uniformity. The content of the sites is also of paramount importance: what if confidential or simply wrong information gets into the site and out into the public domain. So far everything has been very pragmatic and handled in an ad hoc fashion. Mistakes have been made, and sensitive material has been pulled back once a major mistake has been identified. Some TUs are, however, opposing IT controls that are too stringent and preventive. Basically, the success of a site is linked to the freshness of its content, its relevance, and its uniqueness (it must not be found elsewhere, at least for a while). Any form of (self)-censorship subtracts from the attractiveness of the site, and thus pre-empts the pool of potential users.

A dilemma emerges at this point which poses more strategic implications than one would at first suppose. It concerns the public nature of knowledge in a knowledge-intensive company, and the scope for those tools that support the knowledge management and communication processes versus the hierarchical or competitive reasons that oppose the free circulation of knowledge. The Internet fits the formative context of a highly distributed, loosely coupled knowledge community and hence its development and diffusion is conditioned by how strategic trade-offs in knowledge management are handled. So far the 'logic of the infrastructure' has prevailed. In fact, when MedNet was still in existence, the Internet was kept at bay, precisely because of security concerns in a company known for its secrecy and high level of confidentiality. Still, the Internet prevailed in the long term, because its use both was and is supported by scientific communities who normally cross firm and institutional boundaries when they need to exchange knowledge.

Standards are going to be set by the Marketing IT Service, but how well they will be followed or enforced seems to be an open question, at least in the short term. What characterizes the initiatives of the various TUs is a policy of 'let the thousand flowers bloom'. Hence, creativity, variety, and multiplicity of initiatives abound in a landscape that contrasts sharply with the one enacted by MedNet, despite being based on the same underlying technical infrastructure.

The level of use of the Intranet in the headquarters varies. Sometimes there are issues related to the overlapping and substitutability between what can be found on the Net and what can be obtained from more established sources such as the bulletins and newsletters of the TUs. On the other hand, some Internet sites, such as the one about AIDS, received more than 500,000 hits in their first months of existence and have won prizes from the business press. This is probably the first time such a broad impact has been achieved with such a relatively small amount of money. If nobody seems to have a clue where all this will lead to, nobody seems to be panicking about it either. MedNet was the source of many more sleepless nights than any failure, misuse, or lack of use of an Internet or Intranet site. As an aside, note that the management approach of 'releasement' impedes the observer to identify a clear trend in any of the directions discussed so far.

Both Internet and Intranet sites carry the mark 'made in Basle', which at local, country level may be perceived as the stigma that caused the long-term failure of MedNet. Hence, one of the big challenges for the new infrastructure is determined by what happens at the periphery. Are the Basle sites accessed and used? Are there local developments of the infrastructure in the various countries? And what logic drives them?

The Affiliates: Varying Web Practices

To a varying degree the Internet and Intranets are diffused in the national affiliates and acquired companies. The range of variation is considerable. In California, the company Syntex gives access to its Intranet sites to every employee, including shop-floor workers. In Roche, Italy, only one-tenth of the workforce has access to the Web. But the situation is rapidly changing: even relatively backward country organizations are setting out very ambitious plans regarding the internal development and use of the Internet and Intranets.

While MedNet was perceived at the periphery as a burden imposed from Basle—something people had to use and pay for without getting much benefit— the Intranet is lighter and more accessible. As mentioned above, the Net works as a *template* in two ways: it allows material prepared in Basle to be downloaded and customized. But, most importantly, it provides a point of reference and a model to start similar or different initiatives at a local level. In Roche Schweiz these have already been turned into something that is becoming 'the' new information system for the Swiss affiliate. The local site fits nicely with and builds on the sites of the headquarters. The global content is used and filtered to become part of the contents of a national site. The local user can navigate across material that is partly national, while still having reasonable and relatively easy access to the international sites.

In Italy, it is envisaged that the local Intranet will become the backbone information and communication system to support the merging of Roche Italy and Boehringer Italy (a merger that has come up against obstacles because of the integration of the pre-existing SAP administrative systems).

At the time of the study, there were no explicit edicts or standards imposed from Basle (either from Strategic Marketing or from corporate IT) to constrain or regulate local developments and initiatives. Rather, limitations were just as likely to stem from the local context. These limitations could be due to the users' level of skill or openness; to the role played by the local IT department (in some cases this is a severe limiting agent); to the presence of local change agents (experts in documentation, knowledge-management units who promote the use of the new tool), and so on.

In contrast with the MedNet experience, it seems that there are no sources of local resistance or opposition to the 'systems invented in Basle'. Local Intranets cannot be seen as centrifugal in respect of a network of applications (the TUs) that are already loosely coupled. The experience of MedNet was not completely negative, however. In some at least of the national companies MedNet provided a fresh alternative to the rather conservative and inward-looking data-processing practice. It prepared the terrain, so to speak, and helped some of the local lead users to grow in their networking experience, making them ready for the new environment of the Internet and Intranet.

A country survey

A sample of European affiliates has been investigated to appreciate the diffusion of the Internet and Intranet in a variety of contexts. Such a study cannot be representative of the state of the diffusion and use of the technology within Roche as a whole, since the focus is only on Europe, and so there are significant users—for example, in the USA—that are not considered; nor does it indicate any best or worst practice. The sample of countries examined here just suggests the extant variety in styles of adoption and implementation. A brief comparison between the four countries examined—France, Italy, Sweden, and the UK—is carried out to discuss the relative differences, again without expecting to evaluate the absolute state of progress of each country, since no reference standard is yet available within the company.

It must be added that in most of the affiliates, the Internet and Intranet have been seriously developed only since 1996–7, and are inevitably considered a low priority, or a 'luxury' application, when compared to the installations of SAP. The latter attracts most of the resources, including management attention. Finally, it is worth noting that an overall sharing of information *between* affiliates is low, while sharing with Basle is uneven (depending upon country and TU).

Roche France was one of the more systematic users of MedNet (two information librarians were using it to access information to be provided to the affiliate); and was also able to set up its own version in French on the Minitel (Medtel (see Ciborra 1996*b*)). The transition to the new Internet/Intranet environment is taking place steadily. The framework of deployment is, however, mixed. On the one hand, top management agreed on a strategic plan to establish the Internet and the Intranet at Roche France, just after the discontinuation of MedNet. An Internet site for the new cardiovascular drug was built rapidly, as part of the pre-marketing campaign and as a differentiating factor to penetrate the new (for Roche) cardiovascular medical community. The deployment of 'deeper' sites like the one on AIDS is taking much more time, and one wonders about the actual backing from senior management of such an initiative (even the gathering of the funds needed is done through the goodwill of individual product managers). In general, whenever the Internet resembles any other media for a marketing campaign, its adoption is fairly straightforward. When it is perceived as something different attitudes are more lukewarm. This does not obstruct the building of the new sites: it just subtracts momentum. For the rest, the Internet and the Intranet are being used by the two librarians very much as MedNet substitutes (with some significant advantages in respect to the latter, such as access, user friendliness, content, and so on).

The relative lack of strategic intent is matched by continuing difficulties or delays in internal communication. In order to foster cooperation and teamwork, local marketing has been reorganized around product teams. Even so, communication is not fully developed, and there is little common memory or established ways to share and transfer knowledge. The use of the Internet and the Intranet does not seem to be perceived as the ultimate solution or support to this kind of problem. Potential users still do not have, or know how to achieve, full access to the Internet (often because of PC configuration problems), and, even then, they point out the lack of effective navigation tools to guide them or help them search for content related to their specific domains.

The AIDS site will represent the template for the future sites of local TUs. Its development is taking place according to a participatory approach, whereby leading internal stakeholders, from Marketing, to Sales, Legal Affairs, and Clinical Developments, apart from the IT specialists and the librarians, are involved. However, outside stakeholders have been left out of the development process. Not only are doctors, and patient associations, not involved, but there has also been no reference or connection to the Basle AIDS site. On the basis of the idea that 'France is different', and in any case Roche France collects so much national material that can be put on a French web site, there seems to be no urgency to learn from what other countries have done previously.

The resulting picture is of a relatively fragmented organization and development, where the infrastructure has not really affected deeply the way knowledge is shared or developed, at least so far. Moreover, development does not show a great momentum, despite being embedded in an overall dynamic business. Things may change and speed up in response to external pressures—for example, the French government has approved the launch of a National Internet site supporting the creation of a gigantic Intranet servicing the whole National Health Service. Through its various initiatives Roche is experimenting and bringing up to speed its Internet/Intranet infrastructure in preparation for such a new public infrastructure.

Roche Italy is a less advanced user of IT as a communication tool. Few people used to have access to MedNet or the Internet. But at the time of the study the situation was changing dramatically, at least as far as the planning stage was concerned. Top management had become aware of the potential of the Internet as a marketing tool, and resources were put in place for building a marketing site for the cardiovascular TU: it was to be a site aimed at cardiology experts. The initiative was reputed to be so urgent that resources for a (slower) development plan for the Italian Intranet site were given lower priority (even the newly appointed, dynamic IT manager was taken off guard). Though delayed, the strategy for the Intranet was no less interesting and momentous. The Intranet was seen as becoming the new management information system. Specifically, the delicate process of merging with Boehringer Italy was to be supported by a newly created common Intranet backbone.

Preparations for the launch of the new cardiovascular drug involved starting a series of collateral initiatives, such as epidemiological research projects in collaboration with university research centres. The Internet plays a role here, for example, as a means of collecting data from the doctors participating in the study. For the local AIDS TU, external research centres were contacted, together with managers and doctors involved with the Basle site. The possibility of building an Italian site aimed especially at GPs was being considered. For other TUs, like antibiotics, the traditional marketing organization seemed to prevail, formed by the so-called Medical Advisers. Here, there was a project to connect the 800 Italian advisers through the Internet and the Intranet in their homes.

The tools available are mostly used internally—for example, for literature retrieval and access to market data. It is envisaged that intermediary roles will still be needed between the final user, say the Medical Adviser or the Product Manager, and the Intranet—people who are able to navigate and summarize useful information for certain classes of usage. It is expected that the building of a fully Italian Web site could reduce the role of such human intermediaries, but only in the medium term. The diffusion of the Internet can also be constrained by local company approaches and legislation. Thus, in Italy, the use of the Internet for certain drugs like the anti-AIDS ones is seen as less strategic and relevant, given the still low numbers of external users (for example, GPs) on the Internet, and the strict regulations regarding how pharmaceutical companies are allowed to communicate to the public.

Finally, a series of compatibility and standard problems were plaguing the progress of the technical infrastructure at the time of our interviews. In the past these problems had not been felt, since Internet access was strictly limited by management in the first place. With the new free access, technical infrastructure issues were coming to the surface: despite the advanced plans, very few of the PCs in the company's offices had compatible platforms to exchange data and navigate the Web.

Roche Sweden is also in the early stages of developing its own site. It will be designed by product, and moreover will be differentiated internally according to the target audience—doctors or general public (patients). The Internet is seen essentially as a marketing and communication tool for the local market. Thus, it is not linked to the Intranet, nor is it based on what the other affiliated headquarters do: it is rather developed autonomously. The Intranet, specifically the Drug Product Information System, is used in a way similar to MedNet, as a retrieval engine to access information held centrally about product information, corporate data, or press clips. Another data set frequently accessed is the clinical trial status (which definitely works more smoothly than MedNet: updating is better and it is more user friendly). MedNet was good as a concept (the idea actually started in Roche Sweden), but it was mismanaged during development and use. The Internet and the Intranet are appreciated because they leave ample room for local, autonomous development. The Basle home page is used as basic input, and the Internet philosophy has subsequently caught on in a natural way, being fairly well integrated with everyday activities. Less emphasized is the use of the Internet and the Intranet as strategic tools. The new media are left free to develop and diffuse naturally rather than being targeted as a weapon endowed with strategic potential. Concerns for further strategic implications of the Internet—for example, the issue of security, or the 'informating' effect of the technology (Zuboff 1987)—are not high: what prevails is the here and now, ad hoc development, and problem solving.

Roche UK has in general an advanced level of development and use of Internet and Intranet technology. At the time of the study it had around 600 users, of which about 100 were in the marketing area: these numbers were substantially higher than those found in the other countries. What was envisaged at that time was to link the entire sales force (300 people) with portable computers from which they would be able to access the various web sites. It must be noted that UK marketing has the advantage of contact with a heavy and competent Internet user and developer in the R & D centre 'Discovery'. This potentially facilitating factor is not available to the other affiliates examined here, since they tend to be large or small sales organizations, with some production facilities.

Once again, web sites differ according to products. For the over-the-counter (OTC) ones the Internet provides product information, which is basically consumer information on a brand basis, similar to what can be found on comparable sites developed by competitors especially in the USA. For the younger customers' OTC products, MTV-style home pages have been created, which include some forms of data capturing and interactivity. The development is usually triggered by the initiative of the product manager, while the IT department plays a supporting role. The Internet site is managed by an outside agency, very much like an advertising campaign project. There is no specific strategic linking internally or with what Basle is doing (in any case, that is not seen as relevant for OTC). Overall, the Internet has a purely add-on role for such products, other media, such as TV and popular magazines, still being very important.

In a typical TU the Intranet may be used once a day to access clinical trials, competitive analyses, and activity plans, and is also frequently utilized for training. The Internet page has two levels of access: for health professionals or for outsiders, like journalists.

The pages are built by a public relations agency, according to a well-defined strategy framework (valid for the specific TU). Since the trend in the National Health Service is to give all GPs computers, the Internet is going to become a powerful tool for speciality target advertising: doctors may well be using the Internet for communications with the company. A first stage will be carried out through the Medical Advisers, who will give GPs a CD-ROM that includes various bookmarks pointing to Roche sites. Other developments envisaged will concern pharmacists, for the actual handling of prescriptions and specific enquiries.

Though the Internet is perceived as 'working better than MedNet', its diffusion is the result of a grass-roots development. In general, the development of the Internet and the Intranet is not coordinated centrally, nor does it depend on the dp service: it is an infrastructure that unfolds almost naturally and is driven by the flow of daily work.

The diffusion of the Internet is taken seriously by management: the issue is how to reach a critical mass of users. An idea is to distribute access terminals to make the Internet a means of ubiquitous communication (apart from the distribution of laptops to the sales force, there will also be booths on the shop floor and in the canteens). Also in Roche UK, it is assumed that the Intranet will eventually become the backbone information system for the entire firm. Still, at the time of the study, for some segments of the workforce (members of production especially, but also the sales force), although the use of e-mail had caught on rapidly and steadily, the actual level and quality of use of the Web were not clear, at least for those managers who were interviewed. It has been noticed, however, that access to the Intranet is frequently triggered by e-mail: a message arrives and refers to the content of a page, so that the recipient is induced to go to that site to get all the information the message is referring to.

Table 11.1 summarizes the qualitative comparisons between the different situations observed at the four affiliates. Recall that the evaluations at the time of the study were impressionistic and do not refer to any standard: they suggest only a *relative* ranking.

In general, the highly unregulated Internet/Intranet approach seems to pay off, at least in terms of diffusion at local level. There are no signs of opposition: on the contrary, new, local initiatives are flourishing in ways that are always (loosely) connected to the headquarters' initiatives. This is the logic of a 'cultivating' approach. Basle sites are the seeds that work as models, templates, and content repositories, around which local initiatives can be developed independently, possibly relying on the headquarters for advice. The 'Basle template' is diffused and made accessible through local adaptations and applications. It is a process of 'loose cloning' accompanied by local transformation and creation. Headquarters relinquish control, giving up the idea of any enforcement of standard (at least so far). The main worry is the diffusion of the infrastructure and its actual use. But even there, the approach seems to be different from the heavy 'internal marketing' campaigns that characterized the 'forced' diffusion of MedNet. Promoting the Intranet is done by example, by choosing some content (like the latest news) that can be found only on the Intranet, by word of mouth and by free imitation, rather than by 'pushing'.

Infrastructure and Knowledge

What has been learnt from the study of the diffusion of the Internet and the Intranets in the different TUs and affiliates can hardly be squeezed into a unitary or coherent framework. It is a characteristic of the approach of loose coupling or releasement that what happens in one area or one country may not happen in, or fit with, the rest. Rather, it reflects (even enhances) the diversity of approaches and styles within the company. The more the infrastructure is embedded in the business, be it product-related aspects or market aspects, the more the applications it supports will vary along the relevant dimensions of embeddedness.

During the study of how the Internet and the Intranets are harnessed to support marketing in a specific TU and in a specific country, evidence was gathered of the various stages of progress and the plans to use the infrastructure.

On the basis of such evidence, it is possible to abstract from local circumstances and the varying levels of implementation, which are influenced by contingent factors such as management awareness or technology readiness. The data can then be

Table 11.1. *A first comparison between the four affiliates*

Internet/Intranet aspects	Affiliates			
	France	Italy	Sweden	UK
Top management support	Medium	High	Medium	High
Technical platform readiness	Low	Low	High	High
Allocation of funds	Low priority	High priority	Low priority	Medium priority
Perceived strategic value	Low	High	Low	Medium/ high
Development of local sites	Medium	Starting	Medium	High
Speed of implementation	Low	Fast (planned)	Medium	Medium/ high
Converns over security (development)	Medium	Medium	Low	Medium
Cooperation with Basle (development)	Low	Low	Low	Medium
Stage of other (Roche) sites	Medium	Starting	Early	Medium
Range of applications (external)	Medium	Low	Medium	High
Range of audience (external)	Medium	Low	Low	High
Reach of audience (internal)	Medium	Low	Low	High
Reach/range of future applications	Medium	High	Medium	High
Sales-force connection	—	Planned	—	Soon implemented
Internet editorial committees	Yes	—	Yes	Yes
New organization	Yes	Yes	—	—
User awareness/ acceptance	Low	Low	Medium	Medium

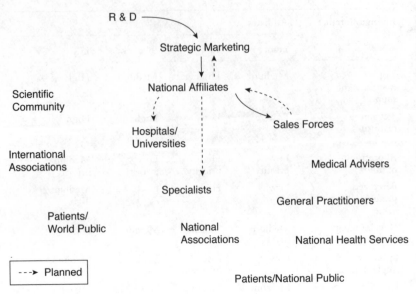

FIG. 11.2. MedNet main linkages

FIG. 11.3. OTC main linkages

used to show at least qualitatively the correlation between different types of knowledge-processing support needed to market 'simple' or 'complex' products, or 'emergent' or 'mature' products.

A first attempt in this direction is carried out in Figs. 11.3–11.6, where the following product categories are taken into respective consideration: OTC, cardio-

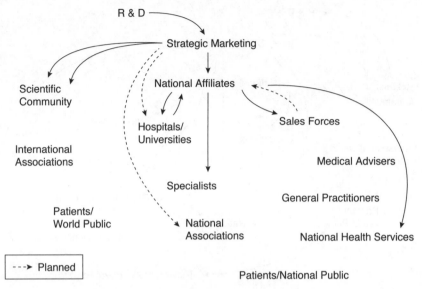

FIG. 11.4. Cardiovascular therapy main linkages

vascular, AIDS, and antibiotics. Each figure contains the main linkages that current or planned Internet or Intranet applications are offering between important stakeholders related to the marketing business function, connecting headquarters and affiliates with outside institutions, customers, and practitioners. The linkages are the 'sum' of what is being implemented or planned in the various locations visited during the study (that is, the Basle headquarters and Schweiz, plus the four other European affiliates). Each picture should give a sufficiently reliable indication of what kind of effort is being put globally into each product category, and what is the emerging pattern or configuration of linkages for the marketing of that product. In other words, Figs. 11.3–11.6 represent a country-independent, overall picture of infrastructure in use by product. Finally, Fig. 11.2 envisages which linkages MedNet was supposed to support in term of a corporate marketing network.

Comparing the 'maps' among them, the following two main considerations can be put forward:

- The Internet and Intranets provide a much more extended and interlinked support to marketing than MedNet (as consistently emerged from the various interviews: nobody seems to regret MedNet, not even at headquarters!) (cf. Fig. 11.2 with the others);
- However, the support sought from infrastructure is *selective*. Specifically, the more the product is complex, emergent, and of 'high social impact', the more extensive and ramified the network (cf. Fig. 11.5 on AIDS with the others; or conversely Fig. 11.3 on OTC with the rest).

FIG. 11.5. AIDS therapy main linkages

FIG. 11.6. Antibiotics therapy main linkages

The main conclusion that can be drawn from this rudimentary comparison is that the deployment of the technical infrastructure, especially in the absence of any strong constraint in terms of business process design enforcement, is shaped by the requirement set by the knowledge intensity of the product. Knowledge intensity depends both upon the number of actors, which are sources, or recipients, of product-related knowledge, and upon the amount/complexity of the knowledge generated or required at each stage of the development, launch, and marketing of a product (Ciborra and Hanseth 1998*b*).

Concluding Remarks

Beyond the differences that emerge from a comparison of the infrastructures supporting the different products, the Roche case also exemplifies an alternative model of infrastructure development and diffusion from the one of top-down, strategic alignment (see Chapter 2). Indeed, in this case there is no strong top-down direction, but rather releasement; no alignment *by fiat*, but rather a loose coupling between local context and technology initiatives. Thus, the infrastructure expands by the decentralized linking of local initiatives that are born as spin-offs of headquarters' initiatives. The latter constitute a reference model for imitation, and provide the content, so that local web sites can be built with an initial minimal (critical mass) content. The 'grass-roots' initiatives enjoy two key features: they are local (and sometimes expressed in local language—while MedNet was always at fault in this respect), and they retain a link with the headquarters' content. Navigation allows the user to cross the local/global boundaries seamlessly, though in practice this is not done as frequently as might be expected.

The power of the periphery is harnessed to support the diffusion of the infrastructure, and not as a source of resistance. The process of infrastructure building becomes self-reinforcing, albeit to some extent centrifugal. All this seems to fit nicely with the way knowledge is managed in Roche marketing activities: key knowledge is created centrally around the development of the product, but a lot of complementary knowledge is generated and resident close to local markets. The use of the Internet and the Intranet as a technical infrastructure, and the present management approach—a mixture of releasement and cultivating strategies—seem to fit the loosely coupled nature of the distribution of knowledge within and across the business. It is a case of a surprising 'alignment and fit' through the decoupling of tools, processes, and local and central practices, in the aftermath of the hard and costly lesson learned through MedNet: the impossibility of enforced, top-down alignment.

12

Postface: From Infrastructure to Networking

Bo Dahlbom

The Internet is often described as an infrastructure for information society, but it is not immediately obvious that the notion of infrastructure, originally introduced to describe the foundation of industrial society, is useful in an analysis of the role of information technology. In this final chapter we will question the idea of information technology as foundational infrastructure, and suggest that this technology is best understood as a flexible medium by which social structures are formed, re-formed, and dissolved, in a continuous process of networking.

A Paradox?

The standard introduction to management literature in the early 1990s told about how things were changing. In the past, they would say, it was possible for companies to rely on a stable market with faithful customers. But all that is different now, they went on to say, with global competition on a global, deregulated, and open market, empowered customers demanding tailor-made products and services of high quality, a shorter product lifespan, a rapidly developing information technology, more knowledge-intensive work, and, therefore, a more educated workforce demanding empowerment (Drucker 1988).

In the past, the most successful organization was the huge factory, mass producing one and the same product to the same customers year after year, but now we were entering a situation in which the only surviving companies would be the ones that were able to adjust quickly to an increasingly changing market with changing demands for new products and services. The recommended recipe for survival always involved moving away from the industrial factory organization towards a more loosely organized, networked enterprise, with alliances, external networking, and outsourcing as major ingredients (Peters and Waterman 1982).

At the same time, in the early 1990s, the US government launched an inspiring programme for a national information infrastructure that drew the attention of media to information technology: 'Coming Soon to Your TV Screen: The Info Highway—Bringing a Revolution in Entertainment, News and Communication' (*TIME Magazine*, cover, 12 April 1993). Just as Vice-President Al Gore's father had once contributed to taking the USA out of the Depression by a huge infrastructure project including automobile highways, so his son would now help increase economic growth with an infrastructure project for electronic highways. A well-tested industrial society (Keynesian) method for ending economic depression was to lay the foundation for post-industrial society.

The Clinton administration programme for information highways not only created an information technological media boom; it also helped to initiate a more general interest in infrastructures. Politicians and researchers got involved in building and examining the infrastructure for information society. So successful was this latter project that it did not take long before management theory also picked up the notion of infrastructure. So, while there was a general impression, expressed in popular management literature, that industrial society with its stable infrastructures was being replaced by a *panta rhei* society of highly flexible and mobile organizations, management theory began to speak of the need for corporate infrastructures, especially in connection with processes of globalization. This seems paradoxical. Why build infrastructures for a society without infrastructure?

One reaction to this paradox is to question the entrenched notion of infrastructure in favour of a more flexible and complex notion better suited for analysing the role of information technology in information society. This line of argument can be found in the work of Susan Leigh Star (Star and Ruhleder 1996) and Ole Hanseth (Hanseth 1996, and Chapter 4 above). Here a slightly more radical remedy will be suggested. There is nothing wrong (or not very much wrong) with the received view of infrastructure as applied to a typical mid-twentieth century industrial society and its companies, we will argue. So, let us keep the notion of infrastructure more or less as it is, but instead realize that the new social structures we are now building are different enough from the industrial organizations we are leaving to be best characterized as a society with no infrastructure.

Thus, in this chapter, the notion of infrastructure and its role in our understanding of society and company structures will be analysed, comparing and contrasting the society and organizations we are leaving, dominated by machine technology, with the society and organizations we are entering, built by information technology. It will be argued that the notion of infrastructure, useful as it is in theorizing about machine technology, can be very misleading when used in theories about information technology. In particular, we will concentrate on what seems to be the four central ingredients in the notion of infrastructure, which together give us an illuminating analysis of modern, industrial society:

- the idea of infrastructure as a foundation underlying society;
- the idea of infrastructure as a stable structure;
- the idea of infrastructure as a common resource;
- the idea of infrastructure as a common standard.

It will be argued that these four ingredients, when used to understand the role of information technology, will lead us seriously astray. We will try to show that information technology, rather than being a productive foundation, is a flexible means of communication, by which social structures are formed, re-formed, and dissolved, in a continuous process of networking. Information technology is characterized by its lightness rather than by its weight and inertia. It is relatively inexpensive, so that we can afford to compete rather than share, and it is an adapter technology that invites us to experiment with several standards at the same time. Rather than forming a stable infrastructure for information and service production, information technology introduces a more flexible and lightweight, networking, society without infrastructure. We will end by saying something about that society, about its networking, nomadic, enterprises, and about the nomadic philosophy and social science that will make sense of this society.

A Foundation

Infrastructure was introduced during the Industrial Revolution in the nineteenth century as a military term to designate railroads, industries, and other resources behind the actual front, that were necessary to wage war. Today, the term is normally used for the stable structure—roads, harbours, railroads, airports, energy systems, and telephone networks—underlying production and distribution of goods and services in a society. It is common to distinguish three major types of systems within the infrastructure: the system of transportation, the energy system, and the system of communication.

If the term was new a hundred years ago, the concept had a long history in our culture. When Western philosophy began, it was with a quest for foundations. Natural philosophers from Thales to Empedokles asked for the *arché* of the world, for its ground, its foundations. Most of them ended up in one or another version of the four elements—earth, water, air, and fire—as the foundation of everything else.

Cultural historians have argued that this interest in foundations is typical of a young agricultural culture, trying to come up with an ideology legitimizing a lifestyle of staying on the farm rather than roaming the world. Farms are built on foundations, and the whole agricultural society is planted solidly in the ground. So, we get a philosophy concentrating on building stable foundations, sometimes worried by movement and change, but never really taking them seriously, except as aberrations or accidents against a background of stable foundations.

Archaeological excavations in the Mediterranean area typically show layers of buildings on top of each other. New civilizations are built on the old; progress moves upwards from the ground. This whole idea of having something to build on becomes one of the fundamental philosophical ideas of our culture, from the axiom systems of Euclid and classification schemes of Aristotle to the methods of Descartes and Spinoza. The world, and our knowledge of it, are organized in levels, and the philosopher moves, like an archaeologist at work, up and down these levels: analysing, reducing, deducing, and explaining. Classical philosophy is a philosophy for farmers.

Modern philosophy remained, from Descartes to Kant, a quest for foundations. An industrial society needs stable foundations, even more than an agricultural one. But there are important differences. With its huge and complex distributed production system, an industrialized society needs a well-functioning and reliable distribution system. It becomes natural for such a society to think of the distribution system—ports, railroads, highways, and airports—as a foundation for all of society. And thus the notion of infrastructure is formed.

The interest in foundations and levels really increases with the modernization of philosophy. This is especially so in the philosophy that more than any other showed an explicit interest in industrialization. We are thinking, of course, of Marx and Marxism.

In their theory of historical materialism, Marx and Engels distinguished between the basis and the superstructure of a society. In the basis were the material conditions: productive forces and relations of production. In the superstructure were political, legal, and ideological institutions as well as the ideas dominating them. This way of thinking of society, with a material basis of production, and different institutional levels building on that basis, was to become the de facto standard in modern sociological thought.

Marxism is modern in the way it deals with historical change. The material foundations of societies evolve, and sometimes this evolution results in a major social change, a revolution. The so-called Industrial Revolution is such a revolution in Marx's sense. When the tools of traditional societies finally evolve into machines, and the productive forces thus make a leap forwards, they will break through the agricultural ways of organizing work and a revolution will take place changing the very foundations of society. And when the ways of production change, everything else will have to change too: everyday life, politics, the judicial system, institutions of education, health care, art, ideologies, and so on.

Marx's theory is a descendant of the Romantic Movement that around 1800 began to play around with the idea of foundations. Poets and artists began to think of the infrastructure as something underlying the visible social systems and activities—the mysterious sewage systems, water pipes, and so on are the hidden blood and nervous system of society. The infrastructure, when it really is an infrastructure, is subterranean and out of sight, and preferably not only below but also beyond our consciousness. When you are reminded of the infrastructure, it tends to make you nervous: there is something down there making everyday activities possible, but you do not really know what it is, where it is, or how it works, and what will happen, come to think of it, if it breaks down. In the early nineteenth century people began to hesitate to look down into the entrails and subconscious of society for fear of vertigo and unease.

Historical materialism is a useful tool for understanding the changes from agricultural to industrial to information societies. But one has to be aware of the fact that it relies on an understanding of technology that is very much 'historical' in the sense of being based on the technology dominating industrial society, machine technology. Properties of other sorts of technology are not so well accounted for in historical materialism.

There are things we know about technology that a theory of technology must account for:

- Technology is artificial—that is, designed, constructed, made by people. Thus, the modern world is an artificial world.
- Technology plays important roles in our lives, determining our space of possibilities, giving us our identity. With spectacles I can see; without computers I could not dream of a job as a programmer.
- Technology comes in many varieties, as tools, machines, media, and complex systems. New varieties will continue to appear.

Theories of technology typically use one or more root metaphors and expand on its theme. These root metaphors will get their inspiration from one or another preconceived understanding of technology. In the industrial age it is tools and machines that dominate our thinking: tools, when we look back to the craftsmanship that we fear is disappearing as the machines take over; machines, when we look into the future and applaud the automation of labour.

When we think of technology as a social construction (Bijker *et al.* 1987; Dahlbom 1992) we have a romantic notion of technology as tools, made by us, for us to use at our leisure. Technology is an extension of our mind, a prosthetic device, with which we can conquer the world. When we think of technology as a machine, it becomes a form for our life (Winner 1986), an infrastructure for society (Hanseth 1996).

Marx called his theory 'historical' materialism, but of course he used the conceptions of his time to interpret history—that is, he used the notion of technology as a machine in his theory of technology. So, society is organized by forces and relations of production making up a material basis for the rest. But the very notions of force and production are industrial-age notions. In agricultural societies, tools are used to cultivate the land. To think of tools as forces of production is to stretch the imagination. Similarly, in information society the focus of attention will be on transactions (on communications, sales, services) rather than on production. And, information technology is no productive force; it is a medium or an intermediary in a communications network.

We are still waiting for the Marx of post-industrial society. A pretender to this epithet is still stuck in traditional Marxism, defining the information economy in terms of information production (Castells 1996: 67): namely, Castells relies on Marx's notion of mode of production to define information society, and fails to see that this society is not really a production-oriented or production-based society at all. If we want to understand the role of technology in post-industrial society, we have to break out of industrial-age thinking. We can continue to use Marx as an inspiration, but we have to be careful not to use his machine metaphors (like infrastructure) to force information society into an industrial mould. We can continue to be historical materialists, but we have to be careful how we understand the role of the material in a nomadic society, and refrain from thinking of it as a 'basis'. And we have to be careful in our understanding of materialism itself when we go from agricultural and industrial societies creating wealth by moving and transforming matter to information and media societies in which fortunes are made by exploring and exploiting virtual worlds.

A Stable Structure

An infrastructure can be thought of as a platform for implementation that, without interfering with the details, offers the foundation and service needed by the various applications for production, distribution, consumption, and recreation. But an infrastructure can also be a regulating skeleton, providing framework and guidelines for the activity. The infrastructure provides stability and security rather than liberty of action. A rudimentary infrastructure will be a liberating platform, but it will leave a lot of work for you to do. A more developed infrastructure will restrict your choices while at the same time doing most of the work.

The infrastructure of modern industrial society is made up of systems. Thus, if you say 'roads' you will have to add cars, petrol stations, car dealers, garages, traffic regulations, and a lot more that is necessary for roads to be functional. It is important to see that these systems are not just technical systems, but rather socio-technical. If one takes the notion of infrastructure seriously enough, one must therefore add a number of less material systems, social institutions, such as educational systems, monetary systems, and languages necessary to make the technical systems operational. In addition to the systems of transportation, energy, and communication, one had better include in the infrastructure those basic industries on which the majority of enterprises in a society depend, such as banking, steel mills, chemical industry, and food industry. Once we begin to slide down this slope, we will see more and more examples of things to include in the infrastructure. Is not the fact that there is a market for its products as vital to a company as the necessary means of production?

All this makes infrastructure a somewhat slippery notion. Perhaps we should only use it in a relative sense: X is an infrastructure relative to Y, meaning that Y depends for its operation on X, and X is somehow more stable and basic than Y. And yet, the notion of infrastructure works well in industrial society with its predilection for levels: base–super structure, basic research–applied research, basic knowledge, basic technologies, and so on. In comparison, information society seems at first to lack an infrastructure of its own (much of the old infrastructure will still remain, of course), or perhaps, rather, to lack a material infrastructure. The rapid changes characterizing that society and the immaterial nature of information, as well as the very idea of networks, seem incompatible with ontological levels, stable foundations, and infrastructures.

A complex industrial society is impossible without a well-functioning infrastructure of energy, transport, and communications systems. Like the productive forces in Marx's theory, the infrastructure is a stable, inert material foundation for production, social life, and organization. These are illuminating theories of the way a modern, industrial, society works, but, when the distance from natural resource to final product increases, when focus shifts from products to services, when all labour is well educated, and when technology becomes more knowledge intensive, then that society is turned on its head. The nearest we come to a stable foundation of information society is its ideas, its educational institutions, its research organizations, its political and legal system, the software, the habits, and values of its citizens.

This change is similar to the change experienced when moving from an agricultural to an industrial society. In agricultural society it is food production that is the basis of society. Farmers used to warn their sons not to leave the farm to go to the cities, 'because in the cities there is nothing to eat'. To a farmer, the cities depend on the farms for their survival, but with industrialization of agriculture this dependence relation changes. Modern agricultural production units depend on the factories in the cities—on roads, machines, fertilizers, and electricity—for their survival. Similarly, factory thinkers continue to believe that the infrastructure of industrial society will remain the infrastructure of information society.

A Common Resource

The notion of infrastructure is rich in content. Infrastructures are stable foundations for organizations and activities. We have argued above that we should be careful in extending these ideas of infrastructure to information technology. But infrastructures are also shared, common resources, and that idea may, on the other hand, be quite valuable to retain in our understanding of information technology.

Modern organization theory treats the division and coordination of labour as the two fundamental aspects of organizations (Mintzberg 1983). Management information systems, office automation, group-ware, and workflow management is all about controlling these internal aspects of the organization. Infrastructure, in comparison, can be viewed as a public commodity external to the organization. In that sense, it is a shared resource, a stable, long-term investment, preferably paid for by taxes rather than by users, so that it will be used freely without constraints by companies and individuals to increase the wealth of nations.

The infrastructure is what you need to build an organization. In the infrastructure is included technology, personnel with their basic education and competence, buildings, systems of transport, finance, laws, a market, and so on. Organizations are, of course, vitally dependent on such an infrastructure. As they grow in power, they will try to control it, to ensure it is well functioning. They will incorporate aspects of the infrastructure within the organization, or build their own alternative infrastructure, rather than having to depend on public resources partly beyond their control.

When the Internet is introduced to the general public in the Clinton–Gore initiative, it is described as an infrastructure, a shared resource, extending beyond and between companies. But when companies reluctantly begin to use the Internet, they soon find ways to turn it into an internal, proprietary infrastructure. When you decide to use Internet technology internally, enclosed within firewalls, in an organization, it is used as an infrastructure for the organization. If the company has several profit centres with independent economic responsibilities, and it uses an Intranet as a shared resource, then this infrastructure can be said to be internally public.

With companies trying to keep up with the revolution brought on by the Internet, and 'globalizing' in response to the global market made possible by information technology, there is much talk about 'global infrastructures'. So far, this has mostly been a misnomer, however, since what companies do to become global is not to begin to use the Internet as infrastructure, but to introduce global information systems. Just as traditional management information systems were used to support control and standardized conduct in the organizations of the 1970s, so the 'global infrastructures' of the 1990s were really global information systems for standardization and coordination of labour.

Large companies hesitate about how to deal with the Internet as an infrastructure. Should they invest in electronic commerce with the Internet as the marketplace, or should they not? In many ways this can be a much more important decision than it might at first seem. By choosing to use information technology as a public infrastructure, in this case the Internet, the company will open its boundaries to the surrounding world. Instead of using information technology to build information systems to sharpen company boundaries, a process will begin that can eventually turn the old factory companies of industrial society into more distributed, customer-oriented, sales organizations. If the old industrial companies do not do this, there will be other companies who will do so at their expense.

A production-oriented company will focus on its production and distribution infrastructure, while a sales-oriented company will focus on external communication. So far, the public globalization process has been moving much more quickly than companies would normally have expected, and so they have wasted money on internal infrastructure rather than using what has quickly become publicly available. Why build your own roads, when you can use the public roads? Why develop EDI when there is the Internet? A high and reliable quality in production and distribution may demand an internal infrastructure that is yours to own and control. But a powerful sales organization needs to meet the customers where they are, and therefore has to operate on the public infrastructure.

Industrial companies rely on a well-functioning infrastructure for supply and delivery. So dependent are they on such an infrastructure that they try hard to control it, preferably turning it into a company-owned system. Sales-oriented companies in information society rely on a well-functioning electronic market for selling their services. It does not make sense to turn this into a proprietary system, since the very idea of a market is for it to be a shared resource in the sense of being open and accessible to everyone (with enough money).

The conclusion, then, is that the common-resource aspect of the notion of infrastructure remains important as we move into an information society. Information technology is inexpensive enough for big companies to invest in their own infrastructures. They do not need to depend on information technology as a public resource paid for by tax money. And yet, it makes good sense for them to orient their operations towards the publicly available communication network. Information technology will provide the market place for information society by providing the communication medium for a society, increasingly engaged in commerce of all sorts on a global level.

A Common Standard

To think of an infrastructure as a stable foundation, a common resource, to operate upon is to think of it as a material structure. But one of the more important aspects of an infrastructure is immaterial. To build a national, or international, railway system, one has to agree on how wide the rails should be. And the trains need timetables, which presuppose a standard time. An industrial society needs numerous standards for interfaces connecting the modules making up machines. Nuts, bolts, screws, nails, boards—they all need standards and all these standards rely on standard measures. A national market needs a common currency.

All the vehicles that will run on the common infrastructure will have to be adapted to the properties of that structure. So, all the owners, producers, users of vehicles will have to agree on how to design the infrastructure, what standard to choose (see Chapter 4).

Information technology too has its standards, of course. Operating systems, protocols, cables, and interfaces of all sorts characterize this technology. To us they may seem stable and impossibly inert in a world of otherwise flexible technology. And yet we are speaking about standards that rarely survive for more than two decades. More important than this is, of course, the nature of information technology, which makes the relation between vehicles and infrastructure importantly different.

Industrial society solves its problems of incompatibility between flexible vehicle technology and inert infrastructure by means of gateways. The very same gateways can also be used, of course, as the means to combine infrastructures with different standards. When trains cross a border, their wheel width will have to change. But to machine technology, gateways are a problem. They are expensive and cumbersome. They are awkward and inelegant, and something to be avoided as much as possible. Information technology is very different.

Information technology is a gateway, or adapter, technology. Compilers and interpreters are the very essence of information technology. So, the reason for standards is different. Partly, there are hardware reasons but, with increasing softening of the technology, the reasons are more pragmatic than necessary. Why have different operating systems, programming languages, or communication protocols, when they are equal in capacity, and when gateways have to be installed and, of course, draw a bit on time and space resources?

Only gradually are we beginning to understand this newly won freedom from standardization. With information technology we get gateways and do not have to standardize any longer. Why introduce a global currency when all it takes is software gateways in all systems of exchange? When there is no need for standards, then standards will no longer slow down the development of new technology. And the tempo and flexibility of society will increase.

A Nomadic Society

Information technology develops and changes quickly compared to machine technology. Investments in industrial society infrastructures—ports, railroads, highways, airports, traditional telecommunications—are large and typically paid for by taxpayers. Investments in information-society infrastructures—fibre nets, routers, servers, and software—are comparatively small scale, and commercially interesting with many competing alternatives. Even if they continue to be a common resource, it is not because of their monopoly or that they are so expensive, but because the very idea of a public communications network as a global market is commercially appealing. Indeed, even from a security point of view, it makes more sense that we do our transactions on the same communications network than that we drive on the same roads.

In major cities around the world you can buy Gant shirts, jackets, trousers, and sweaters. Perhaps you have seen one of their catalogues, made in a truly American style, with colourful pictures in New England settings on nice, thick paper. When the Gant shirts were becoming popular in Sweden in the early 1980s, Swedes used to look for Gant stores when visiting the USA. They never found any. No wonder, since Gant was not a US shirt-maker. Gant was what Hedberg (1991) calls an 'imaginary organization'. In the 1980s it was a team made up of a few clothes designers, a couple of business people, a copywriter, and some assistants. Altogether there were about a dozen people, operating out of Stockholm.

When they decided to go into the fashion business on their own, they chose not to invest in textile factories, but decided to stick to doing what they knew: designing clothes. So, once they have designed a new collection, they arrange for some textile factory to make a few samples. They take them to the USA and hire photographers and whatever it takes to make the catalogue, and then they return to Sweden. In the beginning, Gant shirts were sold in various high-quality clothes stores, but now there are specific Gant stores selling only Gant. These stores are not owned by the company, of course. They operate on independent contracts. Now, there are even Gant stores in the USA.

Companies like Gant are like the hordes of pre-agricultural, nomadic, societies, as described by Émile Durkheim. According to Durkheim, people then lived in small groups of about twenty-five members (the size of a modern school class), roaming around in the fields and forests, gathering roots and nuts or hunting for small animals. Such a group is a horde. They live off the land, but they never stay very long in one place, nor do they sow to harvest.

If, by infrastructure, we mean the platform or framework, the foundations, making nomadic life possible, we would perhaps find the infrastructure of the hordes in their kinship system, their marital habits, and customs. But that would be silly. We would transport a notion that is really useful in industrial societies (and to a lesser extent in agricultural societies) and use it on a society to which it does not apply. The very idea of nomadic societies is not to rely on infrastructures. If there is anything like an infrastructure in nomadic societies, it is nature itself.

Companies like Gant rely on industrial society in the same way that the hordes rely on nature as a common resource. The society formed by such 'imaginary' or networking organizations does not have an infrastructure in anything like the sense characteristic of industrial society. What they rely on for their operations are, first and foremost, good communications and the possibility to change communicative partners without delay. Such companies do not want information highways in any way like the highways or railroads of industrial society.

What we see around us is the dawn of a nomadic society that, at least to begin with, draws on industrial and agricultural society for its operations, in a way reminding of how the nomadic hordes lived off nature. In a world dominated by such networking, nomadic organizations, there will still be room for industrial-type organizations providing a sort of infrastructure for the networking organizations. There will still be a need for steel production, paper mills, railroads, ports, airports, airlines, and the whole system of industrial production and distribution will be necessary for the networking organizations to operate.

But the communications networks that are so vital for nomadic, networking life will not be part of that infrastructure. The optic fibres, satellites, routers, and hubs necessary for communication will be much too flexible, changing, and makeshift to be anything like an infrastructure for information society. They will be like the Internet of the 1990s.

Information-society hordes are small, mobile companies with good design ideas, such as Gant, Benetton, and Nike, or companies that are simply good at selling, like TV Shop. Good at doing business on the new electronic markets and able to place orders with the old industrial companies, the hordes use their resources, like the nomads used nature, and move on when opportunities are better elsewhere.

The first hordes are already here. And, in some big companies, innovation projects are sometimes set up as hordes. When electronic commerce at last becomes a major factor on the business scene, we can expect to witness an interesting game with the old industrial companies and the new hordes as players. One day there may be an automotive company that is a horde! A small group of automobile designers will develop a car and place the production on contract with different traditional companies (as some automotive companies already do). The horde has the ideas; others can do the low paid, high-quality, routine work for them. Information society will be an idea society.

A Nomadic Philosophy

Most of twentieth-century philosophy remains stuck in infrastructure thinking. This is certainly true of the phenomenological movement, as defined by Edmund Husserl and Martin Heidegger. And it is true of Cambridge analytic philosophy with Bertrand Russell and of the Vienna circle, under the influence of Ludwig Wittgenstein in the *Tractatus*. But there are powerful exceptions, as well, pointing towards a break with traditional and modern quests for foundations. The most influential alternatives to infrastructure philosophy are to be found in American pragmatism, as developed by Peirce, Dewey, and James around 1900, in the Vienna circle's development after *Tractatus*, with Rudolf Carnap as figurehead, in Wittgenstein's later philosophy, and in French poststructuralism.

In his early essays, *From A Logical Point of View* (1953), and in *Word and Object* (1960), W. V. O. Quine developed an influential version of a philosophy without foundations, drawing mainly on Carnap and pragmatism. Quine came to play the central role in modern analytic philosophy in the USA after the Second World War, very much setting the agenda for philosophy there. Quine used a quote from Otto Neurath, a member of the Vienna circle, as the motto for his philosophy: 'Wie Schiffer sind wir, die ihr Schiff auf offener See umbauen müssen, ohne es jemals in einem Dock zerlegen und aus besten Bestandteilen neu errichten zu können.'

For Quine there is no such thing as a first philosophy, a foundation, or a method on which to base one's quest for truth. Philosophy is not prior to science, but rather it is the other way around: philosophy emerges in the midst of the scientific project, drawing on scientific results to explain what knowledge is, what is knowable and what is not. Philosophy is not the foundation of the sciences; instead epistemology is simply a 'chapter of psychology'.

Ancient and modern philosophy, as defined by Plato and Descartes, respectively, can be described as examples of 'vertical thinking', trying to organize knowledge in levels or layers. The philosophical method is typically one of scepticism, of analysing knowledge claims by questioning assumptions, weeding out what is uncertain, doubtful, or contingent in order to reach an unquestionable core. Quine's philosophical position and method are different and truly provisional. Philosophy grows dialectically with science, supporting itself once here, once there, advancing and retreating, building and rebuilding its vessel of knowledge, increasing its understanding by horizontal expansion rather than by vertical restriction.

While ancient and modern philosophy drives poles down into the mud to reach the hard rock underneath, Quine invites us to think horizontally and use the flimsy network of a continuously revised science to stay afloat on the mud, saying, in effect, that there is no rock beneath, that it is mud all the way down.

This is a philosophy for a society without infrastructure. It is a philosophy without foundations, a 'tough-minded' philosophy, to quote William James. It is a philosophy for a society in which life has become horizontal rather than vertical, in which people engage in networking rather than edification, establish multiple connections rather than hunt for Archimedean points, and encourage diversification rather than core activity. In short, it is a philosophy for a nomadic society.

Quine is the most powerful nomadic philosopher on the American scene, but there is a whole group of sympathetic philosophers in his vicinity: Wilfrid Sellars, Nelson Goodman, Hilary Putnam, Richard Rorty, Daniel Dennett. In their different ways they all make their contributions to a philosophy for information society—beginning their work when that society is barely discernible at the horizon.

There are extensive similarities between Quine's philosophy and that of the late Wittgenstein, even if there are also major differences. Instead of science, Wittgenstein relied on everyday experience as his background for philosophical therapy. But the message is very much the same: mistrust in foundations, and in the traditional (and modern) ambitions of philosophy to find an infrastructure on which to place everything else. In practice, Wittgenstein was more of a nomadic philosopher than Quine, roaming from subject matter to subject matter in his attempts to make his point, while Quine has a more restricted view, tending to repeat the same argument, the same illustrations, again and again.

There are relevant similarities, as well, between Quine's philosophy and that of French poststructuralism, especially as expounded by Jacques Derrida in the late 1960s and early 1970s. Derrida's criticism of Husserl's foundationalism and his break with the closed systems of Lévi-Strauss structuralism, in favour of an open-ended, continuously changing networking, have close parallels in Quine's philosophy. We are not saying that these three philosophers, Quine, Wittgenstein, and Derrida, coming out of very different traditions, and with very different agendas, have so much in common that it warrants close comparisons. What we are saying is only that, against a background of traditional and modern infrastructure philosophy, they all share a more horizontal way of thinking, giving, each in his own particular way, a powerful exposition of an alternative, nomadic philosophy.

In the last decades there have been backlashes against the very radical philosophies of Wittgenstein, Quine, and Derrida, backlashes with a more traditional (or modern) approach to philosophy. But it is a safe bet that, when in the new century, the origins of information society philosophy are traced, these are the three major contributors that will be singled out.

The social sciences, too, will have to change, of course, as we leave modern industrialized society behind, entering a post-industrial, networking, nomadic society. The process of modernization, the Industrial Revolution taking us from a traditional, rural, agricultural society into a modern, urban, industrial world, can no longer continue to set the agenda for the social sciences. Marxism, structuralism, Weberian rational organization theory, Parson's universals, systems thinking, Gesellschaft–Gemeinschaft: these can no longer provide the conceptual framework for social theorizing. They all obviously suffer from industrial-age, infrastructural thinking.

We have to realize that the social sciences were established, in the midst of the Industrial Revolution, to explain that revolution, as theories of modernization and industrialization. As we leave industrial society behind, there will need to be a more fundamental rethinking of the conceptual and theoretical frameworks of the social sciences. In informatics, we have to get rid of systems thinking, and we have to develop new ways of thinking about technology. And, we should be very careful when importing such politically loaded, industrial-age, concepts as that of infrastructure to analyse the social role of technology.

With this warning in mind, we will search for metaphors for technology that go beyond the tool–machine discussion typical of industrial-age social science. If we break out of the harness of technology as a system that constrains and controls our every step, an obvious alternative is the idea of technology as a medium, a space for us to meet and in which to interact. It is an attractive metaphor, but we have to realize that we are yet a long way away from that situation. The way we now use information technology involves rather a lot of interaction with the technology itself. Here are some metaphors that try to capture this: technology as stranger (Ciborra 1996*a*); technology as intermediary (Latour 1991); technology as organism (Dahlbom and Mathiassen 1993).

These theories break away from the two-layered theory of society, at least when it comes to understanding technology. It has often been observed that our Western culture has a penchant for nouns. Farmers and factory-owners are people of substance, and processes and change are always secondary to substance. Infrastructure is a very powerful expression of substance thinking. A networking, nomadic society may perhaps be better described with verbs than with nouns. It is a networking society, not a network society. It is activities and actions rather than organizations and agents that make up that society. (Even when we want to use verbs, we find only nouns.) So, we should follow Weick (1969) and study organizing rather than organizations, and Czarniawska (1997) and speak of 'action-nets' rather than 'actor-networks'.

Barbara Czarniawska has been a long-time proponent of an ethnographic approach to the study of organizing (Czarniawska 1997, 1998). Ethnography is, of course, the approach to use when meeting with foreign cultures and social practices. And ethnography, therefore, is the most suitable approach to our own organizations and social practices, when these undergo revolutionary change. We who grew up in an industrial society were, of course, experts on that society, being shaped by it and being responsible for shaping it. But having grown up in an industrial society, we are obviously uncomprehending when confronted with the society coming out of the information-technology revolution. Our conceptual frameworks only hinder. We have become foreigners in our own society, and we have to approach our own society as foreigners.

Eventually there will come a new Marx, Durkheim, Weber, Pareto, and Tönnies, and they will provide the conceptual frameworks needed to understand the information-technology revolution and the new society growing out of it. They will, of course, build on the nomadic philosophy already outlined and on all the ethnographic research going on today as the revolution is unfolding. The general character of their analysis will be to show how information technology takes us out of a vertical society with levels and layers, infrastructures and superstructures, into a horizontal society of networking nomads, a society without foundations.

Conclusion

The modern organization is a creation of the Industrial Revolution. Systems thinking is the adequate foundation for theorizing about that organization. If information technology is really changing the focus of business from production to sales, by automating industrial production, on the one hand, and creating a global market, on the other, then those organizations will have to change too. The opaque factories on the outskirts of society, so typical of industrial society, will change into mobile, distributed sales companies with no clear boundaries to their environment. Rather than using information technology to control their internal organization, they will prefer to use information technology as a public communications medium to participate in the world.

An infrastructure is a stable foundation, a common resource, a standard for business activities. But if you think of IT in this way, you will soon find yourself in trouble. Here we have argued that IT is characterized by its lightness rather than by its weight and inertia. IT is no productive foundation; it is a flexible means of communication. It is relatively inexpensive, so that we can afford to compete rather than share. It is an adapter technology that invites us to experiment with several standards at the same time.

The infrastructure of information society is not the Internet, or information technology more generally. If there is an infrastructure there at all, it is the old industrial society with its industrial production factories and distribution systems. But this is a misleading way of thinking. The lightness and flexibility of information society, made possible by its light, flexible, and inexpensive technology, will spread to the old industrial structures too. They will not serve as an inert foundation for the new society. Instead, they will be transformed by the new social organizations in order to meet new demands for flexibility and change.

Information technology is no infrastructure issue to decide upon and then lay aside in order to attend to business. Information technology is what we make business with. Electronic commerce is not a question of finding a standard for payments on the Internet. It is instead, as the name indicates, the nature of commerce, the market, of electronic society. And it is on this market that we must compete, by experimenting with new technology, new ways of organizing, moving quickly, like nomads.

References

Akrich, M. (1992), 'The Description of Technical Objects', in W. E. Bijker and J. Law (eds.), *Shaping Technology/Building Society* (Cambridge, Mass.: MIT Press).
—— and Latour, B. (1992), 'A Summary of a Convenient Vocabulary for the Semiotics of Human and Nonhuman Assemblies', in W. E. Bijker and J. Law (eds.), *Shaping Technology/Building Society* (Cambridge, Mass.: MIT Press).

Alvesson, M. (1993), 'Organizations as Rhetoric: Knowledge-Intensive Firms and the Struggle with Ambiguity', *Journal of Management Studies*, 30/6: 997–1015.

Andersen Consulting (1997), *Re-Inventing Drug Discovery: The Quest for Innovation and Productivity* (AC Industry Study).

Applegate, L. (1994), 'Managing in an Information Age: Transforming the Organization for the 1990s', in R. Baskerville, S. Smithson, O. Ngwenyama, and J. DeGross (eds.), *Transforming Organizations with Information Technology* (Amsterdam: North-Holland).

Argyris, C., and Schön, D. A. (1996), *Organizational Learning*, ii (Reading, Mass.: Addison-Wesley).

Arrow, K. J. (1994), 'Foreword', in W. B. Arthur (1994)

Arthur, W. B. (1987), 'Self-Reinforcing Mechanisms in Economics', in Philip W. Anderson, Kenneth J. Arrow, and David Pines (eds.), *The Economy as an Evolving Complex System* (Reading, Mass.: Addison-Wesley).
—— (1988), 'Competing Technologies: An Overview', in Giovanni Dosi *et al.* (eds.), *Technical Change and Economic Theory* (New York: Pinter Publishers).
—— (1989), 'Competing Technologies, Increasing Returns, and Lock-In by Historical Events', *Economic Journal*, 99: 116–31.
—— (1990), 'Positive Feedbacks in the Economy', *Scientific American*, 80: 92–9.
—— (1994), *Increasing Returns and Path Dependence in the Economy* (Ann Arbor: University of Michigan Press).
—— (1996), 'Increasing Returns and the Two Worlds of Business', *Harvard Business Review* (July–Aug.), 100 ff.

Bancroft, N. H., Seip, H., and Sprengel, A. (1998), *Implementing SAP R/3: How to Introduce a Large System into a Large Organization* (Englewood Cliffs, NJ: Prentice Hall).

Bangemann, M., da Fonseca, E. C., Davis, P., de Benedetti, C., Gyllenhammar, P., Hunsel, L., Lescure, P., Maragall, P., Thorn, G., Velazquez-Gastelu, C., Bonfield, P., Davignon, E., Descarpentries, J.-M., Ennis, B., Henkel, H.-O., Knutsen, A., Makropoulos, C., Prodi, R., Timmer, J., and von Pierer, H. (1994), *Europe and the Global Information Society: Recommendations for the European Council*, http://www2.echo.lu/eudocs/en/report.html.

Barnard, C. I. (1968), 'Mind in Everyday Affairs', in C. I. Barnard, *The Functions of the Executive* (Cambridge, Mass.: Harvard University Press).

Bartlett, C. A., and Ghoshal, S. (1998), *Managing across Borders: The Transnational Solution* (Boston: Harvard Business School Press).

Beck, U. (1992), *Risk Society: Towards a New Modernity* (London: Sage).
—— Giddens, A., and Lash, S. (1994), *Reflexive Modernization* (Cambridge: Polity Press).

Beniger, J. R. (1986), *The Control Revolution: Technological and Economic Origins of the Information Society* (Cambridge, Mass., Harvard University Press).

Berg, M. (1997), 'Of Forms, Containers, and the Electronic Medical Record: Some Tools for a Sociology of the Formal', *Science, Technology & Human Values*, 22/4: 403–33.

Berg, M., and Timmermans, S. (forthcoming), *Orders and their Disorders: On the Construction of Universalities in Medical Work*.

Bijker, W. E. (1993), 'Do not Despair: There is Life after Constructivism', *Science, Technology & Human Values*, 18: 113–38.

—— and Law, J. (eds.) (1992), *Shaping Technology/Building Society* (Cambridge, Mass.: MIT Press).

—— Hughes, T. P., and Pinch, T. (eds.) (1987), *The Social Construction of Technological Systems* (Cambridge, Mass.: MIT Press).

Bikson, T. K. (1996), 'Groupware at the World Bank', in C. U. Ciborra (ed.), *Groupware and Teamwork: Invisible Aid or Technical Hindrance* (Chichester: J. Wiley).

Bloomfield, B. P., Coombs, R., Knights, D., and Littler, D. (1997), *Information Technology and Organizations* (Oxford: Oxford University Press).

Borstad, A. J., Hepsø, V., Onarheim, J., Tvedte, B., Aune, A. B., and Engelsen, K. (1993), 'Experience Transfer in Statoil', *Proceedings of IPCC '93—IEEE International Professional Communication Conference, October 1993, Philadelphia* (New York: ACM Press).

Boston Consulting Group (1999), *The Pharmaceutical Industry into its Second Century: From Serendipity to Strategy* (BCG Industry Study).

Bowker, G., and Star, S. L. (1994), 'Knowledge and Infrastructure in International Information Management: Problems of Classification and Coding', in L. Bud-Frierman (ed.), *Information Acumen: The Understanding and Use of Knowledge in Modern Business* (London: Routledge).

Boyton, C., Victor, B., and Pine, B. J., III (1993), 'New Competitive Strategies: Challenges to Organizations and Information Technology', *IBM Systems Journal*, 32/2: 40–64.

Braa, J. (1997), 'Use and Design of Information Technology in Third World Context with a Focus on the Health Sector: Case Studies from Mongolia and South Africa', D.Phil. thesis (Oslo).

Broadbent, M., and Weill, P. (1993), 'Improving Business and Information Strategy Alignment: Learning from the Banking Industry', *IBM Systems Journal*, 32/1: 162–79.

—— —— (1997), 'Management by Maxim: How Business and IT Managers can Create IT Infrastructures', *Sloan Management Review* (Spring), 77–92.

—— —— and St Clair, D. (1995), *The Role of Information Technology Infrastructure in Business Process Redesign* (CISR WP No. 278, Sloan WP No. 3824; Centre for Information Systems Research, Sloan School of Management).

Callon, M. (1991), 'Techno-Economic Networks and Irreversibility', in J. Law (ed.), *A Sociology of Monsters: Essays on Power, Technology and Domination* (London: Routledge).

—— (1994), 'Is Science a Public Good?', *Science, Technology & Human Values*, 19: 395–424.

—— and Latour, B. (1981), 'Unscrewing the Big Leviathan: How Actors Macro-Structure Reality and how Sociologists Help them to Do So', in K. Knorr-Cetina and A . V. Cicourel (eds.), *Towards an Integration of Micro- and Macro-Sociologies* (London: Routledge & Kegan Paul).

—— —— (1992), 'Don't Throw out the Baby with the Bath School! A Reply to Collins and Yearley', in A. Pickering (ed.), *Science as Practice and Culture* (Chicago: University of Chicago Press).

Castells, M. (1996), *The Information Age: Economy, Society, and Culture*, i. *The Rise of the Network Society* (Oxford: Blackwell).

Ciborra, C. U. (1993), *Teams, Markets, and Systems. Business Innovation and Information Technology* (Cambridge: Cambridge University Press).

—— (1994), 'From Thinking to Tinkering: The Grassroots of IT and Strategy', in C. U. Ciborra and T. Jelassi (eds.), *Strategic Information Systems: A European Perspective* (Chichester: J. Wiley).

—— (1996*a*), 'Introduction: What does Groupware Mean for the Organizations Hosting It?', in C. U. Ciborra (ed.), *Groupware and Teamwork: Invisible Aid or Technical Hindrance?* (Chichester: J. Wiley).

—— (1996*b*), 'Mission Critical: The Use of Groupware in a Pharmaceutical Company', in C. U. Ciborra (ed.), *Groupware and Teamwork: Invisible Aid or Technical Hindrance?* (Chichester: J. Wiley).

—— (ed.) (1996*c*), *Groupware and Teamwork: Invisible Aid or Technical Hindrance?* (Chichester: J. Wiley).

—— (1996*d*), *Teams, Markets and Systems*, 2nd edn. (Cambridge: Cambridge University Press).

—— (1997), 'De profundis? Deconstructing the Concept of Strategic Alignment', *Scandinavian Journal of Information Systems*, 9/1: 67–82.

—— (1998), 'Crisis and Foundations: An Inquiry into the Nature and Limits of Models and Methods in the IS Discipline', *Journal of Strategic Information Systems*, 7: 5–16.

—— (1999*a*), 'Notes on Improvisation and Time in Organizations', *Accounting, Management and Information Technology*, 9: 77–94.

—— (1999*b*), 'Hospitality and IT', in F. Ljungberg (ed.), *Informatics in the Next Millennium* (Lund: Student Litteratur).

—— and Hanseth, O. (1998*a*), 'From Tool to Gestell', *Information Technology and People*, 11/4: 305–27.

—— —— (1998*b*), 'A Contingency View of Infrastructure and Knowledge', ICIS Proceedings, Helsinki (Dec.).

—— and Lanzara, G. F. (1994), 'Formative Contexts and Information Technology', *Accounting, Management and Information Technology*, 4: 611–26.

Clark, K., and Fujimoto, T. (1991), *Product Development Performance: Strategy, Organization, and Management in the World Auto Industry* (Boston: Harvard Business School Press).

Collins, H. M., and Yearley, S. (1992), 'Epistemological Chicken', in A. Pickering (ed.), *Science as Practice and Culture* (Chicago: University of Chicago Press).

Cordella, A., and Simon, K. (1997), 'The Impact of Information Technology on Transaction and Coordination Cost', in K. Braa and E. Monteiro (eds.), *Sociaol Informatics: Proceedings of IRIS 20* (Oslo: Department of Informatics, University of Oslo).

Cussins, C. (1998), 'Ontological Choreography Agency for Women Patients in an Infertility Clinic', in A. Mol and M. Berg (eds.), *Differences in Medicine: Unravelling Practices, Techniques and Bodies* (Durham, NC: Duke University Press).

Czarniawska, B. (1997), *Narrating the Organization: Dramas of Institutional Identity* (Chicago: University of Chicago Press).

—— (1998), *A Narrative Approach in Organization Studies* (Thousand Oaks, Calif.: Sage).

Dahlbom, B. (1992), 'The Idea that Reality is Socially Constructed', in C. Floyd, H. Züllighoven, R. Budde, and R. Keil-Slawik (eds.), *Software Development and Reality Construction* (Berlin: Springer-Verlag).

—— (1996), 'The New Informatics', *Scandinavian Journal of Information Systems*, 8/2: 29–48.

—— and Janlert, L. E. (1996), 'Computer Future', mimeo, Department of Informatics, Göteborg University.

Dahlbom, B., and Mathiassen, L. (1993), *Computers in Context* (Oxford: Blackwell).

Davenport, T. H., and Short, J. E. (1990), 'The New Industrial Re-engineering', *Sloan Management Review*, 32/1: 11–27.

David, P. A. (1986), 'Understanding the Economics of QWERTY', in W. N. Parker (ed.), *Economic History and the Modern Economist* (Oxford: Blackwell).

—— (1987), 'Some New Standards for the Economics of Standardization in the Information Age', in P. Dasgupta and P. L. Stoneman, *Economic Policy and Technical Performance* (Cambridge: Cambridge University Press).

—— and Bunn, J. A. (1988), 'The Economics of Gateway Technologies and Network Evolution: Lessons from Electricity Supply History', *Information Economics and Policy*, 3: 165–202.

Davis, G. B., and Olson, M. H. (1985), *Management Information Systems: Conceptual Foundations, Structure and Development* (New York: McGraw-Hill).

Davis, S. M. (1987), *Future Perfect* (Reading, Mass.: Addison-Wesley).

De Certeau, M. (1984), *The Practice of Everyday Life* (Berkeley and Los Angeles: University of California Press).

Dicken, P. (1998), *Global Shift: Transforming the World Economy*, 3rd edn. (London: Paul Chapman Publishing).

DiMaggio, P., and Powell, W. W. (1983), 'The Iron Cage Revisited: Institutional Isomorphism and Collective Rationality in Organizational Fields', *American Sociological Review*, 48: 147–60.

Doz, Y. (1986), *Strategic Management in Multinational Companies* (Oxford: Pergamon Press).

Dreyfus, H. L. (1994), *Being-in-the-World* (Cambridge, Mass.: MIT Press).

Drucker, P. F. (1988), 'The Coming of the New Organization', *Harvard Business Review*, 88: 45–53.

Duncan, N. B. (1995), 'Capturing Flexibility of IT Infrastructure', *Journal of Management Information Systems* (Autumn), 12/2: 37–57.

Earl, M. J. (1996) (ed.), *Information Management: The Organizational Dimension* (Oxford: Oxford University Press).

Essler, U. (1998), 'Analyzing Groupware Adoption: A Framework and Three Case Studies in Lotus Notes Deployment', Ph.D. thesis (Stockholm).

Farrell, J., and Saloner, G. (1985), 'Standardization, Compatibility, and Innovation', *Rand Journal of Economics*, 16: 70–83.

—— —— (1986), 'Installed Base and Compatibility: Innovation, Product Pre-announcement, and Predation', *American Economic Review*, 76: 940–55.

—— —— (1992), 'Converters, Compatibility, and the Control of Interfaces', *Journal of Industrial Economics*, 40/1: 9–36.

Feigenbaum, E. A., and McCorduck, A. (1984), *The Fifth Generation: Artificial Intelligence and Japan's Computer Challenge to the World* (London: Michael Joseph).

Feldman, M. S. (1987), 'Electronic Mail and Weak Ties in Organizations', *Office, Technology and People*, 3: 83–101.

Giddens, A. (1991), *Consequences of Modernity* (paperback edition; Cambridge: Polity Press).

Grindley, P. (1995), *Standards, Strategy, and Policy: Cases and Stories* (New York: Oxford University Press).

Grudin, J. (1988), 'Why CSCW Applications Fail: Problems in the Design and Evaluation of Organizational Interfaces', *Proceedings CSCW 88* (New York: ACM).

Guralnik, D. B. (1970) (ed.), *Webster's New World Dictionary of the American Language* (New York: World Publishing Company).

Hagström, P. (1991), *The 'Wired' MNC: The Role of Information Systems for Structural Change in Complex Organizations* (Stockholm: Institute of International Business, Stockholm School of Economics).

Hammer, M. (1990), 'Reengineering Work: Don't Automate, Obliterate', *Harvard Business Review* (July–Aug.), 104–12.

Hammer, M., and Champy, J. (1993), *Reenginering the Corporation: A Manifesto for Business Revolution* (New York: Nicolas Brealey).

Hanseth, O. (1996), *Information Technology as Infrastructure* (Gothenburg Studies in Informatics, Report 10; Department of Informatics, Göteborg University).

—— and Monteiro, E. (1996), 'Inscribing Behaviour in Information Infrastructure Standards', *Accounting, Management and Information Technologies*, 7/4: 183–211.

—— —— (1998), 'Changing Irreversible Networks', in W. R. Baets (ed.), *Proceedings of the 6th European Conference on Information Systems* (Granada, Spain: Euro-Arab Management School).

—— Thoresen, K., and Winner, L. (1993), 'The Politics of Networking Technology in Health Care, *Computer Supported Cooperative Work*, 2/2: 109–30.

—— Monteiro, E., and Hatling, M. (1996), 'Information Infrastructure Development: The Tension between Standardization and Flexibility', *Science, Technology and Human Values*, 21/4 (Fall), 407–26.

Haraway, D. (1988), 'Situated Knowledges: The Science Question in Feminism and the Privilege of Partial Perspective', *Feminist Studies*, 14: 575–99.

Hedberg, B. (1991), 'The Role of Information Systems in Imaginary Organizations', in R. K. Stamper, P. Kerola, R. Lee, and K. Lyytinen (eds.), *Collaborative Work, Social Communications and Information Systems* (Amsterdam: North-Holland).

Heidegger, M. (1959), *Gelassenheit* (Tübingen: Neske).

Henderson, A., and Kyng, M. (1991), 'There is no Place like Home: Continuing Design in Use', in J. Greenbaum and M. Kyng (eds.), *Design at Work: Cooperative Design of Computer Systems* (Hillsdale, NJ: Lawrence Erlbaum Assoc. Publishers).

Henderson, J. C., and Venkatraman, N. (1993), 'Strategic Alignment: Leveraging Information Technology for Transforming Organizations', *IBM Systems Journal*, 32/1: 4–16.

Hepsø, V., Borstad, A. J., and Midtlyng, J. O. (1997), 'CSCW—Design and Implementation Compromises: An Example from the Implementation of Experience Transfer in Statoil', *Group Bulletin ACM SIGGROUP*, 18/3: 56–60.

Hood, W. F. (1983), 'The Aristotelian versus the Heideggerian Approach to the Problem of Technology', in C. Mitcham and R. Mackey (eds.), *Philosophy and Technology* (New York: Free Press).

Hughes, J., Randall, D., and Shapiro, D. (1993), 'From Ethnograpic Record to System Design', *CSCW Journal*, 1/3: 123–41.

Hughes, T. P. (1983), *Networks of Power: Electrification in Western Society, 1880–1930* (Baltimore: Johns Hopkins University Press).

—— (1987), 'The Evolution of Large Technical Systems', in W. E. Bijker, T. P. Hughes, and T. Pinch (eds.), *The Social Construction of Technological Systems* (Cambridge, Mass.: MIT Press).

—— (1994), 'Technological Momentum', in M. R. Smith and L. Marx (eds.), *Does Technology Drive History? The Dilemma of Technological Determinism* (Cambridge, Mass.: MIT Press).

Husserl, E. (1970), *The Crisis of European Sciences and Transcendental Phenomenology* (Evanston, Ill.: Northwestern University Press).

Introna, L. (1997), *Information, Management and Power* (Basingstoke: Macmillan).

Itami, H., and Numagami, T. (1992), 'Dynamic Interaction between Strategy and Technology', *Strategic Management Journal*, 13: 119–35.

Itami, K. (1988), 'The Corporate Network in Japan', *Japanese Economic Studies*, 26/2.

Ives, B., and Jarvenpaa, S. L. (1991), 'Applications of Global Information Technology: Key Issues for Management', *MIS Quarterly* (Mar.), 33–49.

Joerges, B. (1988), 'Large Technical Systems: Concepts and Issues', in R. Mayntz and T. P. Hughes (eds.), *The Development of Large Technical Systems* (Frankfurt-am-Main: Campus Verlag).

Jones, M. (1998), 'Information Systems and the Double Mangle: Steering a Course between the Scylla of Embedded Structure and the Charybdis of Strong Symmetry', in T. J. Larsen, L. Levine, and J. I. DeGross (eds.), *Information Systems: Current Issues and Future Changes: Proceedings of the IFIP WG 8.2 and 8.6 Joint Working Conference on Information Systems (Helsinki)* (Laxenburg, Australia: IFIP).

Kahin, B., and Abbate, J. (eds.) (1995), *Standards Policy for Information Infrastructure* (Cambridge, Mass.: MIT Press).

Kaplan, R., and Norton, D. (1993), 'Putting the Balance Scorecard to Work', *Harvard Business Review*, 71: 5.

Katz, M., and Shapiro, C. (1985), 'Network Externalities, Competition and Compatibility', *American Economic Review*, 75/3: 424–40.

—— —— (1986), 'Technology Adoption in the Presence of Network Externalities', *Journal of Political Economy*, 94: 822–41.

Keen, P. W. (1991), *Shaping the Future: Business Redesign through Information Technology* (Boston: Harvard Business School Press).

Klein, H., and Myers, M. (1999), 'A Set of Principles for Conducting and Evaluating Interpretive Field Studies in Information Systems, *MIS Quarterly*, 23/1: 67–93.

Kling, R. (1991), 'Computerization and Social Transformations', *Science, Technology and Human Values*, 16/3: 342–67.

Knights, D., Noble, F., and Willmott, H. (1997), ' "We should be Total Slaves to the Business": Aligning Information Technology and Strategy—Issues and Evidence', in B. P. Bloomfield, R. Coombs, D. Knights, and D. Littler (eds.), *Information Technology and Organizations: Strategies, Networks, and Integration* (Oxford: Oxford University Press).

Konsynski, B. R., and Karimi, J. (1993), 'On the Design of Global Information systems', in S. P. Bradley, J. A. Hausman, and R. I. Nolan (eds.), *Globalization Technology and Competition: The Fusion of Computers and Telecommunications in the 1990s* (Boston: Harvard Business School Press).

Korpela, E. (1994), 'Pates to Notes: A Networked Company Choosing its Information Systems Solution', in R. Baskerville, S. Smithson, O. Ngwenyama, and J. DeGross (eds.), *Transforming Organizations with Information Technology* (Amsterdam: North-Holland).

Latour, B. (1987), *Science in Action* (Milton Keynes: Open University Press).

—— (1988), 'The Prince for Machines as well as Machinations', in B. Elliott (ed.), *Technology and Social Change* (Edinburgh: Edinburgh University Press).

—— (1991), 'Technology is Society Made Durable', in J. Law (ed.), *A Sociology of Monsters: Essays on Power, Technology and Domination* (London: Routledge).

—— (1996), *Aramis or the Love of Technology* (Cambridge, Mass.: Harvard University Press).

—— (1999), *Pandora's Hope: Essays on the Reality of Science Studies* (Cambridge, Mass.: Harvard University Press).

—— and Woolgar, S. (1986), *Laboratory Life: The Construction of Scientific Facts* (London: Sage).

Law, J. (ed.) (1991), *A Sociology of Monsters: Essays on Power, Technology and Domination* (London: Routledge).

—— (1992), 'Notes on the Theory of the Actor-Network: Ordering, Strategy, and Heterogeneity', *Systems Practice*, 5/4: 379–93.

—— (1999), 'After ANT: Complexity, Naming and Topology', in J. Law and J. Hassard (eds.), *Actor Network Theory and After* (Oxford: Blackwell).

Levitt, T. (1983), 'The Globalization of Markets', *Harvard Business Review* (May–June), 92–102.

Lévy, P. (1996), *Essai sur le cyberculture: l'universel sans totalité. DiversCité Langues. En ligne*. i. *1996–1997*, www.uquebec.ca/diverscite.

Luftman, J. (ed.) (1996), *Strategic Alignment* (Oxford: Oxford University Press).

Lyytinen, K., and Damsgaard, J. (forthcoming), *What's Wrong with the Diffusion of Innovation Theory?—The Case of Complex and Networked Technology.*

McKinsey & Co. (1999), *Raising Innovation to New Heights in Pharmaceutical Research* (McKinsey Industry Study).

Mason, R. O., McKenney, J. L., and Copeland, D. G. (1997), 'Developing an Historical Tradition in MIS Research', *MIS Quarterly*, 21: 257–78.

Mintzberg, H. (1980), *The Nature of Managerial Work* (Englewood Cliffs, NJ: Prentice-Hall).

—— (1983), *Structure in Fives: Designing Effective Organizations* (Englewood Cliffs, NJ: Prentice-Hall).

Misa, T. (1994), 'Retrieving Sociotechnical Change from Technological Determinism', in M. R. Smith and L. Marx (eds.), *Does Technology Drive History? The Dilemma of Technological Determinism* (Cambridge, Mass.: MIT Press).

Monteiro, E. (1998), 'Scaling Information Infrastructure: The Case of the Next Generation IP in Internet, *Information Society*, 14/3: 229–45.

—— and Hanseth, O. (1995), 'Social Shaping of Information Infrastructure: On Being Specific about the Technology', in W. Orlikowski, G. Walsham, M. R. Jones, and J. I. DeGross (eds.), *Information Technology and Changes in Organizational Work* (London: Chapman & Hall).

Normann, Ricard, and Ramirez, Rafael (1994), *Designing Interactive Strategies. From Value Chain to Value Constellation* (Chichester: J. Wiley).

Orlikowski, W. J. (1991), 'Integrated Information Environment or Matrix of Control? The Contradictory Implications of Information Technology', *Accounting, Management, and Information Technology*, 1/1: 9–41.

—— (1992), 'Learning from Notes: Organizational Issues in Groupware Implementation', in J. Turner and R. Kraut (eds.), *Proceedings of the Conference on Computer-Supported Cooperative Work 92* (New York: Association for Computing Machinery Press).

—— (1996a), 'Improvising Organizational Transformation over Time: A Situated Change Perspective', *Information Systems Research*, 7/1: 63–92.

—— (1996b), 'Evolving with Notes: Organizational Change around Groupware Technology', in C. U. Ciborra (ed.), *Groupware and Teamwork: Invisible Aid or Technical Hindrance* (Chichester: J. Wiley).

—— and Robey, D. (1991), 'Information Technology and the Structuring of Organizations', *Information Systems Research*, 2/2: 143–69.

Palvia, S., Palvia, P., and Zigli, R. M. (1992), *The Global Issues of Information Technology Management* (Harrisburg, Pa.: Idea Group Publishing).

Peppard, J. (1999), 'Information Management in the Global Enterprise: An Organizing Framework', *European Journal of Information Systems*, 8/2 (June), 77–94.

Peters, T. J. (1989), *Thriving on Chaos: Handbook for a Management Revolution* (London: Pan Books).

—— (1992), *Liberation Management: Necessary Disorganization for the Nanosecond Nineties* (New York: Alfred A. Knopf).

—— and Waterman Jr., R. H. (1982), *In Search of Excellence: Lessons from America's Best-Run Companies* (New York: Harper & Row).

Pfaffenberger, B. (1988), 'Fetished Objects and Humanised Nature: Towards an Anthropology of Technology', *Royal Anthropological Institute*, 23: 236–52.

Piore, M. J., and Sabel, C. F. (1984), *The Second Industrial Divide. Possibilities for Prosperity* (Basic Books).

Postman, N. (1992), *Technopoly: The Surrender of Culture to Technology* (New York: Random House).

Powell, Walter W. (1990), 'Neither Market nor Hierarchy: Network Forms of Organization', in B. M. Straw, and L. L. Cummings (eds.), *Research in Organizational Behavior* (Greenwich, Conn.: JAI Press).

PriceWaterhouseCoopers (1999), *Pharma 2005: An Industrial Revolution in R&D* (PWC Industry Study).

Prusak, L. (1997), *Knowledge in Organizations* (Boston: Butterworth-Heinemann).

Quine, W. V. O. (1953), *From a Logical Point of View* (Cambridge, Mass.: Harvard University Press).

—— (1960), *Word and Object* (Cambridge, Mass.: MIT Press).

Reich, R. (1991), *The Work of Nations: Preparing Ourselves for Twenty-First Century Capitalism* (London: Simon & Schuster).

RFC (1994), 'The Internet Standards Process—Revision 2', *RFC 1602, IAB and IESG* (Mar.).

Rice, R. E., and Rogers, E. M. (1980), 'Reinvention in the Innovation Process', *Knowledge*, 1/4: 488–514.

Roche, E. (1996), 'Multinational Corporations—the Emerging Research Agenda', *Journal of Strategic Information Systems*, 5: 129–47.

Sauer, C., and Burn, J. M. (1997), 'The Pathology of Strategic Alignment', in C. Sauer and P. Yetton (eds.), *Steps to the Future* (San Francisco: Jossey Bass).

Scott Morton, M. S. (1991), *The Corporation of the 1990s* (Oxford: Oxford University Press).

Shapiro, C., and Varian, H. R. (1999), *Information Rules: A Strategic Guide to the Network Economy* (Boston: Harvard Business School Press).

Smith, M. R., and Marx, L. (eds.) (1994), *Does Technology Drive History? The Dilemma of Technological Determinism* (Cambridge, Mass.: MIT Press).

Star, S. L., and Griesemer, J. R. (1989), 'Institutional Ecology, "Translations", and Boundary Objects: Amateurs and Professionals in Berkeley's Museum of Vertebrate Zoology, 1907–1939', *Social Studies of Science*, 19: 387–420.

—— and Ruhleder, K. (1996), 'Steps towards an Ecology of Infrastructure: Design and Access for Large Information Spaces', *Information Systems Research*, 7/1: 111–34.

Steinmueller, W. E. (1996), 'Technology Infrastructure in Information Technology Industries', in M. Teubal, D. Foray, M. Justman, and E. Zuscovitch (eds.), *Technological Infrastructure Policy: An International Perspective* (Dordrecht, The Netherlands: Kluwer Academic Publishers).

Suchman, L. (1987), *Plans and Situated Action* (Cambridge: Cambridge University Press).

Thompson, J. (1967), *Organizations in Action* (New York: McGraw-Hill).

Timmermans, S., and Berg, M. (1997), 'Standardization in Action: Achieving Universalism and Localization in Medical Protocols', *Social Studies of Science*, 27: 273–305.

—— Bowker, G., and Star, S. L. (1995), 'Infrastructure and Organizational Transformation: Classifying Nurses' Work', in W. Orlikowski, G. Walsham, M. R. Jones, and J. I. DeGross (eds.), *Information Technology and Changes in Organizational Work* (London: Chapman & Hall).

Turner, I., and Henry, I. (1994), 'Managing International Organizations: Lessons from the Field', *European Management Journal*, 12/2 (Dec.), 417–31.

Venkatraman, N., and Henderson, J. (1999), 'Business Platforms for the 21st Century: Mastering Information Management', *Financial Times*, Supplement (Mar.).

Walsham, G. (1993), *Interpreting Information Systems in Organizations* (Chichester: J. Wiley).

—— (1997), 'Actor-Network Theory and IS Research: Current Status and Future Prospects', in *Proceedings of the IFIP TC8 WG 8.2 International Conference on Information Systems and Qualitative Research* (London: Chapman & Hall).

Weick, K. E. (1969), *The Social Psychology of Organizing* (Reading, Mass.: Addison-Wesley).

—— (1976), 'Educational Organizations as Loosely Coupled Systems', *Administrative Science Quarterly*, 21: 1–19.

Weill, P., and Broadbent, M. (1998), *Leveraging the New Infrastructure: How Market Leaders Capitalize on Information* (Boston: Harvard Business School Press).

—— —— and St Clair, D. (1996), 'IT Value and the Role of IT Infrastructure', in J. Luftman (ed.), *Strategic Alignment* (Oxford: Oxford University Press).

Willcocks, L., and Lacity, M. (eds.) (1997), *Strategic Sourcing of Information Systems* (Chichester: J. Wiley).

Williams, R., and Edge, D. (1996), 'The Social Shaping of Technology', *Research Policy*, 25: 865–99.

Williamson, O. E. (1975), *Markets and Hierarchies* (New York: Free Press).

Winner, L. (1977), *Autonomous Technology: Technics-out-of-Control as a Theme in Political Thought* (Cambridge, Mass: MIT Press).

—— (1986), *The Whale and the Reactor* (Chicago: Chicago University Press).

Winograd, T., and Flores, F. (1987), *Understanding Computers and Cognition* (Reading, Mass.: Addison Wesley).

With-Andersen, H. (1997), 'Producing Producers: Shippers, Shipyards and the Cooperative Infrastructure of the Norwegian Maritime Complex since 1850', in C. F. Sabel and J. Zeitlin (eds.), *Flexibility and Mass Production in Western Industrialization* (Cambridge: Cambridge University Press).

Womack, J. P., Jones, D. T., and Roos, D. (1991), *The Machine that Changed the World: The Story of Lean Production* (New York: Harper Perennial).

Yates, JoAnne (1989), *Control through Communication. The Rise of System in American Management* (Baltimore: Johns Hopkins University Press).

Yin, R. K. (1994), *Case Study Research: Design and Methods* (Thousands Oaks, Calif.: Sage).

Zuboff, S. (1987), *In the Age of the Smart Machine* (New York: Basic Books).

Index

Note: Authors of chapters have the relevant page numbers in **bold** print.